20 Innovative Electronics Projects for Your Home

Joseph O'Connell

TAB TAB BOOKS Inc.
Blue Ridge Summit, PA

FIRST EDITION
FIRST PRINTING

Copyright © 1988 by TAB BOOKS Inc.
Printed in the United States of America

Library of Congress Cataloging in Publication Data

O'Connell, Joseph
20 innovative electronics projects for your home.

Includes index.
1. Household electronics—Amateurs' manuals.
I. Title. II. Title: Twenty innovative electronics
projects for your home.
TK9965.O24 1988   621.381   88-8571
ISBN 0-8306-0947-4
ISBN 0-8306-2947-5 (pbk.)

Questions regarding the content of this book
should be addressed to:

Reader Inquiry Branch
TAB BOOKS Inc.
Blue Ridge Summit, PA 17294-0214

Table of Contents

Introduction   vii

1 Solid State Electric Blanket Controller   1
   Features * About Temperature Compensation * The Circuit *
   Construction * Use * More Uses of the Circuit * Parts List

2 Variable AC Power Controller   11
   Use * Phase Control Circuits * The Components * The Circuit
   * Construction * More Uses of the Circuit * Parts List

3 Regulated Voltage and Current Supply   24
   The Circuit * Construction * Use * More Uses of the Circuit *
   Parts List

4 Infrared Remote Control Relayer   35
   The Circuit * Construction * Installing the Remote Control
   Relayer * Further Use * Parts List

5 Electronic Distance Measuring System   43
   The Circuit * Construction * Use * Going Further * Parts List

6 **Ringing Telephone Alerter**   **56**
The Circuit ∗ Why This Circuit? ∗ Construction ∗ Parts List

7 **Portable Refrigerator**   **63**
Two Methods ∗ Required Materials ∗ Construction ∗ Control
Circuitry ∗ Making a Power Supply ∗ Materials List for the Large
Portable Refrigerator ∗ Materials List for the Small Portable Re-
frigerator ∗ Parts List for a Low Voltage Cutoff Circuit

8 **Remote Volume Control**   **82**
The Circuit ∗ A Note on the Circuit Chosen ∗ Construction ∗
Operation ∗ More Uses for the Circuit ∗ Parts List

9 **Protected Outlet Box**   **90**
The No-Frills Version ∗ Adding the Automatic Power Switch ∗
Adding a Power Inverter ∗ Other Uses of the Outlet Box ∗ Parts
List

10 **Telephone Accessory**   **104**
The Phone Line ∗ The Circuit ∗ Construction ∗ Other Uses ∗
Parts List

11 **Tide Clock**   **111**
The Circuit ∗ Construction ∗ Calibration ∗ Use ∗ Other Uses of
the Circuit ∗ Parts List

12 **Fluorescent Bike Light**   **123**
The Circuit and Parts ∗ Construction ∗ Use ∗ Parts List

13 **Straight Wire Without Gain**
Functions and Operation ∗ Construction ∗ General Construction
Sequence ∗ Adding an Active Stage Sources ∗ Parts List: Straight
Wire Without Gain ∗ Parts List: Separate Power Supply

14 **Portable Xenon Strobe**   **156**
The Circuit ∗ Parts ∗ Construction ∗ Going Further ∗ Parts List

15 **Electronic Incentive**   **163**
The Circuit ∗ Construction ∗ Use ∗ Parts List

16 **Tool Magnetizer and Demagnetizer**   **172**
The Circuit ∗ Construction ∗ Use ∗ Parts List

17 Multi-Sensor Digital Thermometer   180

The Sensors * The Circuit * Construction * Calibration * Building a Digital Panel Meter * Parts List: Multi-Sensor Digital Thermometer * Parts List: Digital Panel Meter

18 Active Minispeakers   193

The Amplifier Circuit * Building the Amplifier Into the Speakers * Adjustment * Constructing the Portable Carrier * Other Accessories * Parts List: Active Minispeakers * Parts List: Speaker-Carrying Handle

19 Plug-in Tester   207

The Circuit * Construction * Calibration * Use * Parts List

20 Electric Hand Dryer   217

Design Considerations * Modifying the Hair Dryer * The Activating Circuit * Constructing the Activating Circuit * Use * An Alternate Activating Circuit * Parts List for the Timed Version * Parts List for the Motion Detector Version

21 Construction Hints   229

Adhesives * Breadboards * CMOS Handling * Construction Methods * Enclosures * Fuseholders * Labeling Project Enclosures * Metals * Odd Component Values * Plastic * Soldering Irons * Soldering Tools * Test Equipment * Test Leads * Tools

22 Electronic Hints and Simple Projects   241

Battery Charger * Capacitor Bypassing * Color Organ * Fast Stop for AC Motors * Flip-Flop * Fuse Monitor * LEDs * LED Variable Color Power Indicator * Neon Light Circuits * Potentiometers * Regulators * Solid State Relay * Voltage Boosters and Cutters * Zero Crossing

23 Parts Sources   257

New Parts * Surplus Parts * What to Buy New * What to Buy Used * Retail Stores * More Sources for Parts

Index   261

Introduction

Building electronic projects isn't the same as it used to be. In the past, experimenters built things that either couldn't be bought or they cost too much. Nowadays, the lowered prices of consumer electronics has changed the game, making it difficult for a hobbyist in his shop to compete with large companies on a cost basis. A wide variety of commercial electronic devices has also become available that challenge the familiar notion that certain odd things have to be made by hand because they're not sold in stores. Today, almost anything that can be built at home can also be bought for a reasonable cost.

But take heart; there is still room for electronic experimenters somewhere. A few opportunities remain to build things that corporate manufacturers have judged unprofitable to pursue on their large scale. Still other opportunities exist to beat the cost of the few overpriced commercial electronic devices. And there will always be a few things that can only be built at home if they are to ever exist—you know, the kind of gizmo that gets retailers to ask "*What* did you say you wanted?" This book explores some of those remaining opportunities for building unique projects. Its 20 projects fit in the cracks between commercially available devices.

One of the niches the hobbyist can fit into is that gap between what is technically possible in electronics and what products actually make it to the consumer market. This gap is mostly the result of the time lag between research and engineering, but sometimes it exists purely because of industry oversight. For example, the Fluorescent Bike Light project in Chapter 12 doesn't depend on any technology that hasn't been around for years, but it is superior in nearly every respect to incandescent bike lights. Nevertheless, almost every manufactured bike light is incandescent—simply because few people seriously think of doing it any other way. By constructing the Fluorescent Bike Light and other projects yourself, you can take advantage of many good ideas industry ignores.

Not all the projects lie in industry's margins though. There are a few projects in this book that are available commercially. But these are projects in which you can really save money when you build them yourself. An example is the Infrared Remote Control Relayer of Chapter 4. Following the directions given in that chapter, it is possible to build for $10 what would cost $50 dollars if you bought it.

Finally, some of the projects in this book have somewhat limited interests that would not be profitable for a mass merchandiser to serve. For example, consider the Tide Clock in Chapter 11. You don't need one if you live inland, but if you happen to need one, you've picked up the right book. The instructions in Chapter 11 enable you to build a project that isn't sold anywhere simply because right now, there is not enough demand for it.

Most of the projects in this book are intended for hobbyists who have had at least a little experience with electronics. All 20 of the projects in this book have been built and tested. Everything learned during the prototyping has been distilled and put into the construction section of each chapter and illustrated with photographs and diagrams. The projects should be easy to build if these instructions are followed, simply because they were so difficult to build as prototypes to *arrive* at those instructions. All the possible bugs have been encountered and squashed more than once to ensure little chance of them cropping up in your version of the projects.

No electronic circuit is entirely original, but those published here approach complete originality as closely as any book. Electronic parts have been around for a long time, and the possible circuits using them have already been invented. Almost no commercial device is designed from scratch but instead uses circuit elements that were designed years ago by other engineers. The skill involved in electronics design is more integrative than creative, but it's just as valid a skill. Like other electronic circuits, those used in this book combine some circuit elements that are not entirely original. Nevertheless, none of the complete circuits appear under anyone else's name and all represent a substantive improvement over previously published work of the same type.

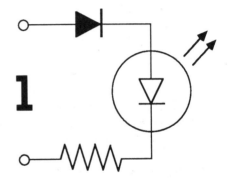

1

Solid State Electric Blanket Control

The electromechanical type of controller that is sold with most electric blankets has a number of disadvantages that this electronic substitute is specifically designed to address. Standard controllers vary the heat output of the blanket by repeatedly cycling it on and off, usually with a long period that you might notice as fluctuations in temperature. This solid-state replacement varies its power output continuously to give a constant temperature. And while most standard electric blanket controllers make a disturbing sound when they come on and have a dial light that's too bright, the electronic project described here has none of those drawbacks. It even adds some features that no commercial electric blanket controllers have (SEE FIG. 1-1).

FEATURES

The design for this electric blanket controller has a few unique features. It's major difference is that it controls the power supplied to the blanket element with a triac that interrupts the AC line voltage at different points in the waveform. This method of controlling power is called *phase control* and is described more fully in Chapter 2. For comparison, a typical output waveform of this control and one from a standard controller is shown in FIG. 1-2. Although both controllers produce the same average output power, the waveform produced by the phase controller is smoother and has no noticeable fluctuations like the standard one does.

The power that the controller supplies to the blanket depends on the amount of time it is ON compared to the amount of time it is OFF. To make setting the control easy, especially in the dark, LED 1 indicates this ratio by its color. When the output is fully

FIG. 1-1. *The finished project shown here is about the same size as the electromechanical controls it is designed to replace.*

off, delivering no power to the blanket, the LED glows green. As the heat control is turned up, the indicator turns slightly yellow in color, changing completely to yellow when the blanket is receiving half power. From there, its color goes through shades of orange and finally becomes red when the heat is turned to maximum. With this type of indicator, the heat setting is visible at a glance. The LED is placed at the index position of the heat control knob so that the knob can be found easily at night.

This project also provides a special switch that makes it easy to warm up a cold bed quickly. This is done by simply bypassing the control circuitry and sending the full 120 VAC to the blanket. Although the heat control could be turned to its maximum position to do the same thing, having a separate switch eliminates the need to frequently reset it. This switch's action is accompanied by a flashing red LED that indicates that the bed is being warmed as fast as possible.

ABOUT TEMPERATURE COMPENSATION

The standard electromechanical controls this design replaces have a rudimentary form of temperature compensation. This means that the power they send to the blanket varies in response to both the dial setting and the ambient temperature of the room. The advantage of temperature compensation is if you went to bed in a house that was warm at first but cooled off at night, the control would automatically increase the power to the blanket as the room got colder.

Although this might sound like a useful feature, it is unnecessary in most cases. For one thing, the temperature sensor is inside the electric blanket controller. Because it is

2

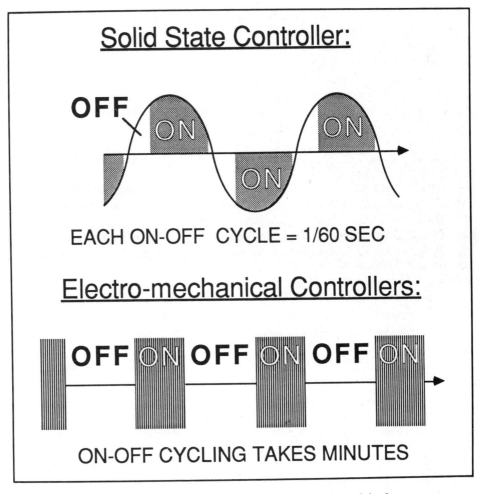

Solid State Controller:

OFF

ON

ON

ON

EACH ON-OFF CYCLE = 1/60 SEC

Electro-mechanical Controllers:

OFF ON **OFF** ON **OFF** ON

ON-OFF CYCLING TAKES MINUTES

FIG. 1-2. *The output of a solid state controller has none of the long-term variations that an electromechanical controller does.*

in a different location than the body of the sleeper, it can't take into account the amount of insulation the bed provides or the amount of heat produced by the body. Even at its best, it will be inaccurate. Another reason that temperature compensation is unnecessary in most cases is that changes in ambient temperature from the time when people go to sleep are usually slight in most houses. But the most important reason temperature compensation is not needed is because of the function of the body itself. During sleep, the body regulates its own temperature throughout wide changes in ambient conditions; it is remarkably tolerant of variations.

Hence, temperature compensation is one feature of standard electric blanket controllers that you can probably do without when you build your own controller. But if the blanket is used in places where there *are* drastic changes in the nighttime temperature due to the lack of heating or to energy-saving measures, then the addition of a thermistor as shown in the schematic will provide temperature compensation. The thermistor specified has a positive temperature coefficient—that is, its resistance increases when its temperature does. The increase in resistance at that point in the circuit has the same effect as turning down the heat control potentiometer.

Unfortunately, thermistors aren't as widely employed in electronic circuits as they once were and are consequently less available. The large manufacturers of suitable thermistors for this project have stopped making them recently. However it could still be possible to obtain a suitable thermistor from the many surplus dealers because they were once a widely used component.

THE CIRCUIT

The circuit for this project is shown in FIG. 1-3. It is essentially a phase controller built around the triac and its associated components. The operation of the triac and the nearby resistors and capacitors is explained in Chapter 2 but is basically similar to a light dimmer. The potentiometer is the heat level control. It sets the output power by determining the ratio of ON to OFF time within the AC waveform sent to the blanket. In series with the potentiometer is the optional thermistor. It serves to compensate the heat control setting for changes in ambient temperature.

The indicator LED 1 is a two-color LED with both red and green elements encapsulated together. The package has three leads: the red and green anodes and a common cathode. When the heat control is all the way down, the triac is effectively open. Current can flow through S1, D1, R3 and the electric blanket element to light only the green LED. The red LED remains off due to the triac's high resistance. But when the heat control is turned up slightly, the triac conducts for a brief period during the beginning of each half waveform. For this short time, the green LED is shorted by the triac and power is switched to the red. Both elements are never on simultaneously. The human eye's persistence combines, in this case, a lot of green and a little red to arrive at a yellowish-green color. As the heat control is increased, the red LED stays on for longer portions of the waveform and the green for less. This yields first a yellow then an orange tint and finally a red color, with smooth changes in between.

With S2 in the FAST WARM position, full power bypasses the triac and flows directly into the blanket. The two-color power indicator light is disconnected and LED 2, a flashing red LED, is connected instead. This LED contains a built-in MOS IC that operates from a three- to seven-volt DC power supply. Components R5, D3, and C7 form the supply for this LED.

Capacitors C1, C4, C5, and C6 are all bypass capacitors that suppress arcing and radio frequency emission. The circuit will operate without these capacitors, but the switches will wear out sooner and nearby radios could pick up noise from the phase control circuit. Chapter 22 has more information about bypass capacitors.

CONSTRUCTION

A suitable enclosure for the solid state electric blanket controller is one of the common plastic project boxes that are usually sold with an aluminum faceplate. But for this project, use the box in the opposite way it was intended to be. Use the plastic bottom as the top, mounting the controls in it—and use the aluminum plate as a base and heatsink for the triac.

4

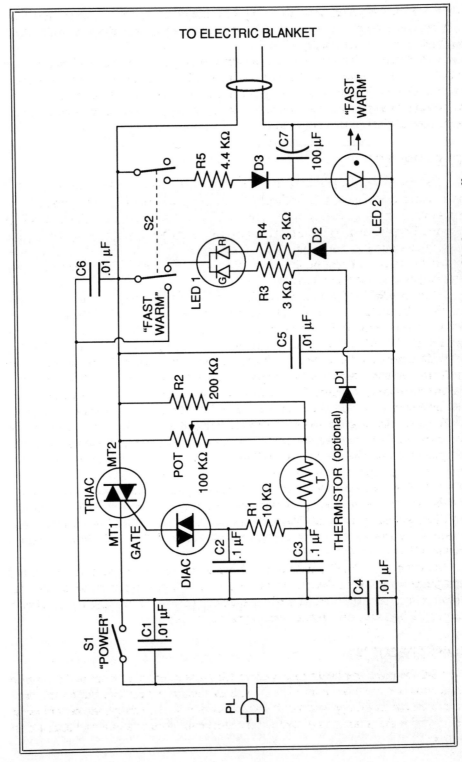

Fig. 1-3. *Complete schematic for the solid state electric blanket controller.*

5

Point-to-Point Wiring

The circuit doesn't lend itself to pc board construction because almost half of its components mount on the panel or to the aluminum plate. A better way to make a circuit of this type is called point-to-point wiring. The place to begin point-to-point wiring for this and similar projects is by examining the schematic and planning the internal layout based on what you know about the parts.

First, notice all the parts that are stably mounted to the enclosure. Place a mark on their terminals since they can serve as tie points for other loose component leads. In this circuit, the potentiometer, the switches, the thermistor, the LEDs, and the triac are stably mounted and provide some of the necessary tie points for the rest of the circuit. See FIG. 1-4 where the leads from these components have been marked by circles.

Then place a different mark at the circuit junctions that still need tie points. Doing this to the controller circuit reveals that at least four more tie points will be needed. Mount terminal strips on the aluminum plate where they will be appropriate for these tie points. Keep in mind that not every connection needs a tie point, though. Between R4 and D2, for example, no separate tie point is needed. Their common leads are simply soldered together securely and the two are from then on treated as one component.

A simple circuit like this lends itself well to point-to-point construction and builds quickly if the above method is followed. Similar projects can benefit from the same method of carefully considering every junction on the schematic before wiring.

Mounting

Mount the LEDs in 13/64-inch holes drilled in the plastic case and secure them with epoxy or hot-melt glue. If you are using a thermistor, mount it outside the case so it is more responsive to air temperature and isn't fooled by heat the triac generates. Like the LEDs, use glue to secure it in place in its mounting holes.

It is important that the triac be insulated from both the aluminum plate and its mounting bolt because it is connected to one side of the AC supply and has the potential to cause shock. FIGURE 1-5 shows how to mount the triac to the aluminum cover of the case. Use thermal grease and a mica washer as the diagram indicates. The washer electrically isolates the triac's tab from the aluminum while still allowing it to dissipate heat. Some mail order parts sources include the necessary mounting hardware with each triac they sell. An alternative to insulating the triac's tab is to use the ISOTAB type, which because of its isolated mounting tab, doesn't require insulating washers.

Finishing Up

With internal circuitry completed, test its operation with an incandescent lamp. The circuit should behave like a light dimmer when the heat output control is rotated. The two-color LED should change colors corresponding to the brightness of the test lamp as indicated previously. With S2 in the FAST WARM position, the test lamp should be at full brightness and LED 2 should blink.

You'll have to cut the wires going to the old controller that came with the blanket you're using before connecting them to this project. Pass the blanket wire and the line cord through grommets in the end of the project's case and knot them inside to keep them there. When they have been wired in place, complete the construction by attaching the

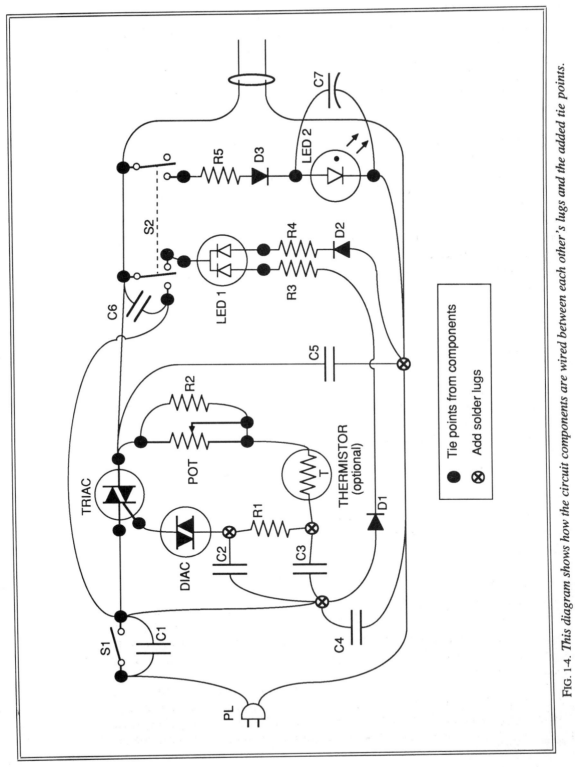

FIG. 1-4. *This diagram shows how the circuit components are wired between each other's lugs and the added tie points.*

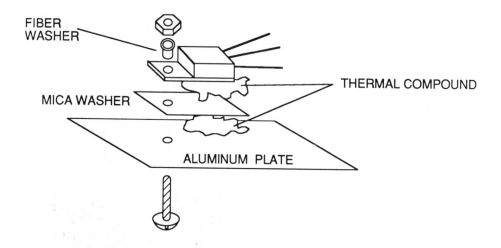

FIBER WASHER

THERMAL COMPOUND

MICA WASHER

ALUMINUM PLATE

FIG. 1-5. *Shown here is the proper way to isolate the triac from its heatsink.*

aluminum place to the plastic box. FIGURE 1-6 shows the completed prototype with its cover removed to reveal the inner wiring. Attach a suitable knob to the shaft of the potentiometer, and label the outside of the case with rub-on lettering.

USE

This controller is a direct replacement for the electromechanical controllers typically supplied with electric blankets. Once the substitution is made, use the electric blanket as you ordinarily would except to take advantage of the added features of this project. Some of the subtle advantages (like the lack of temperature cycling and the silent operation) won't be noticed except by their absence.

Other features can be appreciated more readily. The FAST WARM switch position is useful on cold days when you want to warm the bed as quickly as possible before getting in. Turn this switch on about five minutes before going to bed. If the bed isn't warmed beforehand on cold days, the mattress will cool you from below even if you have an electric blanket warming you from above. Until the mattress warms up from your body heat, it causes the uncomfortable feeling of being too cold on one side and too hot on the other. The FAST WARM switch makes it easy to avoid this.

Take care not to leave the switch in this position too long, however, especially if the electric blanket is covered. Doing this doesn't create an appreciable fire hazard because of the built-in thermal cutoffs that all blankets are required to have, but keeping it fully on for a long period is not good for the blanket's fabric.

When the bed has warmed sufficiently in the FAST WARM position, turn the switch off and set the desired temperature level with the heat control knob. Use the color of the two-color LED as a rough guide or refer to the position of the dial. After a little experience it will become easy to estimate the correct setting for a given room temperature either by color or position.

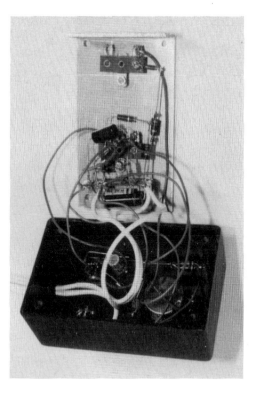

FIG. 1-6. *The finished project with its enclosure opened.*

MORE USES OF THE CIRCUIT

The control circuit presented in this chapter is suitable for other applications as well, particularly those that require an indication of the power output. For example, an electric heater or a remotely controlled device gives no immediate indication of its output level. It needs a monitor like the two-color LED in this project to make setting the control easier. A suitable circuit for a variety of loads can be adapted from FIG. 1-3, keeping in mind that a larger triac is necessary to control loads that draw more power than an electric blanket. Also, the amount of heatsinking that a triac or any semiconductor requires increases as the current it is controlling increases.

PARTS LIST:

Solid State Electric Blanket Control

C1, C4-C6	.01μF, 200V bypass capacitors, value not critical
C2, C3	.1μF, 200V
C7	100μF, 10 V
R1	10KΩ, ¼W
R2	200KΩ, ¼W or whatever gives smoothest response when a light bulb is used to check the output. Omit if thermistor is used.
R3, R4	3KΩ, W (3300Ω 2W resistor in parallel with a 33KΩ, ¼ W resistor)
R5	4.4KΩ, 1W
POT	100KΩ linear taper or 50KΩ linear taper if thermistor is used
TRIAC	2A, 200V or better
DIAC	D-30 or equivalent
D1-D3	200PIV 1A or better rectifier diodes
LED 1	Two-color LED (type with three leads)
LED 2	Flashing red LED (R.S. #276-036 or equiv.)
S1	5A SPST mini toggle switch
S2	5A DPDT mini toggle switch
PL	Line cord and wall plug (take from electric blanket)
THERMISTOR	(optional) PTC thermistor, 25KΩ at 25 degrees Celsius, resistance ratio of about ten

PLUS, suitable enclosure, electric blanket, knobs, grommets, solder lugs, TO-220 mounting hardware, hook-up wire, solder, and rub-on lettering.

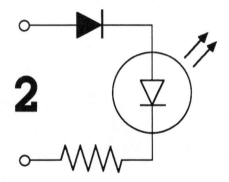

Variable
AC Power Controller

When controlling a motor, light bulb, or other device that draws more than a few watts, it is easiest to turn it fully on or fully off. Otherwise, at any setting less than full power, the controlling circuit has to dissipate the excess as heat. This is why high power loads are controlled by switching them on and off rapidly in a varying on-to-off proportion whenever possible. The average power the load *receives* can be any fraction of its full power, but at any instant, the load is always fully on or fully off.

One practical way of doing this is *phase control*, the method used by light dimmers, motor speed controls, and the project in this chapter. There are two types of phase control circuits built into this project. One is a full-wave controller, providing nearly 0 to 100 percent control of AC output power. It is useful for varying the intensity of lights, heaters, and certain motors. The other circuit forms a half-wave phase controller. It acts on only one polarity of the AC line, yielding a pulsed DC output. This particular approach finds most of its uses with motorized tools because it offers torque compensation to automatically deliver more power to the motor when it is heavily loaded down. This is necessary when a slow but steady speed is required of an electric drill or mixer. See Fig. 2-1.

This project includes building the half-wave and full-wave phase control circuits, described subsequently, into a common enclosure. The two circuits share a number of components that would otherwise have to be duplicated if they were built separately. Together in one project, they should be very useful around your home and shop.

USE

Use the full-wave part of the circuit to dim lights, control heaters, vary the speed of AC motors, and adjust the output of a power transformer for a variable low voltage

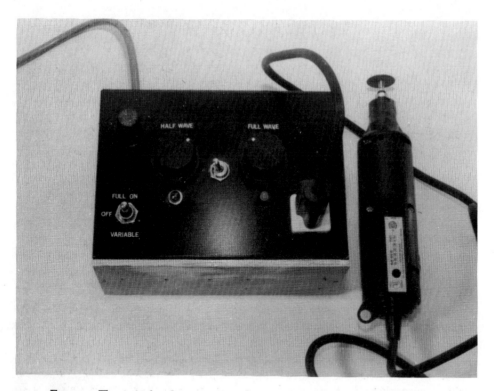

FIG. 2-1. *The completed project is shown here in one of its typical uses.*

supply. Use the half-wave circuit for small power tools like the Dremel Moto-Tool, kitchen appliances, hand drills, or any small power tool without its own speed control. Many tools perform like completely different machines when considerably slowed down and take on quite a lot of additional usefulness. In general, limit your use of the controllers to small motors. Large motors are usually not very useful when slowed down anyway and can draw surges of current that can destroy the SCR or triac. The circuits and their construction are described after some of the basics of phase control are explained.

PHASE CONTROL CIRCUITS

The most efficient power control circuits are those that vary the output by switching the load on and off in differing proportions. Most phase control circuits make use of the fact that an AC voltage already switches on and off twice in each cycle. To vary power, the circuits interrupt a selected part of each waveform and keep it from reaching the load. A typical output would show the 60 Hz AC waveform divided into sections that are either fully on or fully off, as FIG. 2-2 indicates.

The switching is usually done by a thyristor (an SCR or triac) whose gate pulse is derived in some way from the AC waveform itself so it is automatically synchronized with the power being controlled. Let's examine how two typical thyristor phase control circuits work.

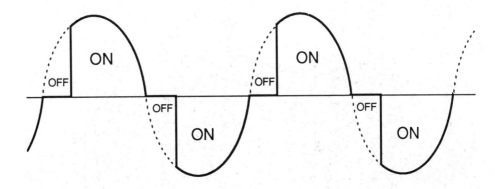

FIG. 2-2. *This is what a typical output from the phase control circuit looks like on a scope.*

Full-wave

FIGURE 2-3 presents a full-wave phase control circuit typically found in light dimmers and some motor speed controls. Two combinations: the potentiometer/C1, and R/C2 form two series RC phase-shift networks. When an AC voltage is applied to a resistor and capacitor connected in series as in the case of these combinations, the voltage appearing at the top of the capacitor is an AC voltage of reduced amplitude that lags the applied voltage by a phase difference of 0 to 90 degrees, depending on the setting of the potentiometer. If you could see both the applied AC voltage and the voltage across C1 on a scope, you'd see the AC line voltage and following it, another delayed AC voltage. With the potentiometer variable from 0 to 100 kilohms, the phase shift is variable from no phase shift at its minimum setting (where the output is essentially connected to the input) to a maximum of about 75 degrees. A second phase-shift network composed of R and C2 extends the total phase shift range at point "T" so that a 0 to nearly 180 degree range is obtainable by varying the potentiometer. It is this phase-shifted signal present at point "T" that is used to trigger the triac and control the AC power to the load.

The diac shown in the schematic is a two-way voltage threshold switch. It conducts when a voltage of about 30 volts of either polarity exists across its terminals. Connected to the triac's gate, it provides a means of setting a triggering threshold at which the triac conducts (the triac is a three-terminal, gate-controlled, AC switching device). The time when the voltage at point "T" reaches plus or minus 30 volts determines when the triac begins conducting power to the load. But remember that the voltage present at "T" is the delayed sine wave. The point in time relative to the AC waveform when "T" reaches 30 volts can be varied by the potentiometer. Consequently, the triggering point where the triac begins to conduct can be varied to take place over a 0 to 180 degree range in the AC waveform. The triac always turns off near the zero point of each half cycle, so by varying the point at which conduction begins, the potentiometer is actually controlling the *interval* it is on for. This conduction interval determines the amount of power the load receives. The waveform drawn in FIG. 2-4 should help you visualize what is happening in this circuit.

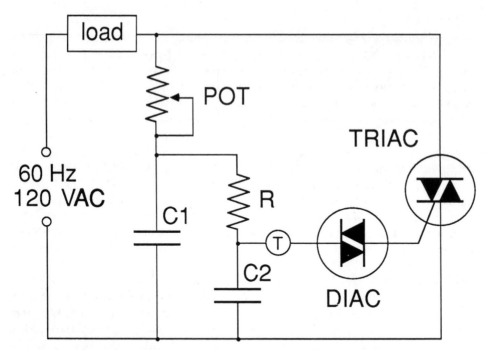

FIG. 2-3. *The full-wave phase control circuit shown here is the type used in light dimmers and similar control circuits.*

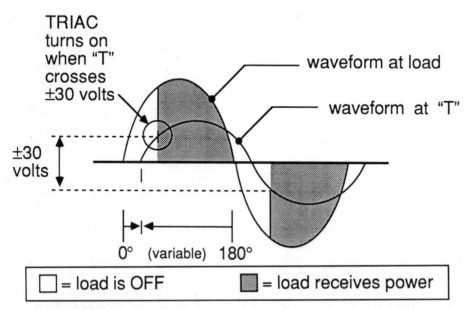

FIG. 2-4. *This diagram shows the voltage at point ''T'' superimposed over the output of the circuit in Fig. 2-3 to indicate their time relation.*

Half-wave

The half-wave phase control circuit used in this project works in a completely different way. The circuit in FIG. 2-5 is a typical example, used in power drills, food mixers, and other variable speed tools that typically have changing loads. It automatically senses and corrects for reduced motor speed due to loading. Because it uses an SCR, conduction is limited to only the positive half of the AC waveform. But since most small series-wound universal motors work well from a DC supply, this is usually not a problem.

The circuit varies the SCR's ratio of on-time to off-time and consequently controls the power the load receives. But unlike the full-wave control circuit that accomplishes this using a delayed gate signal, the half-wave circuit triggers itself by comparing two voltages. One of these voltages is produced by R1, C, D1, and the potentiometer. These components form a DC supply whose output voltage is determined by the setting of the potentiometer. The SCR that is hooked in series with the load begins conducting when the voltage at its gate is higher that at its cathode. When the controller is just turned on, this condition is always met because the gate is hooked to the DC supply and the cathode is at zero potential.

So at first, the SCR conducts full power to the load. But once the motor starts spinning, it acts as a generator, creating its own voltage at the SCR's cathode. This second voltage vies with the voltage of the power supply and tries to turn the SCR off. When the motor is spinning fast enough, it "wins" and the SCR is turned off—unless of course

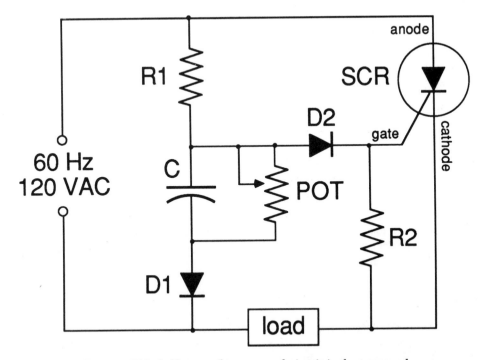

FIG. 2-5. *This half-wave phase control circuit is the type used by small-appliance speed controls.*

the potentiometer is adjusted for an even higher voltage at the gate which the motor will then have to match. Variable speed control is obtained by varying the SCR's gate voltage with the potentiometer, effectively setting the voltage the motor will have to produce in return. The motor is turned on and off repeatedly—allowed to speed up and slow down imperceptibly around an equilibrium position set by the potentiometer. At very slow speeds, where the ratio of off-time to on-time is greatest, you can actually detect the cycling action of the controller by the vibrations the motor produces.

Because the half-wave circuit controls motor speed by *feedback* and not indirectly by varying power, load compensation is automatically included. All possible factors affecting motor speed are considered in the feedback loop, making this type of controller ideal for motors that meet changing load conditions.

THE COMPONENTS

Many hobbyists are unfamiliar with the practical use of the components that are at the heart of these phase control circuits. There are many books, perhaps too many, that explain triac, diac, SCR, and other semiconductor operation and circuit design considerations. Another good source for information on these is manufacturers' data books and applications notes. They are sold at electronics stores, from mail-order houses, and from the manufacturers themselves. You might also find copies at a college or technical library. In addition, the following comments present some useful advice to the experimenter.

Triacs

Triacs are sold in a variety of power ratings and packages. For use in typical AC power control circuits, select one with at least a 200 volt rating and a current rating in excess of the expected load. Often a triac with a higher voltage rating costs no more than a 200 volt triac. Get the highest rated one offered without spending more than a few cents more. The extra voltage "headroom" will provide security against potentially damaging transients.

Triacs in the power range typically encountered by the experimenter are packaged in TO-220 cases. The mounting tab is usually electrically connected to MT2. In a few cases, this is an advantage, but in most it makes mounting difficult because a "live" tab requires careful isolation. At a slightly higher cost, some triacs come in an "Isotab" configuration with the tab electrically isolated.

Many amateur electronics books and magazines try to explain triac operation as if a triac were identical to two SCRs connected back-to-back. Some even go as far as to draw a supposedly equivalent circuit composed of SCRs. This kind of explanation is potentially deceiving. A triac is neither constructed exactly like nor functions like two SCRs. Another often neglected fact about triacs is that MT1 and MT2 are not interchangeable. The load a triac controls should always be placed in the circuit on the MT2 side.

Diacs

A diac is a tiny semiconductor that conducts after a certain threshold voltage has been reached in either direction. It is symmetric; the same voltage of either polarity will turn it on. For the projects in this book, Motorola D-30 diacs were used, but only because they are inexpensive and readily available. Other diacs of about the same voltage should work as well. Although diacs are individually quite cheap, the sum of money you spend on them can become high if you destroy many through careless soldering. Since diacs are so tiny, they are very easily damaged by heat. Use pliers or heat-sink clips to protect them when you solder their leads.

Diacs are used in triac circuits because the gate sensitivity of a triac is not symmetrical. A diac's triggering voltage is symmetrical however, and is well in excess of the triggering voltage of the triac. The use of a diac makes the triac equally sensitive to both polarities of gate signals, because the triac has to wait for the diac to conduct before it can fire. Since a triac and diac combination is common in AC circuits, some manufacturers produce them together in a three- or four-lead package called a "quadrac."

SCRs

SCRs (silicon controlled rectifiers) function somewhat like diodes do but with the addition of a third lead to control their operation. They only conduct in one direction and are either fully on or fully off. When the gate and the anode are positive with respect to the cathode, current flows from anode to cathode. After triggering, for as long as current remains flowing from the anode to the cathode, the gate voltage can be removed; it has served its purpose and is no longer needed. An ordinary SCR turns off only when the anode to cathode current has been reduced to some minimal value (as in the half-wave circuit when the positive-going AC waveform crosses zero and becomes negative).

The latching action of SCRs is both useful and troublesome. In AC phase control circuits, it is useful because once it is triggered, an SCR automatically stays on until nearly the end of the waveform. In DC circuits like the phone hold circuit of Chapter 10, its latching action is also used to advantage. But in many DC circuits, the SCR's stubbornness at turning off is considered a liability, and NPN switching transistors are used instead.

The frequency range at which SCRs are effective extends only to a few hundred hertz, although this is better than the triac, which is hardly useful above 60 hertz. SCRs come in packages similar to triacs, are somewhat less expensive, and generally more available.

THE CIRCUIT

The circuit in FIG. 2-6 combines the two circuits previously discussed. Values have been specified where before there were only theoretical components. One change is the use of a 200 kilohm resistor in parallel with the control potentiometer in the full-wave circuit. This merely provides smoother response to the control knob and permits its full range of rotation to be effective.

Besides the parts of the two phase control circuits, the components in FIG. 2-6 add convenience and suppress noise. Components C1, C2, L, R1, and the MOV form an AC noise and transient suppression network that is effective at reducing the radio frequency harmonics that are a typical complaint of light dimmer users. The choke L (which can either be a commercial 70 to 100 millihenry 5A choke or 18 feet of solid AWG 18 gauge wire wound on a ¼ inch ferrite rod) smoothes the rough output of the controller to give better performance with electric motors at slow speeds. Capacitors C4 and C7 bypass the triac and SCR to keep voltage transients from inadvertently triggering or damaging them. The LED, D3, D4, R5, and R6 form a power output indicator similar to the one discussed

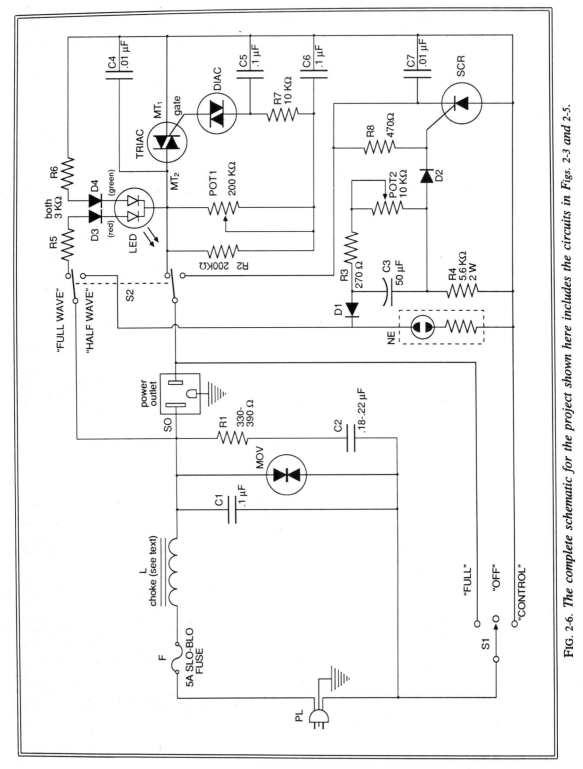

FIG. 2-6. *The complete schematic for the project shown here includes the circuits in Figs. 2-3 and 2-5.*

in Chapter 1 and Chapter 22. Switches S1 and S2 switch between the two control circuits and allow for bypassing either circuit.

CONSTRUCTION

A slightly modified aluminum project box is particularly suitable for the enclosure of this project. These boxes are usually sold as two interlocking U-shaped pieces—a top and a bottom—with four screws to attach the two halves. It is always more convenient if all the parts in a project can fit entirely in one or the other half to avoid stringing wires back and forth between the separate pieces. But this project presents a problem. With two potentiometers, two switches, a neon light, and the LED all mounted in the cover, there is no room left to mount the SCR and triac, which require considerable heatsinking.

The solution is to add another side to the top piece of the aluminum box. Observe in FIG. 2-7 how a scrap piece of aluminum was attached to the top piece of the chassis. The bottom piece is now only needed after the project is completely finished and serves to cover the two remaining sides that the top piece leaves open. The bottom piece should be modified by cutting off its superfluous side to make way for the piece added to the top. The bottom piece also mounts differently; it attaches to the outside of the top piece whereas the manufacturer designed it to mount on the inside. You will need different screws to mount it on the outside because the large and small holes will be reversed.

After preparing the box, the next step in construction is mounting the components in it. The layout of the controls mounted in the top depends what style knobs and switches you use. Large control knobs are best for the two potentiometers since they reduce fumbling and make it easier to vary settings precisely. The switch S2, which selects either the full-wave or half-wave control, should logically be positioned between the knobs so as to make

FIG. 2-7. *A heavy piece of aluminum was added to the cover of the enclosure to heatsink the triac and SCR.*

its purpose immediately apparent. The LED and neon light are effective when placed in the index position of the two knobs. That way they indicate which knob is functioning and the LED gives an idea of the power output. Placing the controls this way reduces the amount of labeling you'll have to do. Switch S1 needs to be labeled separately and each knob should be labeled HALF-WAVE or FULL-WAVE.

Point-to-point wiring is probably the most effective way of wiring this project. Some builders look down on this method of construction, thinking it is haphazard and prone to error. This is not so; there are steps you can take to make it as systematic and trouble-free as printed circuit board construction. The first thing to do when setting out to wire a circuit like the one for this project is to mark where all the tie points exist on the securely mounted components like potentiometers and switches. This has been done with circles in FIG. 2-8. Next, figure where new tie points will have to be added. This has been done with squares on the same diagram. For this project, you'll need about ten additional tie-points, but more or less may be necessary depending on the actual layout of the project. Use solder lug strips for tie points, installing a few more than you think you might need.

Because this circuit has many components and quite a few tie points, it is probably best that you find some way of distinguishing them. Numbering the tie points is an effective way of keeping track of them. Give each point a number on the schematic, as in FIG. 2-8, and number the corresponding solder lugs so you can identify which is which and avoid misconnections. As you wire each component in, lightly draw over it with a pen on the schematic to make it clear what stage you're at. Sometimes this is referred to as "red-lining." By numbering your tie points and "red-lining," you can effectively translate a schematic into a real project without much chance for mistakes.

MORE USES OF THE CIRCUIT

The full-wave control circuit of FIG. 2-3 is quite effective at reducing the AC power that a load consumes without dissipating much power itself. Permanently built into various circuits, it can effectively reduce the electrical size of heating elements, lights, and transformers. A little module like that shown in FIG. 2-9, using the circuit from the full-wave discussion and the component values from the schematic in FIG. 2-6, can be built into a circuit to vary its output. For example, if you need a 500-watt heating element to heat an apparatus but only have a 750-watt element on hand, a small phase control module could effectively reduce the wattage consumed. Keep in mind that for this load, an 8-amp triac would still be needed to maintain an adequate safety margin at 750 watts. Even though the load would only receive 500 watts on the average, there would be times when its full current is drawn through the triac. Thorough heatsinking is necessary when using triacs continuously at high current. Without proper heatsinking, they are only good for a fraction of their full rated current.

Fluorescent Lights

You can dim fluorescent lights with the full-wave phase control circuit, but a dimming ballast is necessary for smooth operation. These ballasts are available at lighting stores, large hardware stores, and the electrical departments of some do-it-yourself stores. They are designed as a direct replacement for the ballast in 48-inch shop lights. A wiring diagram for installing one of these ballasts in an existing light fixture or building your own is often

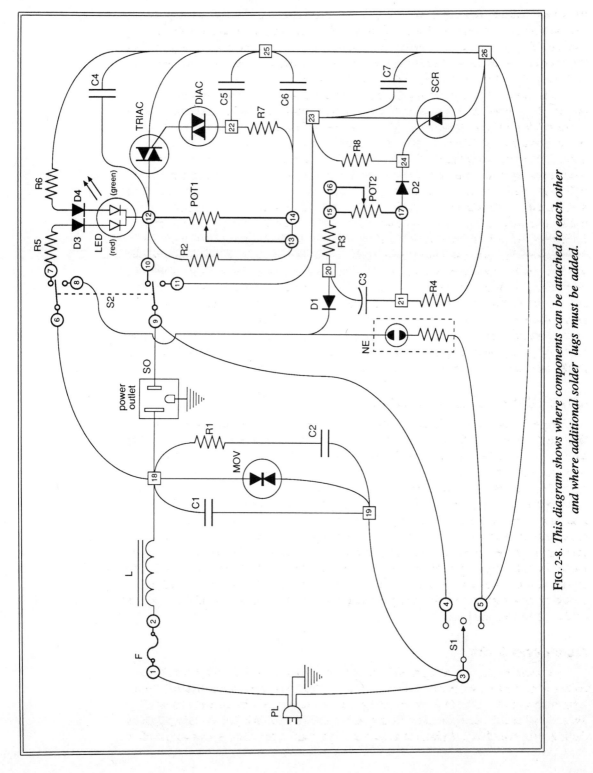

FIG. 2-8. *This diagram shows where components can be attached to each other and where additional solder lugs must be added.*

FIG. 2-9. *A compact phase-control circuit like this has many applications.*

provided in home electrical wiring guides or with the ballast itself. Their installation is mostly a wire-for-wire replacement of the existing ballast. Even without a new ballast though, some dimming control can be obtained over fluorescent lights simply by plugging the light into the controller, but it will probably flicker after awhile.

PARTS LIST:

Variable AC Power Controller

C1, C5, C6	.1μF, 200V
C2	.18 to .22μF, 200V
C3	50μF, 50V or better electrolytic
C4, C7	.01μF, 200V bypass capacitors, value not critical
R1	330 to 390Ω, all resistors ¼W unless indicated.
R2	200KΩ or whatever gives smoothest response
R3	270Ω, 1W
R4	5.6KΩ, 2W
R5, R6	3KΩ, 2W (3300Ω, 2W resistor in parallel with a 33KΩ, ¼W resistor)
R7	10KΩ
R8	470Ω
POT 1	100KΩ linear taper
POT 2	10KΩ linear taper, 1W
F	5A SLO-BLO fuse
NE	Neon panel indicator with built-in dropping resistor
L	18 feet of solid AWG 18, neatly wound on ¼″ ferrite rod or 70 to 100μH, 5A choke
MOV	S10V-S14K130 or equivalent metal oxide varistor
TRIAC	6A, 200V or better triac
SCR	6A, 200V or better SCR
DIAC	D-30 or equivalent diac
D1-D4	200V, 1A or better rectifier diodes
LED	Two-color three-lead LED
S1	Three-position toggle switch, 5A or better
S2	DPDT toggle switch, 5A or better
PL	Line cord and wall plug
SO	Grounded power outlet

PLUS, suitable enclosure, knobs, TO-220 mounting hardware, panel mount fuseholder, solder lugs, rub-on letters, hook-up wire, and solder.

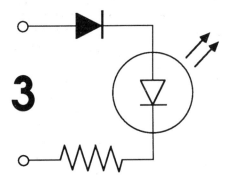

3

Regulated Voltage and Current Supply

This versatile project is a portable device that takes the place of:

→ low-voltage DC adaptors and battery eliminators
→ a bench supply with regulated voltage and current outputs
→ a nickel-cadmium battery charger
→ a trickle charger for car batteries

It has the following specifications:

Inputs: EXTERNAL INPUT binding posts: up to 40 volts AC/DC
                Line cord and wall plug: 120 VAC

Outputs: 3V,6V,7.5V,9V (Adjustable 1.25V to 37V)
                1.5 amps maximum for powering projects and battery-operated devices
                25 mA, 50 mA, 100 mA, 125 mA, 400 mA (Adjustable 12 to 500 mA)
                    for recharging batteries

RIPPLE REJECTION: 80 dB

REGULATION: Line: 0.01%/V, Load: 0.1%

    With these excellent specifications, this project could be very useful around the home and shop. Its output is stable enough and has such low ripple that it would make an excellent piece of test equipment at an electronics workbench. But one of the design goals was for this power supply to be portable and adaptable to different situations away from home.

Physically, it was designed to be rugged and compact. See FIG. 3-1. Electrically, the circuit it uses is protected against short circuits, reverse polarity, overcurrent, and overheating. Its input terminals are indifferent to polarity reversal and can accept AC or DC voltages. For easy connections, the inputs and outputs are all five-way binding posts and are also accessible at a terminal strip for more permanent attachments. These features make the power supply equally useful in remote and mobile applications as it is at home.

THE CIRCUIT

The complete power supply circuit is shown in FIG. 3-2. It is composed of two separate regulators, each with its own output. The voltage regulator is the circuit built around IC1. The current regulator is built around IC2. The input to both regulators is filtered by capacitors C1. Switch S1 selects as the input either the built-in transformer or the binding posts labeled EXTERNAL INPUT. The diodes D1 through D4 form a bridge rectifier that insures the correct polarity from either an AC or DC source plugged into the external input.

The Voltage Regulator Circuit

IC1 is an LM317K adjustable 1.25- to 37-volt regulator chip. It maintains its output voltage constantly 1.25 volts higher than the voltage at its adjust terminal despite any changes in the supply and load. The voltage regulator circuit sets the desired output using this terminal.

Because of its low resistance, R1 tries to pull the IC's adjust pin up to the output voltage. If this were all there was to the circuit, the regulator's output would simply be a little bit less than its full input voltage. This is because the voltage at the adjust pin is not limited in any way and can rise as high as the output voltage.

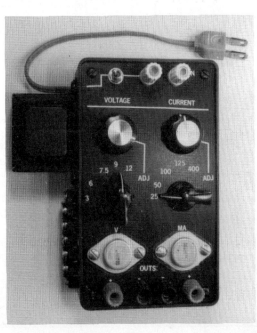

FIG. 3-1. *The small size of the completed project shown here belies its many features and impressive specifications.*

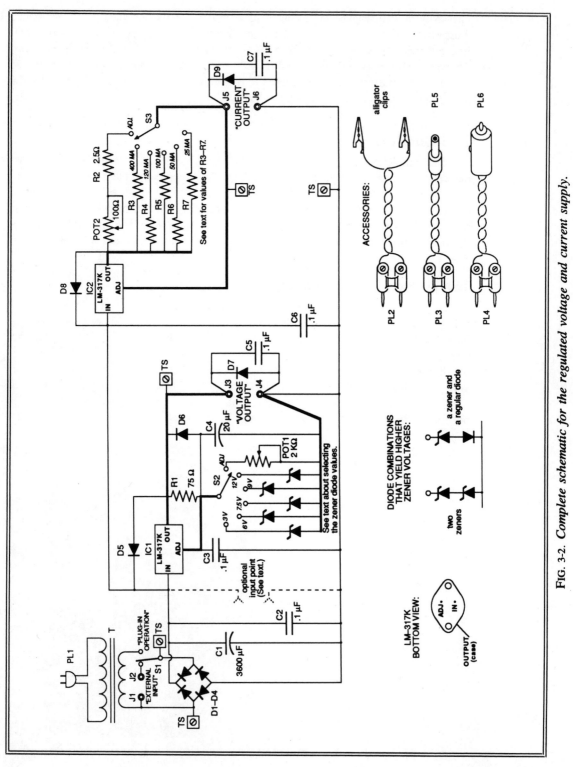

FIG. 3-2. *Complete schematic for the regulated voltage and current supply.*

But with S2 connecting one of the zener diodes to it, the adjust pin is pulled down to the selected zener's voltage. By switching among different zener diodes, different fixed output voltages are possible. When S2 is in the ADJUST position, the potentiometer POT1 forms a voltage divider with R1. The voltage at the adjust pin of the IC depends on its setting and varies from zero to the maximum voltage. The output voltage tracks this voltage, except it is always 1.25 volts higher.

The rest of the components in the voltage regulator circuit improve its performance and provide protection. Capacitor C4 filters out any ripple voltage appearing at the adjust terminal, because ripple at this point would otherwise appear greatly amplified at the supply's output. Capacitors C2, C3, and C5 are bypass capacitors that improve the supply's response to transients, which large electrolytics are sluggish in reacting to.

Diodes D6 and D7 are for protection in case of misconnections. If the output is shorted, D6 provides a discharge path for C2, reducing the voltage at IC1's adjust pin to zero and consequently bringing its output to a low 1.25 volts. Diode D7 provides protection from reverse voltages that might accidentally be placed across the output. Other protection is already built into the IC: automatic output current limiting, power dissipation limiting, and an automatic thermal cutoff to keep the internal temperature of the chip under 170 degrees celsius.

The function of diode D5 is not obvious. It is in the circuit to bypass the IC if the load is momentarily at a higher potential than the supply output, allowing the supply to act briefly as a current sink. The need for this occurs when reactive loads and some audio circuits are driven by this project. The diode is included mainly to improve the supply's operation with high fidelity circuits, presenting them with a low impedance, even when the supply is reverse biased by the circuit it is driving.

The Current Regulator Circuit

IC2 is another LM317K chip, but this time set up as a current regulator. It's output passes through whatever resistor is selected by S3, developing a voltage that is proportional to the amount of current the output draws. Even though it is part of a current regulator circuit, the IC still acts as a voltage regulator. It varies its output voltage to maintain it at a constant level 1.25 volts above its adjustment terminal. If the load attempts to draw excessive current, the increased voltage drop across the setting resistor brings the difference between the output and adjust voltages to more than 1.25 volts. This lowers the output voltage of the IC and limits the current. In actual operation, this doesn't happen as a series of steps of course, but occurs continuously.

The proper resistor value for each fixed current setting is given by the equation $R = 1.25/I$. The adjustable current output is obtained by switching in POT2, a 100-ohm potentiometer. The 2.5-ohm resistor in series with POT2 limits the maximum output current to 500 milliamps.

Diodes D8 and D9 do the same thing for the current supply that D5 and D7 did for the adjustable voltage supply. Capacitors C6 and C7 are bypass capacitors with similar functions to those in the voltage regulator. Bypassing isn't as important in this circuit because it isn't likely to to be used with critical equipment. Still, the capacitors are good at reducing any tendency of the circuit to self-oscillate and will clamp any voltage spikes that occur from switching.

CONSTRUCTION

Before you build the power supply, decide on what preset voltages and currents you want for its output. Select voltages according to the equipment that the supply will be used with. Choose the current presets to correspond to the charging currents of whatever nicad batteries you have. The values chosen for the prototype correspond to the typical charging rates for dry cells and very small nicads (25 milliamps), AA nicads (50 milliamps), some C and D cells (100 milliamps), other C and D cells (120 milliamps), and high capacity D cells (400 milliamps).

Once the choices of preset current and voltage values have been made, don't run out and buy the zener diodes and resistors right away. It's much more practical to get an assorted variety of low voltage zeners and low ohmage resistors and use them in series and parallel to get the exact voltage and current values experimentally.

The output of the voltage regulator will be 1.25 volts higher than the zener voltage and may vary slightly from one IC to another. So the best way to arrive at the correct zeners to use is to connect an accurate voltmeter with a load of about 25 ohms across the output and substitute different zeners into the circuit. Zeners can be put in series to obtain higher voltages. General purpose diodes have a zener voltage too—usually about 0.7 volts for most silicon diodes. Use an inexpensive diode like an IN914 in series with a zener to increase the output voltage slightly. Remember that regular diodes must be connected in the opposite way when part of this circuit though; see FIG. 3-2 for an example. When setting each of the voltage presets, you should be able to come within a few tenths of a volt by connecting two or more zener and regular diodes in series.

Select the current-setting resistors in pretty much the same way. Connect an accurate ammeter to the output of the regulator in series with a load resistor of about 50 ohms for the higher settings and 100 ohms for the lower settings. Using series and parallel resistor combinations, arrive at a value within a few milliamps of the target for each preset. Keep in mind that the output current must pass through the setting resistor and causes it to dissipate heat. Hence, you'll need resistors with power ratings equal to 1.25 times I, but because they will be connected in series and parallel, this shouldn't pose much of a problem. Any setting of less than 200 milliamps should be able to use a ½ watt resistor comfortably. However, using higher wattage resistors will increase the stability of the supply, because their values change less as they heat up.

The prototype fits very nicely into a Radio Shack #270-627 project box. If you use the same type of box, the drilling guide in FIG. 3-3 will be quite helpful. The only disadvantage of this small box is that there is not enough room inside for the transformer; it will have to be mounted on the outside. Even if you use a different sized enclosure and don't take advantage of the drilling guide, make sure to mount the ICs on some form of heatsink and be sure the binding posts are spaced ¾ inch apart to accommodate dual banana plug connectors.

Most of the parts attach either to the aluminum panel or to the parts that do attach to it. As FIG. 3-4 shows, just about all of the project can be constructed by point-to-point wiring among these components. The first step then is to drill all the panel holes in preparation for installing the components. When that is done, you might want to paint the panel flat black to match the rest of the enclosure before mounting the parts. Mount the ICs in TO-3 transistor sockets using a mica washer and thermal compound between the chassis panel and each of them for electrical insulation.

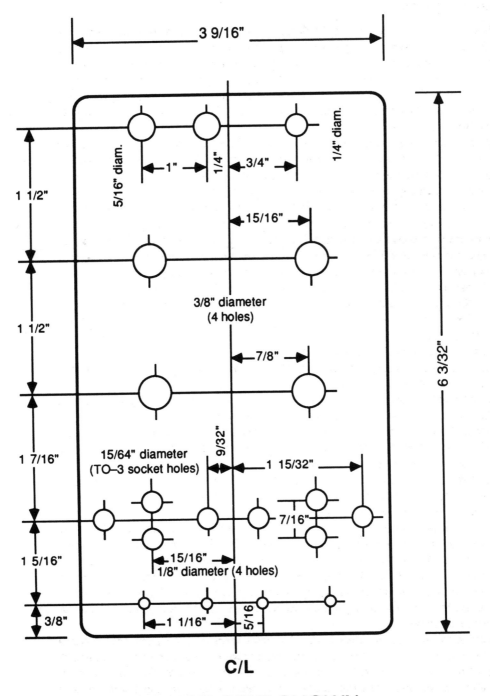

INTERIOR SIDE SHOWN

FIG. 3-3. *This panel-drilling guide makes building the project easier.*

FIG. 3-4. *Most of the circuit was built on the inside front panel as this photograph indicates.*

After installing the panel-mounted components—the switches, potentiometers, and binding posts—do the point-to-point wiring. FIGURE 3-5 is intended as a guide for this step because the physical placement of some of the components will affect their operation. Capacitors C2, C3, and C6 should be mounted close to the ICs and capacitors C5 and C7 at the output terminals. Connect one side of R1 directly to the output of IC1. Use a heavy wire from ground to the tie point that the zeners and POT1 attach to. Heavy wires should also be used from the output connections of the ICs to the output terminals of the supply. All these steps slightly improve load regulation and lower ripple.

The power supply components—the line cord, transformer, bridge rectifier, and capacitor—mount in the bottom half of the chassis wherever they fit best. Unless the transformer is very small, it can only be attached to the outside of the box. The capacitor should fit snugly in the bottom.

This bottom section is also the only place where a terminal strip for inputs and outputs will fit. If you decide to include one of these in your version, you'll need one with five terminals—two for AC/DC input, one for the voltage output, one for the current output, and a common ground for the outputs. A terminal strip will fit nicely along one side of the box next to the transformer as FIG. 3-6 shows. Besides the convenience of accessible input and output terminals it provides, a terminal strip makes constructing this project a little easier by serving as five tie points for the internal wiring.

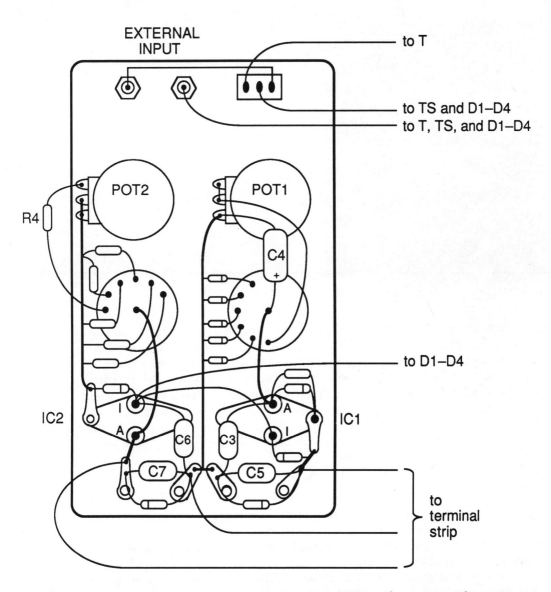

EXTERNAL
INPUT

to T

to TS and D1–D4
to T, TS, and D1–D4

POT2

R4

POT1

C4
+

to D1–D4

IC2

I

A

A

I

IC1

C6

C3

C7

C5

to
terminal
strip

FIG. 3-5. *Follow this diagram for the project's internal wiring and component placement.*

Use foresight in deciding the length of the line cord. It should be long enough to be usable, yet short enough to be uncumbersome when the supply is used in remote applications. Of course, it can be eliminated altogether if you use a removable line cord with a connector.

The final step in construction is wiring together the two halves of the case and attaching the aluminum faceplate to the plastic bottom. To make the power supply useful, construct a number of input and output connectors. In the prototype, dual banana jacks with ¾ inch

FIG. 3-6. *This view of the project shows the five-position terminal strip installed on the outside of the enclosure.*

spacing were chosen. These are good because they are stackable; you can plug one into the other or plug them into five-way binding posts. The common spacing allows the input and output connectors to be interchangeable with each other and other electronic equipment.

Make up a few connecting wires with the dual banana plugs on one end and other connectors on the other according to what the power supply will be used with. Alligator clips are best for battery charging or experiments and can temporarily double for most other connectors. Two sets of wires terminated in alligator clips are a good idea. An additional cigarette lighter plug is a necessity for mobile use. So are power input plugs to fit portable battery operated-equipment.

USE

For high current outputs at low voltage, it's best that the input supply to the ICs does not exceed the expected output by the maximum difference the ICs can handle. This is because the ICs are self-limited to 20 watts total dissipation. Since they are rated at a maximum of 2.2 amps, this isn't a factor unless you have a voltage difference between their input and output greater than about 10 volts. Using a lower supply voltage to the LM317Ks reduces the amount of power they must dissipate, allowing them to run cooler at high current. You can supply a lower voltage through the external input terminals but if you plan on using a lot of low voltage devices that draw a lot of current, use a built-in transformer with a lower voltage secondary or one with a center tap that it can be switched to. Because the ICs require only a two-volt minimum difference between their input and output for operation, the supply voltage can go quite low before performance suffers.

To use this project as a car battery charger, plug the cigarette lighter plug into the car's socket, observing the correct polarity. Plug the banana plugs into the current output of the supply and turn the adjustable current knob to maximum. This will be adequate to charge all but a very dead battery overnight. However, for more than one night or for continuous use, leave the current setting at approximately 100 milliamps.

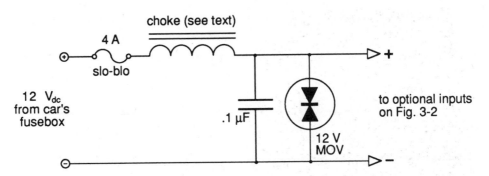

FIG. 3-7. *This circuit allows the circuit in* FIG. 3-2 *to operate from a vehicle's DC supply.*

It is possible to charge nicad batteries according to the directions on their labels. This usually means charging them 12 to 14 hours at a current rate equal to $\frac{1}{10}$ of their amp-hour rating. Dry cells and alkalines can be charged at a 25 milliamps fixed position or with the adjustable potentiometer near its minimum position.

MORE USES OF THE CIRCUIT

A useful application for the power supply circuit is a low voltage outlet built into a car or other vehicle. Combining the circuit in FIG. 3-7 with the one in FIG. 3-2, you can build a permanent low voltage DC outlet and battery charger into your car, boat, or other vehicle. With a 12-volt input, it can only supply outputs up to 10 volts, but that's not much of a limiting factor to portable battery-operated equipment.

The circuit's only purpose is to reduce ignition and motor-induced noise in the vehicle's 12-volt supply. The MOV is optional; use it only if your electrical system is particularly noisy and you're cautious about voltage spikes damaging a sensitive load. The diode provides protection against reverse polarity because the output of this circuit goes right to the input of the ICs, bypassing D1-D4 of the main circuit. The coil is a hash filter. You can buy chokes manufactured specifically for mobile electrical systems, salvage one from a junked car stereo, or wind your own: 100 turns of AWG 18 wire on a ¼ inch ferrite bar.

Build the circuit in FIG. 3-7 onto an aluminum panel and mount it in the door or dash of the vehicle. The IC's can be heatsunk to the panel, but be sure to electrically insulate their cases from the panel with mica washers and thermal compound.

PARTS LIST:

Regulated Voltage and Current Supply

C1	3600μF, 50V or better, electrolytic
C2, C3, C5-C7	.1μF bypass capacitors, value not critical
C4	20μF, 50V, electrolytic, value not critical
R1	75Ω, (all resistors ¼W unless indicated)
R2	2.5Ω, 1W
R3 through R7	See text about determining values experimentally
R3	Approx. 3.13Ω, 1W
R4	Approx. 10.4Ω
R5	Approx. 12.5Ω
R6	Approx. 25Ω
R7	Approx. 50Ω
POT 1	2KΩ linear taper potentiometer
POT 2	100Ω linear taper potentiometer, 1W
T	Step-down transformer with 24V secondary
IC1, IC2	LM-317K adjustable voltage regulator IC
D1 through D4	4A, 50V or better bridge rectifier
D5 through D9	3A 50V or better rectifier diodes
ZENER DIODES	Wattage not critical, see text about values
S1	SPST mini toggle switch, 5A
S2, S3	Six-position rotary switch
PL1	Line cord and wall plug
PL2-PL4	Dual ¾" spaced banana plugs
PL5	Power supply plug to fit portables
PL6	Cigarette lighter plug
J1-J6	Binding posts
TS	5 position terminal strip
ALLIGATOR CLIPS	

PLUS, 6 ¼" × 3¾" × 2" minibox (R.S. #270-627 or equiv.), knobs, TO-3 mounting hardware, solder, hook-up wire, and rub-on letters.

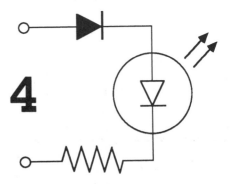

Infrared Remote Control Relayer

This project sends the command signals from any hand-held infrared remote control unit to a remote control VCR, cable converter, or satellite-TV receiver in another room. It's purpose is mainly to save its user from running back and forth between a second TV set and the machine that is controlling it. If you have a VCR or other remote-controllable video source in one room and another TV set installed in a second room, this project is almost a necessity. Without it, you'd have to keep getting up to change channels or operate the VCR. See FIG. 4-1.

The usefulness of this project extends beyond just video systems though, to all devices that use infrared beams to transmit information. Stereo systems that use infrared remote controls can make use of this project if their extension speakers are in another room. Even some computer keyboards, electronic scales, and other household appliances transmit information over an infrared beam to their control console. If this project was added to one of these devices, it could be used in another room or its components could be kept farther apart than they otherwise could.

It's not an entirely new idea. There are commercial devices available that do what this project does, but they cost a lot more. At a lower price than the commercial remote control extenders sell for, you can build yourself this project which has nearly the range and is more versatile.

It's only drawback is the short distance the relayer box requires the remote be held from it. Although the relayer box can be many rooms away from the VCR it is controlling as necessary, the remote control must be within a foot or two of it for the control signal to be relayed properly. The box is very small and easy to place though, so this shouldn't pose much of a problem. The only situation in which longer range would be

FIG. 4-1. *This part of the finished project receives the infrared control signals.*

needed is if there were several viewers watching the second TV at the same time and they all wanted to use the remote control.

The restriction on range is unavoidable. Infrared light emitted from a source point diminishes greatly with distance—just as with any kind of light. A very sensitive receiver is required if it is to be separated from the transmitter by more than a few feet. Commercial remote control extenders and the original remote controlled devices themselves use a shielded assembly containing a photodiode and sensitive high gain circuitry that wouldn't be practical to build yourself. It's much easier to buy the circuitry required for long range than make it yourself. But why buy one? If the limited range of this project is tolerable, then its construction cost of under 10 dollars makes it an attractive alternative to commercial remote control extenders.

Like its commercial competition, this project sends its control signals over the same coaxial cable that carries the video signal to the extension TV. This is a great convenience because it allows you to use a wire that's already installed, rather than bothering putting in a separate one. And like the commercial models, it doesn't interfere with the normal use of the remote control with a VCR or other video source.

But because you build it yourself, this project offers more flexibility than the commercial models. It can also be made to work over an ordinary pair of wires with infrared remote control stereos and other equipment that doesn't use video wiring. This additional possibility makes this project even more attractive since commercial models do not offer it. Now that infrared remote controls are finding their way into more and more consumer electronic products, it is likely that its additional versatility will make this project more valuable as time goes by.

THE CIRCUIT

Because it sacrifices long range, the circuit can be quite simple. FIGURE 4-2 is the complete schematic. When the power switch S in the relayer is on, phototransistor Q

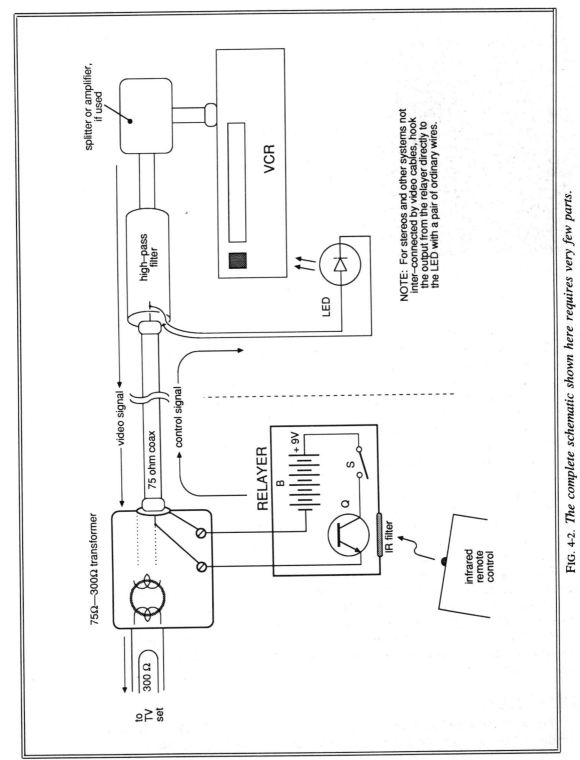

splitter or amplifier, if used

VCR

high-pass filter

LED

NOTE: For stereos and other systems not inter-connected by video cables, hook the output from the relayer directly to the LED with a pair of ordinary wires.

75Ω–300Ω transformer

to TV set

300 Ω

video signal

75 ohm coax

control signal

RELAYER

B

+ 9V

S

Q

IR filter

infrared remote control

FIG. 4-2. *The complete schematic shown here requires very few parts.*

modulates the current that flows through the infrared LED from the battery. Every pulse of infrared radiation received at Q is duplicated by the infrared LED's output.

The phototransistor is shielded from ambient light by a small piece of plastic infrared filter. Infrared filter material looks dark red and is almost totally opaque to visible light. It is sold at low cost by many of the surplus dealers listed in Chapter 23. If you can't obtain the right filter material conveniently though, a thin piece of ordinary dark red translucent plastic can be used instead. The purpose of shielding is so that the infrared phototransistor, whose response to visible light is excellent, doesn't continuously draw current from the battery. Although the circuit draws very little current when shielded this way, the power switch extends the battery's life if it is turned off when the relayer is not in use.

The purpose of the transformer and the high-pass filter shown in FIG. 4-2 is to block the infrared control signals from entering the video equipment. This is necessary so the relayer can use the same wiring as the video signal. There are three circuits that can be used to split off the control signal while passing only video signals. Use whichever of the following approaches is most convenient for you, although the best way is to use a transformer at the TV end and a high-pass filter at the VCR end:

→ A Radio Shack high-pass filter (R.S. #15-579), designed to eliminate amateur radio interference from video signals, can be used (if it is slightly modified).

→ An ordinary 75-to-300-ohm video matching transformer will block the infrared signal to the TV in addition to its usual function. This is a particularly good alternative because transformers are inexpensive, readily available, and often necessary anyway to match the output of modern video equipment to older TV sets.

→ As a third alternative, the circuit in FIG. 4-3 can be built into either the TV set, the video signal source (VCR, cable converter, etc.), or the relayer box.

CONSTRUCTION

Practically any small project box can house the relayer circuitry as long as it blocks visible light falling on the phototransistor. The prototype shown in FIG. 4-1 used one from Radio Shack. It came with a pre-drilled perfboard that fits neatly inside the enclosure and allows the components to be easily mounted. Similar enclosures are available in all parts stores and most of the mail order companies.

Using this enclosure or another suitable one, install the power switch so it is accessible from the front of the enclosure. A piece of infrared filter material should be mounted in a ½-inch hole in the front as well, with the phototransistor right behind it. Observe the designated polarity of the phototransistor and the nine-volt battery, or the project won't work and could be damaged.

Connect the relayer box with thin two-conductor wire to the high-pass circuit used to split the control signal from the video signals meant for the TV. Directions follow for hooking up the relayer box to each of the three alternatives listed previously.

Using a Transformer

Some video-matching transformers provide two screw terminals as an FM output. These are the most convenient transformers to use because the screw terminals provide

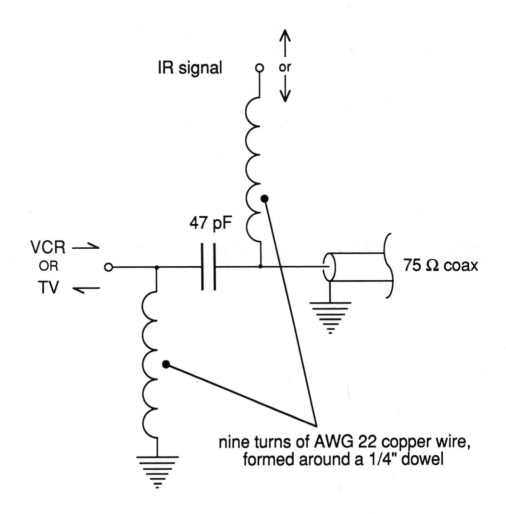

IR signal   or

47 pF

VCR
OR
TV

75 Ω coax

nine turns of AWG 22 copper wire,
formed around a 1/4" dowel

FIG. 4-3. *Use this schematic if you wish to build
the high-pass filter into an existing piece of equipment.*

a place to attach the wire connecting the relayer to the coaxial cable. To modify one of these transformers, open it up by removing the metal ring around the F-connector input. Cut and remove the existing wires to the FM output terminals. Now, wire those terminals directly to the F connector so they go directly to the cable from the signal source. Close up the case, leaving the rest of the internal circuitry untouched. Use the FM output screw terminals to connect the wire from the remote control relayer to the coaxial cable from the VCR.

Modifying a Commercial High-Pass Filter

Using a Radio Shack #15-579 or similar high-pass filter to split the infrared and video signals requires opening its case to connect a two-conductor wire. First remove the outer plastic jacket that encloses the filter. Then use a knife to remove the rubber grommet from around the short length of coaxial cable protruding from one of the ends. This should reveal a metal washer fitted into the aluminum sleeve. Remove the washer with needle-nosed pliers, and set it aside. With a few taps on the F-connector at the other end, slide the inner circuitry out of the aluminum sleeve.

Observe that the circuitry is encased in some kind of potting compound and wrapped in plastic. Cut the plastic wrap off and chip away just enough potting compound around the F connector to make its terminals accessible. Solder a few feet of thin, two-conductor wire to the connector. This wire will later be connected to the infrared LED or to the remote relayer box. Using hot-melt glue or epoxy cement, repot the filter and replace it in its aluminum sleeve. Have the wire leave the case alongside the piece of coaxial cable. It should exit through the washer that previously held the grommet. FIGURE 4-4 shows this type of splitter modified for use in this project and connected to an infrared LED.

INSTALLING THE REMOTE CONTROL RELAYER

Placement of the infrared LED depends on the VCR or other equipment it will be used with. It should be mounted a short distance from the sensing window on the equipment but ideally should be kept as unobtrusive as possible. It also should not block the window totally since you might want to use the remote control directly in the same room with it. One possibility is mounting the LED in a flat piece of clear plastic taped or glued to the side of the equipment. If the equipment is kept in a cabinet, the sides of the cabinet can provide a convenient mounting surface for the LED. Be sure to connect it the right way. The correct polarity can be determined by retracing the wiring back to the relayer box or by trial and error using a regular visible-light LED as an indicator and having someone press the control buttons in the remote location.

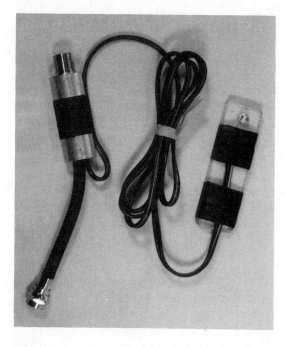

FIG. 4-4. *Radio Shack #15-579 filter modified for use with the prototype.*

Due to its short range, the remote relayer should be kept as close to the favorite viewing position as possible. It's small size should make this easy. Leave the transformer or other high-pass filter mounted on the back of the TV set to keep the video signal path as short as possible. The extra distance should be made up by the wire from the relayer. If this wire is too long, it can get in the way if its not managed neatly. However, a long wire allows the relayer box to be conveniently moved to different locations within the room to overcome the range limitation.

If you have video signal splitters or a distribution amplifier connected to the output of your VCR, be sure to connect the infrared splitter after all that. The coaxial cable that runs between the high-pass filter at the VCR and the transformer at the TV end should have no interruptions. Restricting the control signal to the TV the relayer is to be used with eliminates the possibility of interference with other sets in the video system.

FURTHER USE

More and more stereo systems and other home electronic devices are being sold with infrared remote controls. As it does for video systems, this project can relay the remote control signals to these devices use from another room. The video cable and the splitters aren't necessary. Instead, you need a separate pair of wires connecting the relayer to the LED. The typical frequencies that infrared remote control systems use are in the same range as audio signals, making simultaneous use of speaker wires impossible.

If you have more than one remote TV set, two or more remote control relayers can be used with a single infrared LED. Only the signal splitters and relayer boxes have to be duplicated at the remote ends. Be sure to use the same polarity though when connecting each relayer to the coaxial cable.

PARTS LIST:

Infrared Remote Control Relayer

(Due to certain options, not all parts listed here are required.)

C   47pF ceramic disk capacitor (exact value not critical)
L   (2 required) nine ¼" diameter turns of 24 gauge magnet wire
B   9-volt battery
Q and LED   Infrared emitter/detector pair (R.S. #276-142) [for additional phototransistors, use TIL-414 (R.S. #276-145 or equiv.)]
S   SPST mini toggle switch

PLUS, 75Ω-to-300Ω video matching transformer (R.S. #15-1139 or equiv.), high-pass filter (R.S. #15-79 or equiv.), battery clip, thin two-conductor wire, suitable enclosure, and solder.

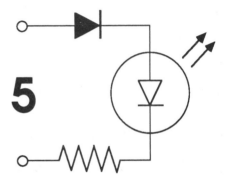

5

Electronic Distance Measuring System

This project is a tool for taking measurements of medium and long distances, around curves, over uneven courses, and in situations where a ruler would be unsuitable. Its heart is an inexpensive calculator, modified to count pulses obtained from two distance measuring devices: a wheel on the end of a handle for medium distances (FIG. 5-1) and an attachment to a bicycle (FIGS. 5-7 and 5-9) for measuring long distances. The distance covered by these devices is continuously displayed by the calculator in your choice of units.

A calculator is used because it is an easy way to get the necessary counting, driver, and display circuitry in a neat and inexpensive package. Also, once a calculator has measured a distance, doing calculations with it is a simple matter because the measurement doesn't have to be entered separately. The project thus takes on a usefulness that a separate calculator and ruler couldn't possibly have.

THE CIRCUIT

The circuit is shown in FIG. 5-2. It is very simple because the calculator does most of the work. The input devices are designed to produce a certain number of pulses per unit of distance they cover. These pulses are used to electrically close the "=" key contacts on the calculator. Assuming the calculator has a constant-add function like most do, it can be set up to add a certain amount to its display with each pulse. The amount it adds with each pulse would be the distance each pulse from the measurer represents.

The calculator obtains its input pulses from two rather similar distance measuring accessories. The wheel with the handle shown in FIG. 5-1 is a wooden disc with a number of holes drilled in its face through which light can pass as it rotates. As it is wheeled over

FIG. 5-1. *The measuring wheel in use with the modified calculator.*

a path to produce a measurement, its rotation interrupts the infrared beam passing between the infrared LED and phototransistor Q1. This causes current from the battery to alternately bias transistor Q2 on and off, electrically closing the "=" key contacts. In the case of the prototype that has four holes in the wheel, the calculator receives four pulses per revolution. The amount it adds to its display for each pulse must therefore be set to one-fourth the circumference of the wheel.

To measure distances of several miles, the calculator is mounted on a bicycle. The bike measures distance with the circumference of its front wheel. Each time the wheel makes a revolution, a small magnet mounted on it passes next to a reed switch, causing transistor Q2 to briefly conduct and adding a count to the calculator display. With each count, the calculator adds the circumference of the wheel to the total distance it displays.

A transistor is connected across the calculator's "=" key to electrically close it. This keeps the actual switching that occurs in close physical proximity to the calculator itself rather than in the reed switch. This is an important consideration because calculators often "look" for a pressed key by using high frequency signals to scan each of the keys in a matrix rather than separately connecting each one to the processor chip. To the high frequencies the calculator uses, a long wire connecting it to the wheel or the bike attachment would present a high impedance which it is best to avoid. So the purpose of transistor Q2 is to keep the switching confined to the vicinity of the calculator.

The transistor can be triggered in two ways so it can be used with the two types of measuring circuits the calculator is likely to encounter. One way to trigger the transistor is with a voltage pulse across its base and emitter, but this requires a triggering circuit

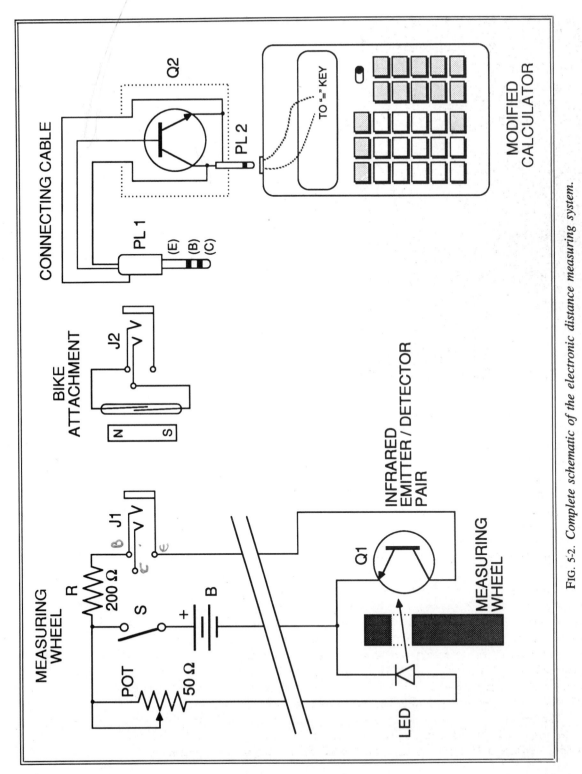

FIG. 5-2. *Complete schematic of the electronic distance measuring system.*

45

with its own source of power. Another way of triggering the transistor is by briefly connecting its base to its collector. This method requires no external source of power.

Since the measuring wheel already uses a battery supply to power the infrared LED, it makes use of the first method and is connected across the base and emitter of Q2. The bike attachment, with no power source of its own, is connected across the base and collector in the second method. The connecting cable makes all three of the transistor's leads accessible at its three-conductor plug. It was designed to interface with the two attachments previously discussed and with any other ones you devise on your own.

CONSTRUCTION

As you might have guessed, building this project involves more mechanical construction than electrical. The place to begin is choosing and modifying the calculator. Then, add one or both of the input devices to make it a complete electronic measuring system.

Modifying the Calculator

The first step is shopping around for a suitable calculator. There are three characteristics that it must have to work with this project: 1) the calculator must have a constant-add function; 2) it must be capable of accepting inputs at a fast rate; and 3) it must have a case that is removable and has room for a small input jack.

Most inexpensive calculators have the constant-add function. They repeatedly add the same number to the display when their "=" key is pressed, accumulating a multiple of that number. However, just to be certain, test any calculator you intend to buy by pressing "1,+,=,=,=." The display should read "4."

The ability to count rapid inputs to the "=" key varies widely among calculators and is harder to test for. A preliminary test can be performed without opening the case by pressing "1,+" and then pressing "=" as fast as you can, making sure that the calculator is registering every entry. If you have an adjustable low frequency oscillator available, you can check the maximum count rate by connecting it to the calculator via transistor Q2. But without recourse to that method, use this general rule that seems to hold over all calculators: the higher the supply voltage that a calculator operates on, the higher its maximum count rate will be. Solar calculators with their very low supply voltage are unsuitably slow. Those that operate on one or two cells are slightly faster but only six-and-nine-volt calculators have a count rate that is suitable. The calculator used in the prototype has a six-volt battery supply and is good for up to 12 counts/second, which is sufficient for this project.

When you have selected a calculator that meets the above two requirements and has a suitable case, open it up. Find the contacts coming from the keyboard. If you can spot the "=" key contacts by inspection, you are fortunate. If not, use a jumper wire and locate the appropriate contacts by trial and error. Find a suitable place to mount a ⅛-inch phone jack. If the calculator has an AC adaptor input, disconnect it and use it for the input jack instead. An adaptor is useless anyway when you're walking around or riding a bike. Carefully wire the "=" contacts to the jack as shown in FIG. 5-3. Finally, close the case, making sure the wires don't obstruct the keys or the display. You might want to label the jack on the outside of the calculator so no one mistakenly plugs an AC adaptor into it.

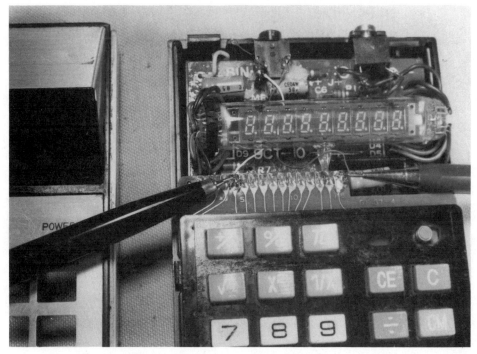

FIG. 5-3. *The two pencils show where thin wires were added
to the keyboard contacts to connect across the "=" key.*

To finish off the calculator part of the electronic measuring system, construct a cable to connect the calculator to the wheel or bicycle. FIGURE 5-2 shows how to wire a suitable cable. Be sure to connect Q2 across the "=" key with the proper polarity. Usually only one way properly registers with the calculator.

Although an attempt was made in the diagram to show transistor Q2 built into the plug, it can be built into the calculator as well. Either way, all three of the transistor's leads will be connected to the cable. Whether you build the transistor into the calculator or into the plug determines whether the calculator needs a three- or a two-conductor plug and jack. The three-conductor wire and plug can be made from store-bought pieces or salvaged from a junked pair of lightweight stereo headphones. The wire should be no more than two feet long or it will get in the way when it is used with the bike accessory.

Making the Measuring Wheel

Construction of the measuring wheel is simplified by the fact that its circumference doesn't have to be a convenient number. Its value only has to be keyed into the calculator once each time it is used. The calculator is as adept at adding messy numbers like 19.226547 inches as it is at adding nice numbers like 20 inches. With this in mind, find a convenient disc with a diameter approximately 5 to 12 inches that you can easily drill holes into. The prototype was made of particle board cut with the circle cutter shown next to it in FIG. 5-4. The side view in FIG. 5-5 is based on this disc but is much the same for anything else you make yours from.

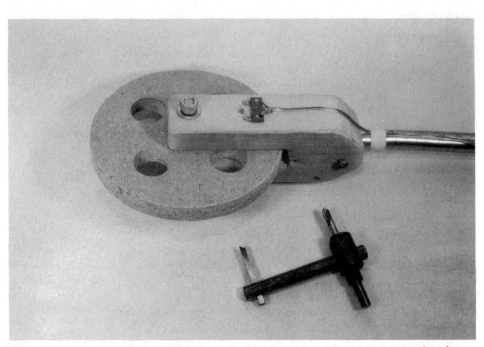

FIG. 5-4. *Shown next to the measuring wheel is the tool used to cut the wooden disc.*

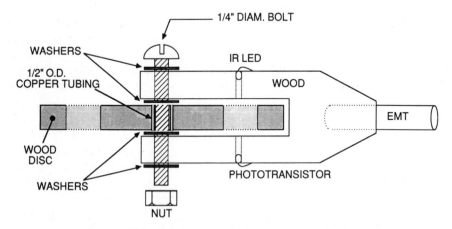

FIG. 5-5. *Side view diagram of the measuring wheel.*

Resolution

The number of holes the wheel has drilled in it determines the measurement resolution and the maximum speed it can be used at. Resolution depends on the number of holes in the wheel because this project doesn't measure distances continuously; it measures them in small digital pieces. The resolution is the size of these small pieces. The minimum distance resolvable is specified by:

$$\text{Resolution} = \frac{\text{Circumference of the Wheel}}{\text{Number of Holes in the Wheel}}$$

The prototype used a wheel with a 20.81-inch circumference that had four holes, so it had a resolution of 5.2 inches.

For finer resolution, more holes could be drilled in the wheel so that the infrared beam is interrupted more often and the calculator receives more frequent updates per distance covered. But since the calculator has a limit to the rate at which it can accept pulses, extra holes in the wheel carry the penalty of reducing the maximum speed it can be walked at. The maximum walking speed of the device can be found by:

$$\text{Max. walking speed} = \text{Resolution} \times \text{Maximum counts/second},$$

which for my prototype works out to be:

$$\text{Max. walking speed} = 5.2 \text{ in.} \times 12 = 62.4 \text{ in./sec. (3.5 mph)}$$

As the simple formula indicates, the appropriate number of holes for any particular wheel depends on its circumference, on the calculator, and how you compromise between resolution and maximum usable speed. The parameters of the prototype wheel represent a useful compromise for the particular calculator it was used with.

The block of wood that holds the measuring wheel and the infrared pair can be made from a single piece of 2-by-4 or by sandwiching three smaller pieces of wood. It's best to drill the mounting holes for the infrared emitter and detector at the same time, straight through the whole block. This assures that the two holes will be aligned. Mount the wheel in the block with a piece of copper pipe, threaded rod, nut, and washers as shown in FIGS. 5-4 AND 5-5.

The handle for the prototype was made from relatively inexpensive EMT tubing available at Channel, Rickel, and similar stores. A bike grip was placed at the top for comfort. The EMT tubing can be bent without kinking if a short piece of BX cable is temporarily inserted where the bend is to occur. A broom stick also makes a nice handle.

Mount the calculator, battery, switch, and the rest of the parts indicated in the schematic on a piece of plastic near the top of the handle, positioned for visibility as shown in FIG. 5-6. The calculator can be held to the plastic by velcro adhesive strips applied to both surfaces. This allows it to be removed and used by itself or on the bicycle.

Connect the LED and phototransistor to the rest of the circuit by running three wires up the tubing. Adjust the potentiometer for about 30 milliamps of current through the LED. Keep this current under 40 milliamps to keep it from burning out. Use the connecting cable described earlier to wire the calculator to the measuring wheel, and be sure that

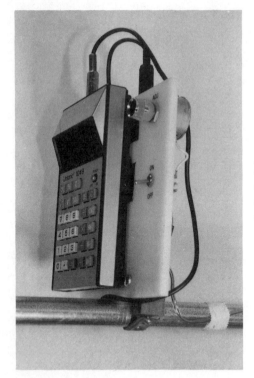

FIG. 5-6. *Mount the calculator to a piece of plastic on the handle of the measuring wheel as shown.*

the cable and J1 are wired so that the measuring wheel circuit is connected to the base and emitter of Q2.

Making the Bicycle Attachment

The bicycle attachment is designed to electrically press the "=" key once for every revolution of the front wheel. With this arrangement, the maximum speed you can ride the bike at and still obtain accurate measurements is given by:

$$\text{Max. speed} = \text{Circumference of wheel} \times \text{Max. counts/second}$$

The prototype was used on a bike with a 26-inch front wheel, yielding a maximum speed of 981 inches/sec. (56 MPH) which is certainly fast enough for a bicycle.

The measurement resolution is the same as the circumference of the bike wheel. For measuring distances of a mile or more, that should be quite adequate. If it isn't sufficient though, an extra magnet can be added to the bike wheel for superior resolution.

Proper operation of the bike attachment depends on a small permanent magnet moving past a reed switch. Because this demands close alignment, careful mounting is important. It's best to mount the magnet at the junction of two spokes for stability as shown in FIG. 5-7. Specific mounting arrangements depend upon the magnets available to you. Look for suitable magnets in toy & hobby shops, Radio Shack, and around the house. Using a magnet with a hole in its center makes mounting easier. As the picture of the prototype shows, the only thing necessary in that case is sandwiching a piece of plastic foam between the

FIG. 5-7. *Notice the small permanent magnet mounted to the spokes of the bicycle. It activates the reed switch mounted on the axle.*

magnet and a piece of circuit board material with a bolt and nut. With other types of magnets you can use tape for mounting. Just keep in mind the vibrations that all the items mounted on the bike will have to withstand.

The reed switch must be mounted so that it can be moved quite close to where the magnet passes but still remain clear of the rotating spokes. In the prototype, a small mounting bracket originally from a cheap bicycle odometer was used as a holder for the reed switch assembly. Using a dremel tool, a small chunk of acrylic plastic was shaped to hold the reed switch and a phone jack as shown in FIG. 5-8. These were held to the plastic with epoxy. The assembly was then grooved to fit the metal bracket and to permit it to slide close to the wheel.

The calculator back was covered with velcro tape as mentioned earlier. This makes mounting it on the bike an easy task. A piece of plastic mounted on the neck of the handlebars and covered with the complimentary pieces of velcro tape permits secure placement of the calculator as shown in FIG. 5-9. The same connecting wire is used to connect the calculator to the reed switch as was used with the measuring wheel. Wire J2 so that the reed switch will close across the base and collector of Q2 when the connecting cable is plugged into it.

USE

The measuring wheel and the bike attachment operate in a similar way. Always start measuring with the wheel of the bike positioned so that the magnet is away from the reed

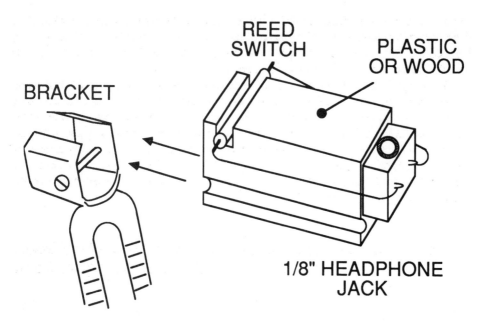

BRACKET

REED
SWITCH

PLASTIC
OR WOOD

1/8" HEADPHONE
JACK

FIG. 5-8. *Shape a piece of plastic or wood to hold the reed
switch and phone jack as this diagram indicates.*

FIG. 5-9. *The modified calculator mounts to the handlebars
of a bike where it records long distance measurements.*

switch—or in the case of the measuring wheel, such that the infrared path is blocked. This is because the calculator won't let you enter numbers while it thinks the "=" key is being held down. Enter the distance that each pulse to the calculator represents in your measurements, press "+," and start measuring.

The proper number to enter is the circumference of the bike wheel or measuring wheel divided by the number of holes it has. If inches are used for this number, the measured distance will read out in inches. But you can easily enter that first input in other units: feet, yards, miles, furlongs, meters, kilometers, or whatever. Some appropriate constants are given in Table 5-1 to convert the wheel's circumference in inches or centimeters to other units. Another alternative is to just enter "1,+," take a measurement, and then multiply the resulting integer output by an appropriate constant to convert it to whatever units you want the distance in.

Table 5-1. List of Appropriate Constants to Convert a Wheel's Circumference in Inches and Centimeters into Other Units.

For an Answer In	Divide Circumference In	
	INCHES BY:	CENTIMETERS BY:
FEET	12	30.48
YARDS	36	91.44
MILES	63,360	160,930
NAUTICAL MILES	72,960	185,320
INTERNATIONAL NAUTICAL MILES	72,913.4	185,200
FURLONGS	7920	20,116.8
METERS	39.37	100
KILOMETERS	39,370	100,000

You can also enter a large value and have the calculator repeatedly subtract a small distance from it. This would be useful if you wanted to set up a 5-mile jogging course, for example. You would enter ''5'' into the calculator before beginning and subtract the fraction of a mile that each revolution of the wheel represented. When the calculator reached zero, you'd have gone the five miles. Along the way, you would always have an indication of just how much further there was left to go.

Another example is if you wanted to see how many uses 100 feet of fencing could be put to in your backyard. The procedure would be to enter ''100'' into the calculator, hook it up with the measuring wheel, and enter the appropriate input to have it subtract the distance it covers from 100. As before, the calculator would always give an indication of how much fence there was left to use.

GOING FURTHER

Other input devices can be added to expand the usefulness of the calculator once it has been modified for counting. In a store, a light beam can be used with a photoelectric detector to count people moving through the door. To count the total number of customers in a day, you would set the calculator to add ''0.5'' to its display each time the light beam was broken. This is because each customer produces two counts—one when entering, and one when leaving. Because it can accept any number as its input and can add, subtract, multiply, or divide repeatedly, a calculator with a counting input is a very useful device.

PARTS LIST:

Electronic Distance Measuring System

R	200Ω, ¼W
POT	50Ω, value not critical
B	two AA batteries
Q1 and LED	Infrared emitter/detector pair (R.S. #276-142)
Q2	General-purpose NPN-type transistor
S	SPST mini toggle switch
PL 1	Three-conductor mini headphone plug
PL 2	Two-conductor mini headphone plug
J1, J2	Three-conductor mini headphone jack
REED SWITCH	Small SPST magnetic reed switch
CALCULATOR	Calculator with fast count rate, constant add, and internal access

PLUS, measuring wheel (5-12 inches diameter, wood suggested), wooden block to mount wheel in, hardware, EMT tubing or broom handle, bike grip, battery holder, flat piece of plastic (2 required) to mount calculator on, bike mounting hardware, velcro, small permanent magnet and hardware to mount it to bike spokes, small piece of plastic or wood (½″ × ½″ × ¾″) to hold reed switch, mounting bracket for reed switch assembly, wire, rub-on letters, and solder.

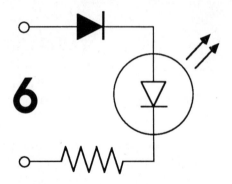

Ringing Telephone Alerter

Here is a project to consider building if you're often in a remote location of your house and can't hear the phone ring. It could also be useful if you occasionally want to turn off the bell on your regular phone so it doesn't ring there but still know from somewhere else when you have a call.

Another feature of the telephone ring alerter comes in handy if you can't hear well or work in a noisy environment. Besides ringing, it has an outlet into which a lamp or some other indicator can be plugged. When your line is called, this project will flash the lamp. This would be good if you wanted to turn off your regular phone's bell for quiet (if a baby is asleep, someone is practicing music, or you have guests) but want a visible indicator that the phone is ringing so you don't miss calls. The complete device prototype is shown in Fig. 6-1.

THE CIRCUIT

The schematic for the ringing phone alerter is shown in Fig. 6-2. It connects to your phone line using a modular phone plug and cord. When you receive a call, the phone company rings your phone by sending 75 to 90 volts AC over the phone line. The ringer voltage passes through C1 which blocks any DC voltage. Diodes D1 through D4 rectify the AC ringer voltage to provide the pulsating DC voltage that drives the ringer and flasher circuits when the phone rings.

When this happens, transistor Q forms an oscillator with R1, R2, and R3 to drive the piezo element. The oscillator circuit can be understood as a single stage amplifier that

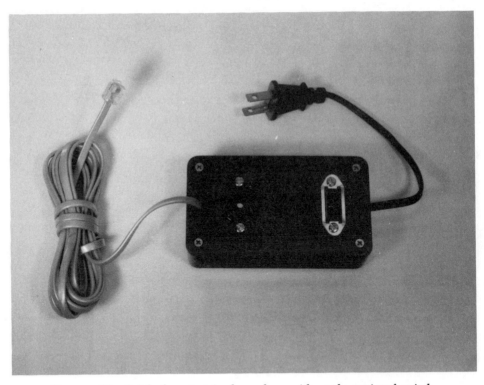

FIG. 6-1. *The finished project is shown here without the optional switch.*

amplifies and inverts the slightly delayed signal produced by the piezo element's feedback lead (blue). It feeds the inverted signal to the drive lead (red), causing it to oscillate.

At the same time, the pulsating supply voltage from the ring signal is applied to the triac driver opto-isolator through current-limiting resistor R4. The triac connected to the opto-isolator flashes the lamp in response to these rapid pulses. If quiet is desired, switch 51 allows just the lamp-flashing circuit to be activated. An opto-isolator like the one used in this project is required by the phone company to keep the 120 VAC from leaking into the phone line if something goes wrong with the circuit.

WHY THIS CIRCUIT?

This project is not unique in what it tries to do. A number of other circuits that provide similar functions have appeared in electronics books and magazines. Most of them use more components than is necessary though, employing a special phone ringer IC to drive the piezo element when a single transistor would work just as well. There are also some devices produced commercially that flash a lamp the way this project does. With so much competition, it seems that a circuit of this type is worth building yourself only if the parts it uses are few and readily available. That is why the simple circuit given in FIG. 6-2 was chosen over more complicated designs that really do no more.

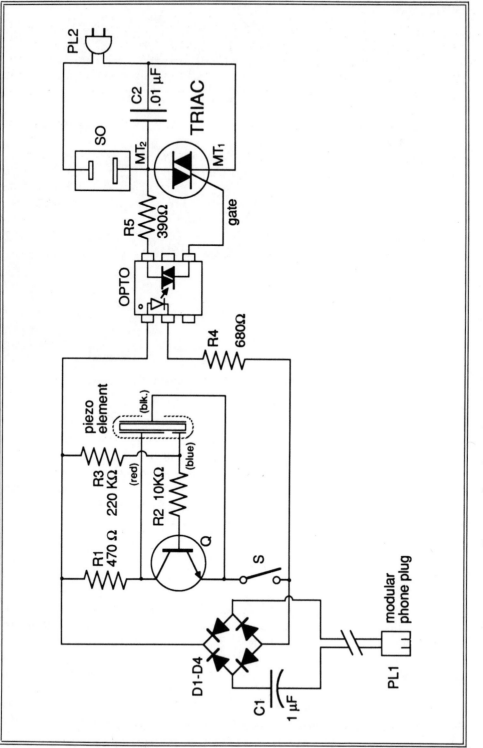

FIG. 6-2. Complete schematic for the ringing telephone alerter.

CONSTRUCTION

A simple circuit like this should translate into a finished project with a minimum of trouble and preparation. Designing and etching a special printed circuit board is too much trouble. A good alternative to etching a PC board is using one of the pre-drilled and pre-etched experimenter boards available from Radio Shack or through some of the mail-order suppliers in Chapter 23. These come with holes already drilled and foil strips interconnecting the holes in a preset but useful pattern.

Rather than designing a unique foil pattern for a particular project, construction with one of these boards is a matter of configuring the circuit to adapt to a universal pattern. Often this is easier than it seems at first. The component placement diagram for a typical board of this sort, the Radio Shack #276-168 Universal PC Board, is given in FIG. 6-3. If you use this board or a similar one, simply plug the components and jumper wires into the indicated holes and solder them on the other side. The finished circuit board should look like the prototype in FIG. 6-4.

Boards such as these, sometimes also called "veroboards," are strongly recommended for similar projects as well. The slight trouble in translating the circuit from a diagram

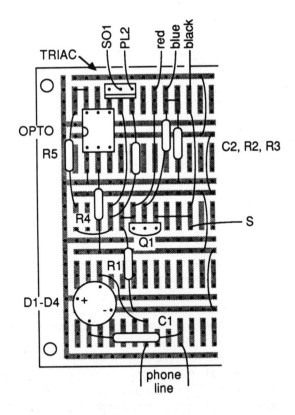

TOP VIEW SHOWN

FIG. 6-3. *The complete circuit for this project fits on half of a Radio Shack #276-168 Universal PC Board following this diagram.*

FIG. 6-4. *The finished circuit board should look like this when all the components have been installed.*

to the pre-etched foil pattern is much less than that of designing and etching a special circuit board. The slight additional cost of the pre-etched boards is offset by the cost of etchant, resist, and tape. More importantly, should later modifications of the circuit become necessary, they are far easier to do on a universal board with many extra holes than on a custom PC board. About the only disadvantage that pre-etched circuit boards have is their unsuitability for high current and high frequency circuits. For circuits that use more than 0.5 amps though, the thin traces can be supplemented with thicker wires. All in all, these project boards represent a significant improvement over standard PC boards for simple circuits like this project.

There are several ways you can elect to enclose the circuit for the telephone ring alerter. Consider some of the alternatives. One way is to build only half of the circuit (the ringer or the lamp flasher part) and permanently install it somewhere. For example, the flasher section would easily fit inside the base of a lamp. A three-position switch could be added to the lamp with options for OFF, ON, and PHONE STANDBY. You might also decide to build the ringer section permanently in a remote location around your house or yard where a regular phone would be too much trouble and expense to install. Or you could build one or both of the circuits inside an existing telephone's chassis.

There are other possibilities as well, but in the construction suggestions that follow, it is assumed that most readers will choose to build a portable version of the project similar to the prototype. A portable version with a modular phone plug is probably the most versatile way to build this project for the average user.

Any small minibox that can comfortably house the circuit board is suitable for enclosing the ring alerter. However, you might also be able to get away without using a commercial project box at all. There are many good substitutes available, like orange juice cans, cassette boxes, or boxes from a 5 & 10 store. If you're truly stuck without a suitable small enclosure for this or another electronic project, try walking through a large department store, keeping the size and type of project in mind. Chances are you'll spot a good enclosure for it masquerading as a package for something else. Cosmetics, cheap jewelry, candy, medicine, etc. all frequently come packaged in suitable enclosures for electronic projects. If you're lucky enough to actually need the thing that the enclosure is enclosing, then there's your chance to make good use of something most people throw away.

Most of the suitable enclosures for this project are plastic, which can make drilling the mounting holes a problem. Although the holes for circuit-board mounting, the phone and power cords, and the toggle switch are small and should be easy to drill without cracking the plastic, the holes for the power outlet and the piezo element can be troublesome.

Most panel-mounted power outlets require rectangular mounting holes that are difficult to cut. To avoid the problem of the rectangular hole, you could use an outlet attached to a short length of wire coming out of a hole in the box. If you'd still prefer to use a rectangular outlet for its neat looks though, start by outlining the exact size of the required hole you need on the plastic. Then select a twist drill of less than ¼ inch and use it to remove as much plastic from inside the outline as possible. Do this by drilling holes inside the rectangle with a drill press. With a sharp knife, cut out the remaining plastic. It helps to have a knife blade attachment for your soldering iron, but these are uncommon; a regular knife heated in a gas flame will also do the job. Shape the hole to its final size with a small rectangular file. If the outlet you have needs holes for additional mounting screws as well, drill them after cutting the rectangular hole, not before. Alignment is much easier when it's done in this way.

The piezo element presents another small problem. It mounts with two screws and could be fastened to the outside of the case in this way, but that would look clumsy. Mounting it from the inside gives a more flush look but requires a 1-inch round hole. A twist drill of that size is hard to come by and will crack the plastic anyway, so don't make the mistake of using one. Instead, use a spade bit of the next smaller size at high speed. Don't let the drill bit break through to the other side of the plastic though, because this would probably crack it. Switch to a knife instead to complete the hole. If the hole is still not large enough, make it bigger with a small diameter drum sander or a piece of sandpaper glued around a dowel. As with the outlet, drill the two mounting holes for the piezo element after the large hole has been drilled, using the piezo element itself to mark the positions for the holes.

The remainder of the construction should present no difficulty. The power cord and phone line should be knotted on the inside of the case to prevent them from being pulled loose accidentally. The power cord need not be longer than a few inches. Because it will presumably be used with a lamp that was already plugged into an outlet, no additional length is needed and would only be bothersome when the project isn't being used in this way.

The recommended circuit board has two holes already. These can be used for mounting or new ones can be drilled if it is more convenient. No heatsinking is needed for the triac, unless you plan on using it with a very large lamp or if your phone rings quite frequently.

PARTS LIST:

Ringing Telephone Alerter

C1	1μF, 100V electrolytic
C2	.01μF, 200V bypass capacitor, value not critical
R1	470Ω, all resistors ¼W
R2	10KΩ
R3	220KΩ
R4	680Ω
R5	390Ω
Q	NPN general-purpose transistor (2N3904 or equiv.)
TRIAC	2A, 200V or better triac to match lamp
D1 D4	1A, 200V bridge rectifier
OPTO	MOC3010 or similar triac driver opto-isolator
S	(Optional) SPST mini toggle switch
PL1	Modular phone plug and wire
PL2	Line cord and wall plug
SO	Power outlet
PIEZO ELEMENT	Three-wire piezoelectric element (R.S. #273-064 or equiv.)

PLUS, suitable enclosure, veroboard, hook-up wire, and solder.

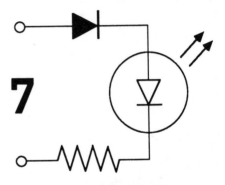

7

Portable Refrigerator

With this project, it is possible to keep food refrigerated in a picnic cooler without using ice. Instead of ice or another frozen substance, thermoelectric cooling modules powered by 12 VDC remove heat from the insulated enclosure. Because no ice is used, the refrigerator can keep food fresh for as long as power is available. Other advantages include less mess than with ice and more room inside the refrigerator. See FIG. 7-1.

The thermoelectric effect that makes this project possible was discovered in 1834 by Jean Peltier, a French watchmaker. He passed a direct current through the junction of two different metals and observed that the junction became either hot or cold depending on the direction of the current flow. What actually happened was that heat was either being transported to or removed from the metal junction to the rest of the wire. As the junction got cold, the wires became warmer and when the junction was warm, the wires were cool. Peltier had found a simple and reversible way to transport heat using electrical power directly.

The discovery didn't find practical applications in cooling until the early 1930's when it was discovered that certain semiconductors make excellent thermoelectric materials. Until the 1950's, thermoelectric refrigeration was limited to satisfying specialized industrial, military, medical, and space flight requirements. But in the late 1950's and early 1960's, a tremendous research boom produced applications such as biological specimen carriers, ambulance drug coolers, and noise-free refrigerators for trucks, airplanes, boats, and luxury hotel rooms. A number of consumer-oriented portable refrigerators were developed and are still manufactured in many countries. Although their use is not as widespread in the United States, portable coolers like this project are very popular in other countries.

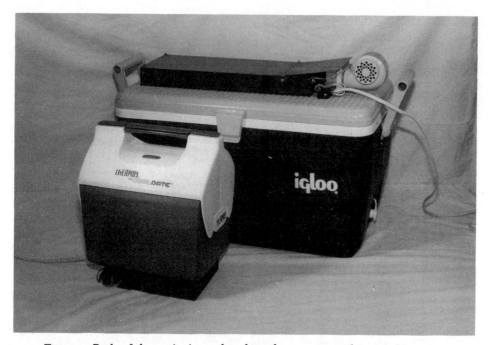

FIG. 7-1. *Both of these picnic coolers have been converted into refrigerators with solid state thermoelectric modules.*

In these and other modern applications, Peltier's thermoelectric effect is put to practical use by semiconductor thermoelectric cooling modules (TEMs). FIGURE 7-2 shows the type of TEM used in this project. It is actually composed of 127 semiconductor junctions between dissimilar materials that have been doped to optimize their thermoelectric effect. The junctions are sandwiched between two thin squares of white ceramic. When current is passed through the module, one piece of ceramic gets hot (called the hot-side) and the

FIG. 7-2. *One of the thermo-electric modules used in this project.*

other (the cold side) gets cold. A more correct description of what happens is that heat flows from the cold side to the hot side.

When the heat at the hot side of a TEM is removed, its cold side can be used to refrigerate the interior of an insulated picnic cooler. Although there are two versions of this project, both use aluminum heatsinks to dissipate the heat from the hot side of the TEMs they use. The heatsinks are helped by a small blower. Although the two versions use the same method to remove heat from their hot sides, there are two different methods of refrigerating the cooler by the cold side of the TEM.

TWO METHODS

Recreational picnic coolers are fairly well insulated. But no insulation is perfect; as long as there is a temperature difference between the inside of the cooler and the outside, some heat will enter. Heat also enters the cooler whenever the top is removed for access to the inside.

The job of a cooling system for such a refrigerator is to remove the heat that enters it as fast as or faster than it leaves. The problem is transporting that heat to the cold side of the TEM where it can be removed. But there are difficulties encountered in transporting heat from all the remote corners inside the refrigerator. Even when it is fully packed with food, a picnic cooler contains mostly air—and air is a good insulator. Unless an effective way of transporting heat is used, the food situated near the TEM will be cool but the rest will stay warm.

There are two effective solutions to the problem of cooling the interior of a refrigerator. Both methods are used on commercial models with varying degrees of success. Both will be presented as options in this project because they are suited to two different types of applications.

An Interior Heatsink and Fan

Air is only an effective insulator when it is not moving. The fact that air tends to insulate between objects in a refrigerator is of little consequence if the air is circulating. With a small fan to blow it around, the air becomes a carrier of heat, removing it uniformly from all places inside the refrigerator. To cool the circulating air in one version of this project, heatsinks are attached to the *cold* side of the TEMs. They remove the excess heat to outside the refrigerator through the TEMs.

This method is especially suited to a large picnic cooler like the 48 quart Igloo ice chest visible in some of the photographs and detailed in FIG. 7-3. Large coolers like it have sufficient room in which to mount the necessary heatsinks and fan. Because they are large, they typically have more air in them than food, making an air-circulation cooling system particularly effective. This type of cooling is best for refrigerators where a number of loose food items must be kept cool.

Drawbacks to this system appear when large amounts of liquid must be refrigerated. For example, if the refrigerator is filled with water to keep bait fish cool, it will lose its effectiveness. The air would only cool the surface of the water while the rest would remain warm. Another situation in which air cooling won't work so well is for a large quantity of 12 oz. cans. Cans have a large ratio of volume to surface area, which makes it difficult for air to cool them. The air also won't circulate freely inside the refrigerator with many

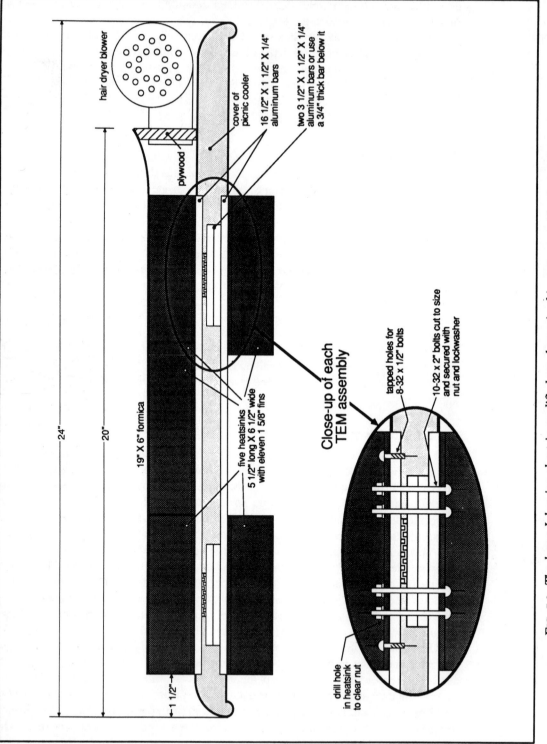

hair dryer blower

plywood

cover of picnic cooler

16 1/2" X 1 1/2" X 1/4" aluminum bars

two 3 1/2" X 1 1/2" X 1/4" aluminum bars or use a 3/4" thick bar below it

24"

20"

1 1/2"

19" X 6" formica

five heatsinks 5 1/2" long X 6 1/2" wide with eleven 1 5/8" fins

Close-up of each TEM assembly

drill hole in heatsink to clear nut

tapped holes for 8-32 x 1/2" bolts

10-32 x 2" bolts cut to size and secured with nut and lockwasher

FIG. 7-3. *The large Igloo ice chest is modified as shown in this cut-away side view of its cover.*

cans to block it. Therefore, the second type of cooling, direct conduction, is used for the smaller version of this project.

Direct Conduction

Liquids are easier to cool by conduction. The portable refrigerator visible in the photographs and drawn in FIGS. 7-4 and 7-5 uses such a method. Three of its five interior sides are replaced with aluminum which is in thermal contact with the cold side of a TEM. Metal cans and other food resting directly on the cool aluminum surface will relinquish their heat more readily than they would to circulating air.

Because there are no heatsinks to take up interior space, the refrigerator can be packed full of food. It even works more effectively when it is full because there are more paths by which heat can be conducted and less air to insulate between objects. In particular, food that is mostly liquid can be cooled more quickly by conduction than through the air.

This cooling method is more suited to small refrigerators because it saves space and because smaller refrigerators are likely to be packed tighter with food. The small prototype is just the right size for cooling a six-pack of cans indefinitely. It is also just right for other specialized uses like keeping chemicals, medicines, or photographic film chilled.

REQUIRED MATERIALS

The first step after deciding which type of refrigerator to make is buying the picnic cooler. Refer back to FIG. 7-1. If you decide to build a large circulation-type one, keep it under 48 quarts. The large prototype represents or exceeds the practical upper limit on size beyond which cooling effectiveness is sacrificed. The small conduction-type prototype shown is typical of the majority of commercial models available. Before buying this type of picnic cooler, inspect it carefully to judge the effectiveness of its insulation. Frequently, the smaller sized coolers skimp on insulation. Their thin walls and almost open tops let too much heat enter the food area.

You then need the TEMs. The smaller size uses one, while the larger size needs two. The best buys in thermoelectric modules are from Melcor (see materials list). Their CP1.4-127-06L module is used almost uniformly throughout the industry in portable cooling applications. It is available for $25.00 in small quantities.

Both versions of this project require heatsinks to remove heat from the hot side of the TEMs. The ones used in both the prototypes were purchased at a good price from one of the many surplus dealers listed in Chapter 23. Their stock of heatsinks changes frequently, so check the current catalog of some of them for heatsinks of a similar size to the ones shown in prototype diagrams.

Most surplus heatsinks are of the extruded aluminum variety because that is the cheapest kind to manufacture. But if you are lucky enough to obtain a built-up heatsink for a low cost, by all means do so. Particularly in forced-air applications, built-up heatsinks offer a number of advantages. Their base plates are often thicker and consequently more rigid and their fins are longer, thinner, and spaced close together so heat can be transferred more effectively to air.

Heatsinks frequently come painted or anodized in a black color for better heat dissipation. Although black heatsinks were used in the prototypes, their choice was a matter of convenience. Their color makes very little difference in the forced-air system that they

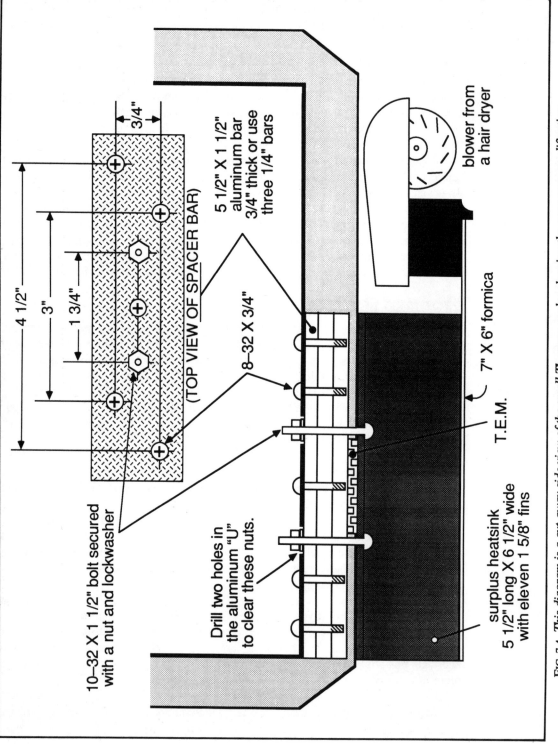

3/4"

4 1/2"

3"

1 3/4"

(TOP VIEW OF SPACER BAR)

5 1/2" X 1 1/2" aluminum bar 3/4" thick or use three 1/4" bars

8-32 X 3/4"

10-32 X 1 1/2" bolt secured with a nut and lockwasher

Drill two holes in the aluminum "U" to clear these nuts.

blower from a hair dryer

7" X 6" formica

T.E.M.

surplus heatsink 5 1/2" long X 6 1/2" wide with eleven 1 5/8" fins

Fig. 7-4. *This diagram is a cut-away side view of the small Thermos cooler showing the necessary modification.*

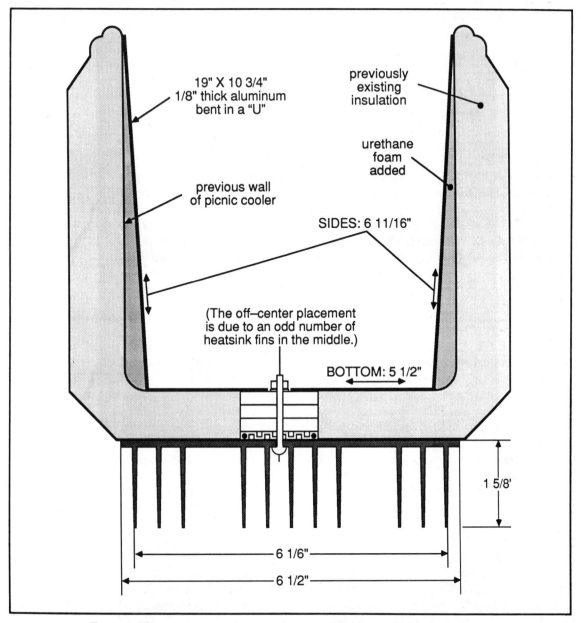

19" X 10 3/4"
1/8" thick aluminum
bent in a "U"

previously
existing
insulation

urethane
foam
added

previous wall
of picnic cooler

SIDES: 6 11/16"

(The off–center placement
is due to an odd number of
heatsink fins in the middle.)

BOTTOM: 5 1/2"

1 5/8'

6 1/6"

6 1/2"

FIG. 7-5. *This cut-away end view of the small Thermos cooler shows how the interior is lined with a U-shaped piece of aluminum.*

both use. Plain, black, and other colors of aluminum offer approximately equal effectiveness when used in this project.

Both versions of the project call for aluminum bar stock. The prototypes were built entirely with pieces sold at a good local hardware store, so locating them yourself shouldn't be much trouble. If hardware shops in your area don't sell the right sized pieces of aluminum, another source is a metal store or a welding shop. Look in the phone book under "Aluminum" or try under "Welding" for a welding shop that specializes in aluminum.

In both options, a certain thickness of aluminum bar is specified. In either case, the bar can be built up from two or more thicknesses of the commonly available 1½ inch by ¼ inch size. But if a thicker bar can be found in the right size, it should be used instead because a solid piece of aluminum conducts heat better than two separate pieces joined together.

The joints through which heat flows in this project depend on heavy pressure to make good thermal contact. Good contacts depend on the smoothness of the surfaces that are joined. Consequently, buy aluminum that is as smooth and flat as possible and be sure the heatsinks have a lapped surface where they will be joined. Melcor recommends using metal surfaces with less than 0.001-inch irregularities where they will contact the TEMs.

But because all metal surfaces have slight aberrations, thermal grease is used in this project between all mating surfaces. The required chemical is Wakefield Engineering type 120, Dow type 340, or an equivalent. Although it is the same stuff used for heat-sinking large semiconductors, the proper use of thermal grease demands more care in this project than it does in that case. The correct procedure is discussed in the next section.

CONSTRUCTION

Because of the different sizes of coolers and heatsinks available, constructing this project is not an exercise in following directions but is rather an individual effort. The method and procedures are the same no matter what the dimensions of your picnic cooler or heatsinks, but exact measurements might not apply. To obtain the correct dimensions for your particular version of this project could mandate that you do some steps out of order. It might be necessary to build this project on many fronts simultaneously rather than strictly following the sequence given here.

For example, in order to know what size hole to cut in the cooler, you might first have to attach the heatsinks to the modules. And deciding where to mount the heatsinks might have to wait until the exact dimensions of the fan is known. The prototypes were built entirely in this way with great success, so be assured it is not difficult.

Cutting the Cooler

Both versions of this project were designed to require as little modification as possible to the picnic cooler they use. This lessens the amount of work required, weakens the cooler minimally, and maintains as much of the original insulation as possible. In both versions, the only major modification is a rectangular hole 1½ inches wide cut in the wall for the TEMs.

The large version that uses circulating air has the hole cut in the cover. It was planned this way because a new cover can be purchased from the manufacturer whenever normal use of the cooler is preferred. Removing four screws allows the covers to be interchanged.

The small refrigerator has its hole cut in the bottom out of necessity. A U-shaped piece of aluminum fits snugly inside the cooler and contacts the TEM through this hole. The hot-side heatsink is on the bottom of the refrigerator to remove heat from the hot side of the TEM. FIGURE 7-6 shows the picnic cooler with a hole cut in the bottom to accept the assembly standing to the left of it.

FIG. 7-6. *The small Thermos cooler is inverted in this photograph. Next to it are the parts for making it a refrigerator.*

The easiest way to cut the holes through the ¾-inch to 1-inch- thick wall of insulating foam and plastic is with a sabre saw. Draw an outline of the hole on the outside of the picnic cooler once the location and length are certain. The large chest used for the prototype had a checkered pattern on the cover that made this particularly easy. Drill at least a ¼-inch hole within the outline to insert the sabre saw. Then cut out the hole using a general-purpose blade. You'll find the urethane foam that picnic coolers are insulated with cuts nicely and leaves a hole with smooth sides.

Installing the Heatsinks, TEMs, and Aluminum Parts

Large Cooler. The large refrigerator has both internal and external heatsinks. Both sets of heatsinks attach to their own 16½-inch-long piece of ¼-inch-by-1½-inch aluminum bar as shown in FIG. 7-3. The flat faces of the heatsinks mount flush to the inside and outside of the cover with the aluminum bars and TEMs between them. Together, the bars occupy only ½ inch of internal space. The TEMs add only about ⅛ inch to the thickness. But the cover of the ice chest is a little less than 1 inch thick. This means that two more ¼-inch thick pieces of aluminum must be inserted between the cold side of the TEM and the long aluminum bar on that side. The extra pieces of aluminum should be put on the cold side of the module, because less heat flows there than at the hot side. The slight thermal resistance of the extra pieces is not as significant as it would be if more heat were flowing through it.

The best way to put the TEMs, aluminum bars, and heatsinks together is to start with the cold-side heatsinks and layer the remaining parts on until reaching the hot-side heatsinks. That way the critical thermal joints can be made before installing anything in the ice chest. The hot-side heatsinks will then be attached to the other parts at a later step and used to sandwich the cover between both sets of heatsinks.

With the aluminum bars cut to size and their rough edges smoothed, lay the cold-side heatsinks down on their fins on a workbench. Plan the alignment of all the parts and drill the necessary holes. To make alignment automatic between separate pieces, it helps to securely tape them together while drilling the first two holes. Then have bolts through those holes when drilling the remaining ones.

When twist drills are used to make holes in aluminum, they leave a burr ring above the surface of the metal. This tendency is lessened when several layers are held together and drilled simultaneously, but it still occurs on the top and bottom surfaces. After drilling the aluminum, use a small metal file to carefully remove the burrs from around the mounting holes. This is an important step for good thermal contact between the flat surfaces.

Now briefly check the TEM to see which side gets cold and which one hot. Hold the TEM between clean fingers. Put a few volts through it in the polarity indicated by the color of its wires. In a few seconds you should know which side is the hot side and which the cold.

After all the aluminum pieces have been cut, smoothed, drilled, filed, and checked again for smoothness, go over them with a wide pencil eraser to remove any pencil marks or deposits that remain from manufacturing. Then take the aluminum pieces and heatsinks to a sink and wash them with detergent (not soap, which can leave a fatty residue). After washing them, lay them on a towel to dry and avoid handling the surfaces that will make thermal contacts.

When they are thoroughly dry, take the aluminum pieces to a clean area to assemble them with thermal grease, again without touching the thermal contact areas. Start by applying a thin uniform layer of thermal grease to the cold side heatsinks where they will be in contact with the aluminum bar. Lay the bar on top of the greased heatsinks and rub it back and forth for about a minute until increased resistance is felt from a large area of direct contact through the grease. Then move on to the 3½-inch-long metal spacers. Attach these in their appropriate locations by a thin layer of thermal grease applied the same way. Follow these pieces with the thermoelectric modules and the remaining aluminum bar, each applied in the same way.

With everything in place, squeeze the assembly together with the eight bolts. Avoid an unbalanced pressure on the TEMs by tightening each bolt a little at a time. Melcor recommends a pressure of 8 to 12 foot-pounds per bolt for every square inch of TEM used, but they are assuming two bolts per TEM, so halve that figure. As the bolts are tightened, excess thermal grease will leak out between pieces of aluminum. Wipe it off with a rag. It is especially important that no thermal grease get between the hot and cold sides or into the TEM where it could conduct heat in the opposite direction.

To complete assembly of the large refrigerator, insert the unit just described into the hole cut in the cover. The top of the aluminum bar should protrude just slightly above the top surface of the cover. If it doesn't, remove some of the plastic liner under the cold-side heatsinks. Lay the fins of the cold-side heatsink on a flat surface. They should be long enough to support everything without any other part of the cover touching.

Because the wires to the TEMs will be inaccessible after the next step, they must be connected now. Choose a location on the outside of the cover to attach a terminal strip for electrical connections. Solder wires to the TEMs that will reach this location. Because of the current involved, use at least 16 AWG. Route the wires up from between the aluminum bars to the terminal strip location. It might be necessary to cut notches in the cover for the wire to exit the hole.

Before attaching the hot-side heatsinks, the gap left when the cover was cut must be sealed to prevent heat or water vapor from entering. Sealing between the hot and cold pieces of metal increases efficiency by keeping the heat that is pumped out of the refrigerator from coming back. A more important reason for sealing between the inside and outside though is to keep the TEMs dry. Because the inside of the refrigerator is cooler than the surrounding air, there is a vapor pressure that tries to force moisture into it. It is the same as if the inside of the cooler were at a partial vacuum; the smallest crack would let air through. The reason moisture must be kept from entering the cavity where the TEMs are is that it will condense on their cold side and form water. Water on the TEMs will soon destroy them. Electrolysis acting between the elements eats them away until they fail, so complete sealing is important.

The urethane foam insulation sold in aerosol cans by home improvement stores is ideal for sealing around the elements. It expands to fill cracks, forms a moisture-proof seal, and is an effective thermal insulator. Applying it is tricky, but a mess made with it is never permanent. After it dries, a knife can easily remove it from places it shouldn't have gotten.

Using the applicator tube included with the urethane foam, practice dispensing it on a scrap piece of cardboard. When you have acquired enough skill at that, apply the foam to the refrigerator. Seal first around the TEMs so that no vapor could possibly get to them. Even the place where the wires from the TEMs leave their insulation must be sealed against vapor. Then place the heatsink and aluminum unit in the hole in the ice box cover with the wires from the TEMs correctly positioned. Seal the gap between the metal bars with urethane. Because the foam expands forcefully after it is dispensed, it should be possible to fill every nook and cranny by working only from the top. When you are satisfied that the gap is completely sealed, let the foam cure for 12 hours or whatever the directions say. Don't worry about excess foam coming over the tops of the metal; it will be much easier to remove when it dries.

After the foam has dried, trim the excess with a sharp knife. It should now be possible to bolt the hot-side heatsinks to the top of the aluminum bar just above the top of the cover. After washing and drying the bar, apply thermal grease where the heatsinks will go and fasten them using the oscillating motion discussed earlier to squeeze extra thermal grease from out of the joint. Tighten the bolts holding the heatsinks to the aluminum bar as tightly as possible with a screwdriver. FIGURE 7-7 shows some of the hot-side heatsinks on the cover of the large refrigerator.

Small Cooler. Building the small refrigerator involves a similar procedure. The hot-side heatsink, TEM, and aluminum bar are assembled as a unit and built into the cooler as a last step just as in the large refrigerator. The only difference in the small refrigerator is that a U-shaped piece of aluminum is used to line the inside of the cooler instead of the cold-side heatsinks that the other version has.

Picnic coolers like the small prototype are covered with a swiveling plastic shell that will only get in the way if it is left on while building the project. So before doing anything to it, pry off the caps that retain the cover and slide it off. If you're careful, it can be replaced without damage when the project is complete.

The first step is bending the piece of aluminum that will line the interior of the cooler. Sheet aluminum is usually bent in a bending brake but two pieces of wood carefully aligned and clamped in a vise will also ensure a straight bend. With the two necessary bends made, slip the "U" into the cooler. Don't worry if the angle of the bends doesn't follow the angle of the cooler's interior walls. That won't matter when the aluminum is later held to the inside of the refrigerator by urethane foam.

The holes in the aluminum bar (or bars, if several thin ones are stacked) must now

FIG. 7-7. *The large Igloo ice chest has a plastic cover
and three heatsinks through which air is blown.*

be drilled so that the U-shaped piece can be marked with their location. Drill and tap those holes and insert the bar into the hole in the bottom of the cooler. With a pencil or pointed object, mark the U-shaped piece in the location of the holes to ensure alignment when it is later bolted to the bar. Five of the necessary holes are for mounting, while two more large ones are required to clear the nuts that hold the rest of the assembly together.

At this point, the heatsink, TEM, and aluminum bar can be assembled. Carefully flatten all rough edges on the aluminum bar and heatsink. Remove the rings that formed around the holes when they were drilled. The mating surfaces should be as flat as possible for good thermal contact. Wash all the aluminum and let it dry thoroughly. Then sandwich the TEM between the heatsink and aluminum bar using thermal grease and the technique described previously for the large cooler. Bolt the sandwich together and torque the nuts to 20 to 30 inch/pounds.

Test fit the assembly to ensure that the surface of the aluminum bar is slightly above the bottom of the cooler. If it doesn't clear the top, you'll have to remove some of the plastic under the hot-side heatsink. Now use the aerosol urethane foam to seal around the TEM and in the gaps left in the cutout. It is best to apply more foam than is needed around the TEM and aluminum bar and then insert the assembly into the hole. The extra will squeeze out and create a mess, but at least you will be sure all the cracks have been filled. When the foam hardens the next day, the excess can be neatly trimmed off.

After the assembly has been sealed to the cooler, attach the U-shaped piece of aluminum to the top of the bar. Thoroughly wash and dry the surfaces that will be joined. Then spread a thin layer of thermal grease on the bar and bolt the ''U'' to it. Tighten the five screws as hard as you can with a screwdriver and wipe up the excess grease that squeezes through the holes.

Complete this part of the construction by sealing the aluminum liner to the inside of the cooler wall. Pull each piece of aluminum away from the side and fill the cavity with urethane foam. Push the aluminum back till it touches the side at the top. Use clothespins or small C-clamps to hold the aluminum to the side as the urethane dries overnight. Trim the excess when the foam hardens.

Incorporating a Fan

Adding a fan to either of the possible versions of this project is a necessary step for satisfactory performance. The TEMs generate and remove a considerable amount of heat to the hot-side heatsinks. Forcing air through those heatsinks will bring their temperature down and make the TEMs operate with greater efficiency. Although a few commercial models operate without a fan, they are missing the opportunity for a great jump in performance at a small cost.

The fans used in this project can be added at nearly the last step. Rather than attaching to the heatsinks or aluminum bars, they mount directly to the ice chest in the large prototype or to the bottom plate in the small version. As long as the size of the fan is considered when the layout of the project is designed, its installation can be left until the initial, more critical and tricky steps are completed.

Besides salvaging one from junked equipment, the most inexpensive source for a small powerful blower is a hair dryer. Although hair dryers operate off 120 VAC, their blower motors are supplied with 12 VDC by four diodes in series with a heating element. With sales and rebates, hair dryers typically cost just five or six dollars. They can be taken apart simply for their fans and for the other useful parts they contain and be worth more than they would as hair dryers. As FIGS. 7-1 and 7-8 show, both prototypes used blowers removed from hair dryers. The large refrigerator took a blower from the turbo-style hair dryer which is the most common type, while the smaller one used a flatter one to save space. Both types of hair dryers are sold in department stores and shouldn't be difficult to obtain.

FIG. 7-8. *The small Thermos cooler shown here uses a blower from a hair dryer.*

Because the blower includes the case as an integral part of it, removing it means destroying the dryer. To obtain the blower, take out the screws holding the dryer together and observe what parts of the plastic case are necessary to guide the air. Cut the rest of the dryer away with a saw and use a power sander to smooth the edges. On the turbo-type dryers used in the large prototype, it might be necessary to wrap the blower assembly with some tape to prevent air from escaping through the center seam. Disconnect the motor from the electrical part of the dryer, noting the polarity of its diodes so it can be hooked up again correctly. The line cord, switch, diodes, and heating elements should all be saved for other projects.

Mounting the blower to the large refrigerator requires a piece of wood and some right-angle brackets. The nozzle of the blower fits snugly into a hole in the wood which relies on two aluminum right-angle brackets to hold it to the cover. A piece of thin, flexible plastic (Formica) covers the heatsink fins to direct the air through them. The Formica is attached at four points to the heatsinks and with two screws to the piece of wood that holds the blower.

The small refrigerator also uses a piece of Formica over its heatsink to confine the airflow to where it is most effective. It is attached by four bolts to holes tapped in the heatsink. In this instance, the cover is also used to support the blower with two bolts. Because the refrigerator uses it as a base, small rubber feet could be added to the Formica heatsink cover to prevent it from marring delicate surfaces.

The large refrigerator needs an additional fan inside it to circulate cool air but it need not have much power. It could be a tiny hobby motor with a plastic fan blade attached or it could be another hair-dryer blower. In any event, space constrictions inside the cooler suggest as small a fan as possible. One possibility is one of the small and quiet DC computer-cooling fans that have recently appeared on the surplus market.

CONTROL CIRCUITRY

Although home refrigerators have a thermostat to cycle their compressor on and off, it is unlikely that this portable project will need one. In most situations, a thermostat would end up leaving the TEMs on nearly all the time and wouldn't justify its expense. There is little danger of the refrigerator becoming too cold if the TEMs aren't cycled on and off, because as the temperature difference between their hot and cold sides increases, they become less efficient and consequently pump less heat. In this way the refrigerator is self-regulating.

Neither of my prototypes used a thermostat. The TEMs and fans are simply connected in parallel, observing the proper polarity. Heavy gauge wiring is used where a high current is expected, and connections are soldered or held securely by screw terminals for good contacts. A thermal cutoff switch is placed in series with the 12 VDC supply and attaches to the hot-side heatsink with thermal grease. This is a precaution against overheating that could occur if the fan failed or if the airflow was blocked. The TEMs can be damaged by extreme heat. Thermal cutoffs are common on surplus equipment and Radio Shack sells a suitable one for 79¢ (R.S. #270-1320).

The most likely power source for this project is a vehicle's 12-volt battery. The large refrigerator with two TEMs and two fans draws 11.5 amps, while the smaller one draws 5.8 amps. With its engine running, a car or boat should have no trouble supplying this current, but if the refrigerator is left connected to only the battery for long periods, it

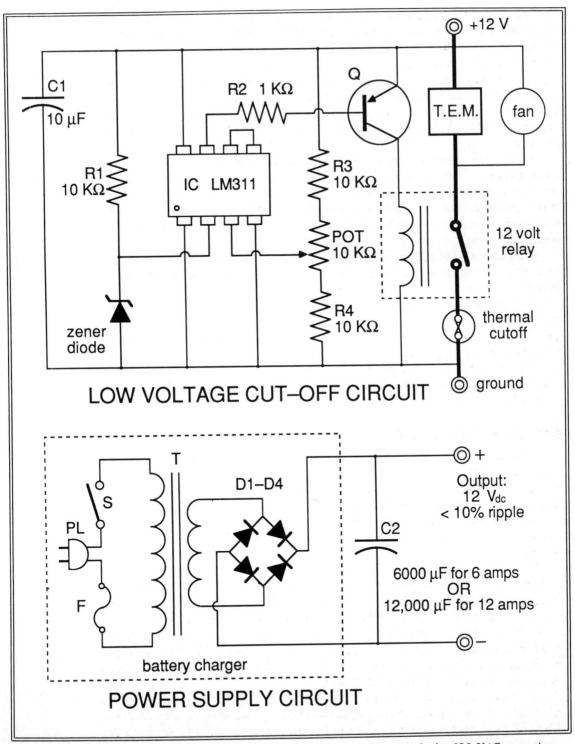

LOW VOLTAGE CUT–OFF CIRCUIT

POWER SUPPLY CIRCUIT

FIG. 7-9. *This is the optional low voltage cutoff circuit and a power supply for 120 VAC operation.*

will discharge it. In uses where the refrigerator may indeed be left connected to a battery for several hours, a low voltage cutoff is essential so the battery doesn't become too weak to restart the engine. FIGURE 7-9 (top) is a simple circuit that switches the refrigerator off if the supply voltage drops below a preset point.

The circuit uses a 12-volt relay with heavy duty contacts to control power to the refrigerator. The relay is energized through Q when the output of the IC is high. The IC is an LM311 comparator whose output goes high when the voltage at its pin two exceeds the voltage at pin three. The voltage at pin three is constant and determined by the zener diode that can be any value from 4 to 7 volts. The voltage at pin two is a fraction of the supply voltage determined by the potentiometer. The potentiometer can be set so that when the supply voltage falls below a certain level, the comparator output goes low and disconnects the refrigerator.

The low voltage cutoff circuit is simple enough to build in a variety of ways. A small piece of a pre-etched PC board or a perfboard can hold all the parts except the relay, which comes with its own mounting hardware.

Once the circuit is built, the potentiometer must be set to turn the relay off at a suitable voltage level. Without the TEMs or fans in the circuit, connect it to a variable supply and measure the voltage on an accurate meter. Set the potentiometer on the cutoff circuit so that the relay drops out when the supply voltage goes below about 10 volts. This keeps the battery it is connected to from discharging below that level.

MAKING A POWER SUPPLY

To use the refrigerator at home or wherever AC power is available, build a 12 VDC power supply or adapt a car battery charger to work with it. Most car battery chargers have sufficient current capacity to power the refrigerator, but check the specifications to be sure. If a battery charger isn't available, a transformer and bridge rectifier will do the same thing as indicated in FIG. 7-9 (bottom).

In both cases, adequate filtering is important. The ripple (the AC component in the DC output) should be kept below 10% for the modules to operate efficiently. This requires a large filter capacitor in parallel with the DC supply. Fortunately, at the low voltage the refrigerator operates from, a sufficiently sized capacitor isn't terribly bulky. The simple circuit shown in FIG. 7-9 indicates the minimum values depending on the expected current draw.

MATERIALS LIST:

Large Portable Refrigerator

HEATSINKS	The prototype used five identical heatsinks from a mail-order surplus dealer. They were 5½" long, 6½" wide at the base, and the eleven fins stood 1⅝" high. Other similar ones are suitable.
ICE CHEST	A 48 quart Igloo brand ice chest was used in the prototype, although a smaller one would probably be best for thermoelectric cooling.
TEMs	Two Melcor CP 1.4-127-06L thermoelectric modules ($25.00 ea.) (Melcor, 990 Spruce St., Trenton, NJ 08648)
ALUMINUM BARS	Two 16½" × 1½" × ¼" aluminum bars and four 3½" × 1½" ×¼" bars, OR use a ¾" bar on the cold side, a ¼" bar on the hot side, and dispense with the smaller bars in between.
THERMAL GREASE	Wakefield Engineering type 120, Dow type 340, or equiv.
URETHANE FOAM	Commonly available expanding urethane insulation (sold in home improvement stores)
BLOWER	Blower salvaged from a compact turbo-style hair dryer (see text)
FORMICA	19" × 6" Formica or other thin plastic as a heatsink cover (size to fit particular heatsinks.)
WIRE	AWG 16 copper wire to carry high current
THERMAL CUTOFF	Radio Shack #270-1320 or other suitable high temperature cutoff switch
TERMINAL STRIP	Screw terminals or solder lugs for secure connections.

PLUS, solder and hardware.

MATERIALS LIST:

Small Portable Refrigerator

HEATSINK	The prototype used a heatsink 5½" long, 6½" wide at the base, with eleven 1⅝" high fins. Other similar ones are suitable.
PICNIC COOLER	Small Igloo or Thermos brand picnic cooler
TEMs	Melcor CP 1.4-127-06L thermoelectric module ($25.00). Refer to Melcor 990, Spruce St., Trenton, NJ 08648.
ALUMINUM BARS	Three 5½" × 1½" × ¼" aluminum bars OR a single ¾" thick bar.
U-SHAPED PIECE	19" × 10¾" × ⅛" piece of aluminum bent in a "U" shape
THERMAL GREASE	Wakefield Engineering type 120, Dow type 340, or equiv.
URETHANE FOAM	Commonly available expanding urethane insulation (sold in home improvement stores)
BLOWER	Blower salvaged from a flat-style hair dryer (see text)
FORMICA	7" × 6" Formica or other thin plastic as a heatsink cover (size to fit particular heatsinks.)
WIRE	AWG 16 copper wire to carry high current
THERMAL CUTOFF	Radio Shack #270-1320 or other suitable high temperature cutoff switch
TERMINAL STRIP	Screw terminals or solder lugs for secure connections

PLUS, solder and hardware.

PARTS LIST:

Low Voltage Cutoff Circuit

C1	10μF, 16V, value not critical
R1, R3, R4	10KΩ, $\frac{1}{4}$W
R2	1KΩ, $\frac{1}{4}$W
POT	10KΩ trimmer
Q	PNP general-purpose transistor
IC	LM311 comparator IC
ZENER DIODE	4 to 6-volt zener diode, value not critical
RELAY	Radio Shack #275-226 Automotive Lighting Relay or equiv.

PLUS, suitable board, hook-up wire, and solder.

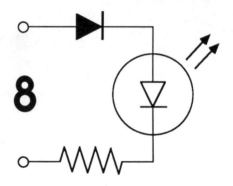

8

Remote Volume Control

The way most people hook up extension speakers to a main stereo system is by switching them in parallel across their existing speaker outputs. But this isn't necessarily the best way of doing things. There are a number of disadvantages in connecting two sets of speakers to one amplifier. For one thing, with two parallel speakers loading it down, the amplifier is presented with a lower impedance which it might have trouble driving. Also, since the two sets of speakers probably differ in sensitivity, impedance, and power handling, their volume levels will be difficult to match. Unless you use an L-pad, the volume of the extension speakers depends on the same control used by the main speakers. But then with an L-pad, the usable power is limited and the amplifier still sees a lowered impedance. Either alternative results in a disagreeable compromise.

These problems can be avoided by driving the extra speakers with a separate amplifier. Because the extra speakers will be driven separately, they can be controlled separately. Their volume can be independent of the main speakers, because it is controlled by varying the input to the additional amplifier. Therefore, this project is a remote volume control for the extra speakers. It is designed to allow you to control the volume of the signal sent to a power amplifier but *from the location of the extension speakers*. It also remotely switches the amplifier on when the extension speakers are being used. See FIG. 8-1.

FIGURE 8-2 is a block diagram that should make it clear how this remote volume control project can be used to hook up extension speakers to a main stereo. The stereo signal is taken from the master system through its tape output jacks. Almost all receivers and preamps have these jacks. A signal obtained at the tape output jacks is independent of the volume setting of the main speakers. The remote volume control takes that signal, varies it over a wide range depending on the setting at the remote potentiometer, and sends

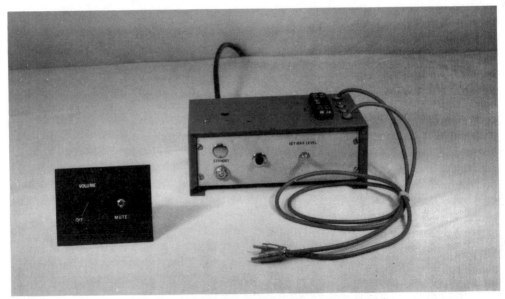

FIG. 8-1. *The finished project has two parts—the
base unit and a remote control panel.*

it to a separate amplifier that drives the extension speakers. The amplifier is plugged into
an outlet in the controller where it receives power when the remote switch S1 is turned
on. That way it is only on when you want it to be.

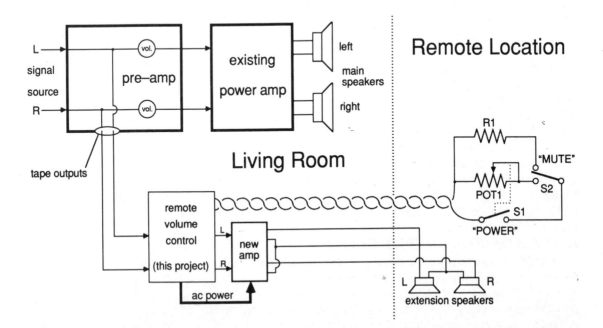

FIG. 8-2. *This block diagram shows how the remote volume control is added to a typical stereo system.*

THE CIRCUIT

The complete circuit for this project is shown in FIG. 8-3. The Motorola MC3340P it is designed around is an inexpensive IC made especially for applications like this. It has a maximum control range of −90 to +13 dB and contributes a maximum total harmonic distortion of 0.6 percent. The volume at its output (pin seven) depends on a variable resistor placed between its control (pin two) and ground. A separate IC is used for each channel in the remote volume control circuit, but both are controlled simultaneously by a single potentiometer.

Potentiometer POT1 is the remote volume control. It determines the ICs' output volume. Back at the base station, POT2 is connected in series with it to limit the maximum volume level allowed. This feature is optional but might be desirable if the extension speakers are particularly sensitive or if you want to keep people from raising the volume past a certain point.

The attenuation of the MC3340P ICs is not linear in response to changes in control resistance. Nor does it have a logarithmic response (called an *audio taper*) to compensate for the way the ear perceives sound levels. Rather, it is somewhat in-between, making a compromise inevitable. It was discovered experimentally that a linear taper potentiometer gave the best results when used with two ICs in the parallel configuration required for stereo. Combined with the particular response of the ICs, a 10-kilohm linear taper potentiometer obtained a semi-logarithmic response from the volume control which was quite acceptable.

When the remote power switch is turned on, current flows from pin two of the ICs, through the remote circuitry, and through the transistor to ground. This causes the transistor to conduct, powering the triac driver opto-isolator. It switches the extension amplifier on via the triac connected to the outlet it's plugged into. Switch S1 can be ganged with POT1 so both power and volume can be controlled with a single knob.

Capacitors C1 and C2 block the DC voltage at the ICs from leaking back into the stereo system. Capacitors C4 and C5 create a high frequency rolloff; this is a common feature of linear IC circuits, because they usually have extremely high frequency response. The remaining capacitors are bypass and filtering capacitors.

An optional muting switch was provided on the remote panel of the prototype and is indicated in the schematic. When activated, it switches from the control potentiometer to a fixed resistor pre-selected to give a low volume level. You might not want to include a mute switch on your project, but if you do, select the muting resistor R1 according to your own preferred sound level.

Muting could also be activated in a similar way at the base station by a switch or a relay. The relay could be connected to automatically mute the volume level in response to a phone call, ringing doorbell, or when a receiver is being tuned.

A NOTE ON THE CIRCUIT CHOSEN

There are other ways to control volume levels by a remote DC voltage, but I chose this circuit over them. For years, light-modulated photocells have been commonly used in similar applications. Originally, this circuit was also going to incorporate a variable intensity light source shining on two light-dependent resistors. While that approach does use fewer parts and looks simpler on paper, it was abandoned because it is actually more

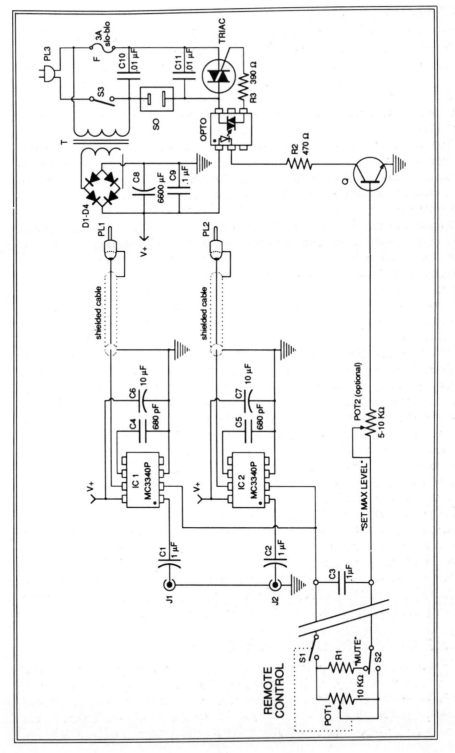

Fig. 8-3. *Complete schematic for the remote volume control.*

expensive and depends on tricky optical alignment of the photocells for good stereo balance. The ICs used in this circuit are less expensive, more rugged, and can provide some gain if needed—something a photocell circuit cannot.

CONSTRUCTION

None of the parts used in this project are difficult to obtain. While the ICs and the triac driver opto-isolator are not everyday items, they are available from most of the mail order parts sources in Chapter 23. The potentiometer POT1 can be purchased with a ganged switch from Radio Shack or the mail order houses. Transistor Q1 can be any general-purpose NPN type.

The circuit is easily built on one of the pre-etched project boards available from Radio Shack or from mail order companies. The component placement diagram for a typical board, the Radio Shack #276-168 Universal PC Board, is given in FIG. 8-4. Using the pattern shown, construction of the audio section is a simple matter of dropping components into the correct holes and soldering them to the board. The AC components and the power supply are best located on a separate circuit board for isolation and because of the larger components used.

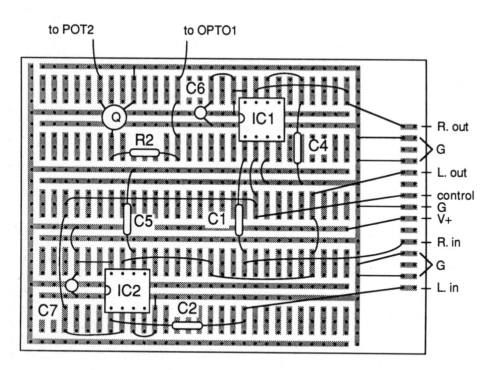

TOP VIEW SHOWN

FIG. 8-4. *Use this diagram with a Radio Shack #276-168 Universal PC Board to simplify construction of the project.*

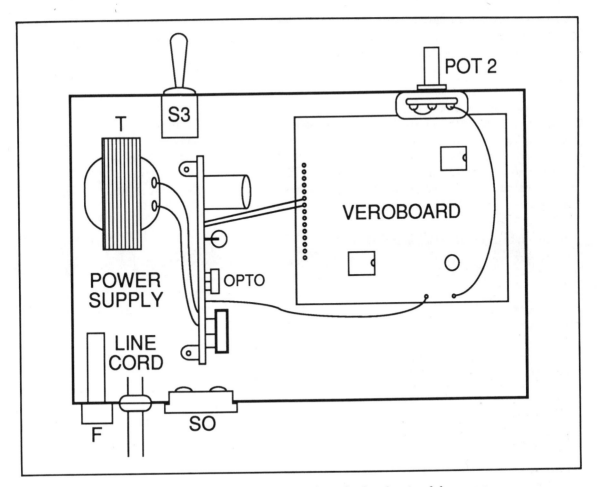

FIG. 8-5. *This is how parts were arranged inside the chassis of the prototype.*

The project should be built in a metal box to shield the audio circuit from hum pickup. As with all audio circuits, try to physically separate the audio portion of the controller from the AC wiring and power supply components as much as it's possible. Other than these considerations, construction should present no special difficulties and depends mostly on the dimensions of the enclosure you obtain. The internal layout of the prototype, built in a surplus steel enclosure, is shown in FIG. 8-5. The power supply circuit is not very critical since the ICs can operate over a supply range of 9 to 18 volts. The relaxed requirements make it possible to use whatever power supply parts are readily available at the time of this project's construction. The appearance of the base unit is not important since it is intended to be tucked away somewhere and forgotten.

How you build the remote station depends on where it will be used. For installation in a wall, POT1 can be mounted in a faceplate without the need for a complete enclosure. Or a small minibox could be used if it must stand alone. Use an ordinary two-conductor wire to connect the remote to the base station. Although a twisted pair of wires is often used to connect low voltage control circuits, it really isn't necessary for this circuit. The base station is insensitive enough to hum so that precautions like twisted wires don't have to be used.

OPERATION

The remote volume control should be left switched on all the time and connected to your stereo as shown in FIG. 8-2. Until the remote switch is turned on, it remains in a standby condition. Only when switch S1 is turned on is the extension amp activated. The power that the remote volume control draws during standby is not significant and the part of the circuit connected to the stereo is isolated from the 120 VAC power line for safety. If you do not wish to leave it on all the time though, plug the remote volume controller into one of the switched convenience outlets provided by the components in your main system.

MORE USES FOR THE CIRCUIT

The MC3340P IC with its wide control range can serve as an inexpensive preamp for line level signals. Connected between a tuner or tape deck and a power amp, it is easy to set up a simple stereo system without a preamp. Because the circuit is so compact and its power supply requirements are easily met, it could probably be built inside the tuner, tape deck, or amp chassis without much trouble. It could then obtain the power supply it requires from the equipment it is operating in. Since the automatic power-on function wouldn't be needed, those components could be eliminated by routing the return wire from the volume potentiometer directly to ground and leaving out Q.

PARTS LIST:

Remote Volume Control

C1, C2	1μF
C3, C9	.1μF bypass capacitors, value not critical
C4, C5	680pF
C6, C7	10μF, 16V or better, electrolytic
C8	6600μF, 16V or better, electrolytic
C10, C11	.01μF, 200V bypass capacitors, value not critical
R1	(Optional, for muting) Determine value experimentally.
R2	470Ω, $\frac{1}{4}$W
R3	390Ω, $\frac{1}{4}$W
POT 1	10KΩ linear taper
POT 2	(Optional) 5 to 10KΩ potentiometer
F	3A, SLO-BLO fuse
T	Step down transformer with 7V to 12V secondary
Q	2N3904 or equivalent general-purpose NPN transistor
IC1, IC2	MC3340P (Motorola) volume attenuator IC
TRIAC	200V or better, current rating to match amplifier's
D1 through D4	50V, 1A or better bridge rectifier
OPTO	MOC3031 zero-crossing triac driver opto-isolator
S1	Mini toggle switch or part of POT 1
S2	(Optional) SPDT muting pushbutton or toggle
S3	5A SPST or better mini toggle switch
PL1, PL2	RCA phono plugs
PL3	Line cord and wall plug
J1, J2	RCA phono jacks
SO	Power outlet

PLUS, panel-mount fuse holder, suitable enclosure, shielded audio cable, heatsink, TO-220 mounting hardware, pre-etched experimenter board (R.S. #276-168 or equiv.), hook-up wire, and solder.

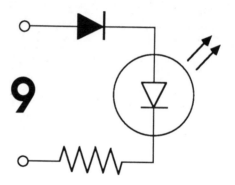

9

Protected
Outlet Box

As computers have become more common, many devices to protect them from line voltage surges, spikes, transients, and interference have appeared for sale. They range from simple ones that don't inspire much confidence to others that are elaborate and cost more than some computers themselves. These powerline protectors, often built into outlet boxes, usually offer additional convenience features. Some allow you to switch power to several outlets together or separately, some automatically do the switching themselves when you turn on a particular device plugged into them, and some even supply backup power during an outage.

The project described in this chapter can be built with or without most of these features found on commercial models and allows you to strike a reasonable compromise between performance and cost. In all respects, it offers a better value for your money than what you can buy.

There are three levels of complexity that this outlet box project can be built with. The simplest is a no-frills computer protector with seven outlets. See FIG. 9-1. It does a good job of eliminating spikes, transients, line noise, radio frequency interference (RFI), and electromagnetic interference (EMI). It offers two banks of outlets, individually protected and somewhat isolated from each other. This is a desirable feature if you have a printer or disc drive that produces electrical noise that could disrupt other sensitive equipment. It allows you to separate components that would otherwise interact. If the power goes out while you're using your computer and then comes back on, this outlet box keeps power off until you manually reset it. The logic behind this is that although any data the machine held at the time is forever lost, this project at least tries to save the equipment from the surges and irregularities that often occur when the power comes back onto the line. This simplest level of the outlet box project also includes a power switch to control its output. See FIG. 9-1.

The second way you can build the outlet box has all the features of the no-frills design but adds an automatic power switch. One of the seven outlets is set aside as a control. When the device plugged into it is switched on, the outlet box senses the current drawn and turns on the rest of the outlets. They stay on as long as the selected device is kept on. This simplifies powering up multi-component systems. Of course this feature can be manually overridden by the master power switch.

The third way the outlet box can be built allows you to hook up a 12 VDC to 120 VAC power inverter to keep your computer going if the power line goes out. This method is not for everyone because not all computers work with common power inverters. Some computers (IBMs and others that use switching power supplies) won't work reliably unless powered by a more sophisticated battery back-up device that generates a true sine wave (or a close approximation of one) at an accurate frequency. But the computers that use transformer-input linear power supplies (most inexpensive computers like Atari, Commodore, some TRS-80s, etc.) can get away with using a power inverter. This third alternative is intended mainly if you already have a 12 VDC to 120 VAC power inverter. If you don't, investing in one to protect a computer that's relatively inexpensive to begin with hardly seems worth it. If you do have a computer that justifies the expense, it probably requires a more sophisticated battery-backup anyway. But still, this alternative is probably useful to some computer users.

FIG. 9-1. *The three possible versions of this project all look like this when finished.*

These three versions of the same project are cumulative. The second or third versions can be added after you've built the first if you later decide you want the features they provide.

THE NO-FRILLS VERSION

The circuit in FIG. 9-2 is for the simplest version of the power outlet project. To appreciate its operation, consider what it's faced with. Transients as high as 1000 volts aren't unusual on an average power line. They are caused by heavy industrial equipment in the neighborhood, lightning, and even household appliances switching on and off. Don't look for them with a voltmeter though; these momentary voltage spikes are too quick to be noticed by ordinary meters. Your computer knows they exist though because transients of high enough voltage can flow right through its power supply to the sensitive IC's.

The Circuit

The metal-oxide-varistors MOV1 through MOV3 in this circuit are there to clamp brief voltage transients to a level of around 180 volts which seems to be tolerable by computers. There are three of them because transients can occur across any pair of the three power line wires. Many commercial "spike protectors" overlook this, featuring only one MOV across the line that can't offer the complete protection of three.

Line voltage spikes are short in duration and though they might be of a high voltage, have little energy. Their energy is absorbed and dissipated by the MOVs easily. If a truly massive surge of any duration should occur though, the MOVs would attempt to clamp it and in doing that would blow out one of the fuses. Fuse F1 is necessary for this reason. Fuse F2, on the other hand, is really optional. It is included as protection against extreme spikes appearing only across the neutral wire and ground, which are rare. Such a spike could occur in the case of a nearby lightning strike but in that case it's doubtful whether a fuse would be all that much protection anyway.

The two EMI/RFI filters are low-pass LC filter modules that protect equipment from the high frequency noise commonly present on power lines. They also keep any RF generated by your computer out of the powerline where it could cause interference with other equipment. These filter modules are sold by Radio Shack and mail order dealers for a few dollars each. Common ratings are three, five, and 10 amps. The higher rated filters cost more so its better to split up the load among two separate filters each with lower ratings as this circuit does. One set of outlets can be isolated from another this way. Often the source of problems in a computer system can be traced to interactions between components rather than to something external to the system.

TRIAC 1, the opto-isolator, and their associated components form an electronic latching relay. When the RESET pushbutton is pressed, the opto-isolator is powered from the supply formed for it by D1, R2, and C2. This switches the triac on, powering the computer equipment, NE1, and the opto-isolator through D2. If power fails even briefly though, the opto-isolator loses its supply and TRIAC 1 reverts to its off state until the RESET pushbutton is pressed again.

There's not much to the rest of the circuit. When switch S is on, NE2 comes on and the outlets are powered. Capacitor C3 connected across the switch suppresses noise and arcing when the switch is operated. This is good both for its sake and the computer's.

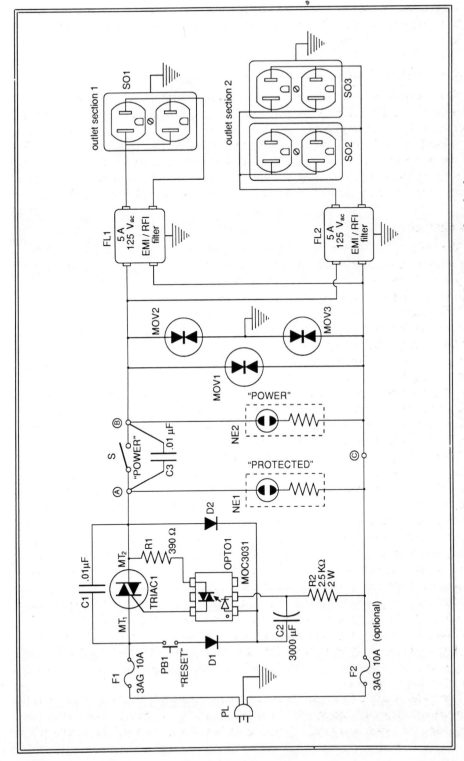

FIG. 9-2. *This schematic is for the simplest version of the protected outlet box.*

FIG. 9-3. *The EMI/RFI filters and the MOVs fit in one side of the outlet box as shown here.*

Less arcing prolongs the switch's life and radiates less noise to the equipment it controls. Capacitor C1 across the triac suppresses high frequency noise that could damage or inadvertantly trigger it. The points "A," "B," and "C" in the diagram are where the circuit for the automatic power switch in FIG. 9-4 attaches. If you're not building that, just ignore these points.

Construction

The easiest and cheapest way to build an outlet box is to use steel junction boxes for the enclosure with duplex outlets mounted in the covers. This method eliminates the need to cut rounded outlet holes in metal and also makes the outlet box easily expandable by the addition of more junction boxes. For the average computer system you need no more than seven outlets, so two boxes should suffice to start with. If you need more later they can always be added. Bolt the junction boxes together with lock washers under the nuts to keep them from loosening. With the boxes so close together you might have to file one edge of each outlet cover slightly so they both can fit without overlapping.

Build the filters and the MOVs into one box as shown in FIG. 9-3. Mount two pairs of outlets in the cover of this side. The other box should contain the triac-latching circuitry for this version of the project and the automatic power switch circuitry for the second option if you decide to add that. In the cover of this second box, mount a duplex outlet and an outlet/switch pair. Mount the neon lights and RESET pushbutton between the outlet holes in the cover of this side as in FIGS. 9-1 and 9-3.

Because the power line to a computer should be free of all interruptions, make sure you wire the circuit securely. Taking the extra precaution of solidly mounting and connecting the components will ensure that momentary dropouts don't occur accidentally if the box is kicked or dropped.

One of the best ways to build neat, high reliability circuits is by building on the copper side of singled-sided PC board stock. This method is described shortly in the suggestions for building the automatic power switch circuit. If you're building only the first version described so far, simple point-to-point wiring can be used with solder lugs. But when you add more components to the circuit, you'll need a more compact way of mounting parts or they won't all fit. A PC board is also the easiest way of mounting the opto-isolator.

If you use point-to-point wiring, use small bolts to attach the solder lugs to the small holes pre-drilled in the bottom of the outlet box. Attach component leads securely by looping them around the lug strips. You might find it easiest to mount the opto-isolator in a small DIP socket with wire wrap leads.

ADDING THE AUTOMATIC POWER SWITCH

The circuit in FIG. 9-4 can be added to the previous circuit at the points A, B, and C. Then whatever device is plugged into its sensing outlet, SO4 will control the other outlets' power. When the controlling device is turned on, current flows through its power switch and circuitry by passing through the pair of diodes D3 and D4. Any silicon diode causes a voltage drop of about 0.7 volts across its junction when current passes through it. Therefore, when the device is turned on, 0.7 VAC is developed at the base of the transistor Q. This makes it conduct, completing the circuit along with D5, R5, and C4 that drive OPTO2, a triac driver opto-isolator. This switches on TRIAC2 which is connected as a power switch for the rest of the outlets. When the controlling device is turned on, the current it draws turns the rest of the system on. When it is turned off, there is no more voltage induced across the diodes so the triac is turned off.

Capacitors C5 and C6 suppress power line glitches, keeping them from triggering the transistor. The transistor can be almost any general-purpose NPN type with a collector-emitter reverse breakdown voltage of 85 volts or greater. Diodes D3 and D4 should have a current rating safely in excess of whatever load is expected to be plugged into the sensing outlet. If one of them opens, the transistor can be damaged. The sensing outlet used should be the one that is part of the switch/outlet combination. These combination units typically have three terminals because one side of the switch and outlet are usually permanently connected. The circuit is designed with this in mind though. Point "A" is common to both the switch and sensing outlet. This is the reason for using that particular outlet for the sensing function.

With the second circuit added to the previous one, you will notice that there are two series-connected triacs in the circuit. Somehow, even though the voltage drop they impart is insignificant, having two triacs in the circuit doesn't seem "elegant." Although they and their opto-isolators cost little and take up almost no space, it just seems redundant to use two in series. And yes, the circuit could be designed differently and the two could be replaced by one with their switching function handled by low-voltage logic ICs. But that design, while more elegant and better looking on paper, would require the addition of a power supply and circuit board and wouldn't allow the circuit to be built in two cumulative steps. The use of two triacs, which admittedly looks clumsy and awkward,

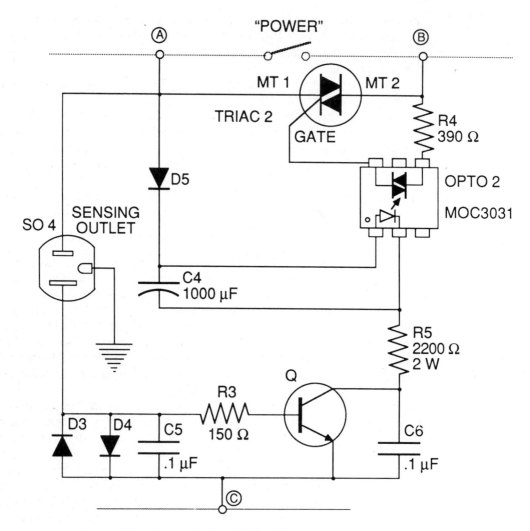

FIG. 9-4. *This circuit can be added to the circuit in Fig. 9-2 at the points* Ⓐ, Ⓑ, *and* Ⓒ *to make an automatic power switch.*

is a case where an effective design just happens to be unelegant on paper.

Construction of the Automatic Power Switch

The best construction method for the automatic power switch is building on the foil side of a sturdy circuit board. A thick, single-sided epoxy-fiberglass board is ideal; suitable stock can be purchased from electronic surplus dealers and sometimes found in the scrap bins of circuit board manufacturers. The reasons for building on circuit board stock are obvious—stability and compactness among others—but the reasons for building on the *foil* side may not be that apparent. They are:

→ Areas of the foil can be used as convenient heatsinking for the triacs.

→ This construction method makes it easy to design circuits by placing the components on the board and sketching lines between them—no repeated flipping back and forth.

→ It is not necessary to work with the mirror image of the circuit layout as you would with an etched board.

→ Wires don't have to pass through the board to reach the foil. This requires fewer holes, accommodates odd-sized connectors easily, and allows for stronger connections by laying wires flat.

→ Changes are easy to make because mounting is less permanent than with a standard circuit board.

→ Points in the circuit are easily reached without having to drill through to the other side.

→ The bottom of the board stays insulated, simplifying mounting.

Designing a foil-sided PC board is relatively easy—much more so than designing one where the components mount on the other side of the board. You start with an idea of the board's size. In this case, the board size is limited by the size of the junction box it will be installed in. Plan the mounting points to the board and where all physical obstructions to the board will be first. Cut the blank board to the right size and check that it fits in the enclosure. Drill and check the alignment of the mounting holes. Doing this for the prototype yielded the board shown in FIGS. 9-5, 9-6, and 9-7. The two holes near the middle are for the hardware that mounts the board to the bottom of the box. With the board cut to size, the layout can be designed next.

Plan on mounting the triacs flat so they take up less room, heatsink them, and provide a good electrical contact to their mounting tab (MT2). Place them in an appropriate position on the board and draw the outline of them and their leads. The placement of the triacs and the other components on the board depends on the schematic; component leads that are connected in the schematic should be placed near each other on the board for easiest connections. Place the other components on the board following the circuit and mark where they and their leads go. While you do this, connect the leads by mapping out foil pads to solder them onto. Do this by drawing lines where you will later cut through the foil leaving islands of foil to connect component leads. The result of this activity is shown in FIG. 9-5 where the components are superimposed over the solid lines that indicate where the foil will be cut.

Drill whatever holes you will need for mounting the small components. These include the opto-couplers and perhaps the diodes, small resistors, and capacitors. The leads of the triacs, large resistors, and wired-in connections can be soldered flat to the foil. With all the necessary holes drilled, cut the foil on the lines you previously drew using an emery cut-off wheel in a Dremel Moto-Tool or similar high speed drill. Cutting along the lines is fairly easy with the cut-off wheel, especially if you slow the drill down somewhat. If you are using epoxy-fiberglass circuit board material, be certain to do your cutting in a well ventilated area or with a dust mask. The airborne epoxy and fiberglass dust is quite harmful to the lungs when inhaled. FIGURE 9-6 shows the board used in the prototype after it was outlined by this method.

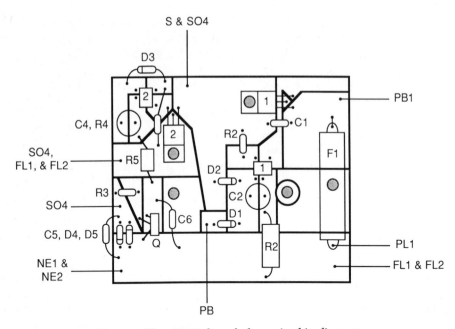

FIG. 9-5. *The circuit board shown in this diagram contains the components in both FIGS. 9-2 and 9-4.*

As a last step and before you mount any components, check the foil pads to see that there are no shorts between them. It could be disastrous if your islands retained a bridge between them. Check this with an ohmmeter or by using a continuity tester like the one in Chapter 19. Although they are very hard to see, in every board I've made this way I've discovered hidden shorts that didn't show up until they were checked electrically.

Mount the components in the order of increasing heat sensitivity. Because the surface of the board is mostly copper, (an excellent conductor of heat) large parts of it get hot when each component is soldered. This can make soldering a little difficult, requiring more time than usual for heating each joint. The opto-isolators and the transistor are the only parts that are particularly heat sensitive. The opto-isolator can be mounted using molex pins or a small IC socket, either of which is a good idea to use anyway even if it were not for the heat. The transistor can be protected from overheating by gripping its legs with pliers or aluminum heat sink clamps. Otherwise, mounting the components is just as easy as mounting them to a regular circuit board—simply a matter of plugging them into the right holes. The completed circuit board is shown in FIG. 9-7.

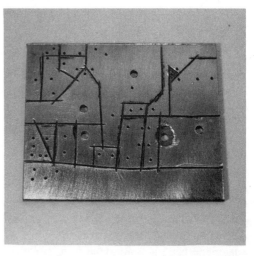

FIG. 9-6. *This circuit board was cut following the guide in FIG. 9-5.*

Install the board in the junction box before wiring connections to it. Be careful when mounting the board that you don't let anything metal touch part of the live copper surface. This can be prevented either by electrically isolating the foil pads around the mounting holes by cutting away the foil around them or by using nylon bushings to isolate the mounting bolts. With the board finally in place, wiring connections to it is simple if enough room was left for wires in the component layout. Bend the ends of wires at a right angle and push them down onto the board with a hot iron while applying solder. Completing the automatic power switch requires only correctly wiring the outlets, switches, and power cord to the board.

Using the Automatic Power Switch

The automatic power circuit is very sensitive; it will respond to currents of only a few milliamps. This can lead to some problems of false triggering. One such problem could be caused by a leaky capacitor connected across the power switch of the piece of equipment used to control the rest of the system. If enough current leaks through, the

FIG. 9-7. *Here the components have been mounted to the foil side of the circuit board.*

circuit might be fooled into turning on. A capacitor this leaky is not common though and should be replaced with a better one anyway.

Another potential problem is equipment that is always on. For example, some computer monitors draw power even when they're off to keep the CRT filament idling so it takes less time to warm up. Also, computers that have separate DC power supplies are essentially "on" all the time they are left plugged in. Their on-off switches are electrically located *after* their power supply, so they can't really be used to control the automatic switcher.

These problems can be overcome if you are willing to modify your equipment. A monitor can be rewired so that its power switch is truly a power switch and not just a switch between halfway on and fully on. This isn't at all that difficult, but it voids the warranty. A power switch can be added to the AC line of a computer's external power supply. This is a good idea because the supply will last longer if it's not left on all the time.

Of course, there are other options as well. The device that switches your system on doesn't have to be the monitor or CPU. It could be the disk drive or even an innocent table lamp that might be switched on when the computer is used anyway. If you do use a lamp, install a long-life bulb in it, because when the bulb burns out, your computer will turn itself off.

ADDING A POWER INVERTER

FIGURE 9-8 is a combined block diagram and schematic showing how to hook up a power inverter with the outlet box to provide backup power for a computer. To eliminate any delay that a switch-over from utility power to battery power might take, the inverter powers the computer all the time it is on.

Only the computer itself is backed up; the other parts of the system plug into the standard outlet box that is dependent on the line. In the case of a power failure, the monitor and storage device can temporarily be plugged into one of the backup outlets to save what's in the computer's memory.

Power to the computer is controlled by the same outlet box that supplies power to the rest of the system. When the system is turned on, a 12 VDC adaptor plugged into the outlet box sends power through D6 to the relay coil. When the contacts of the relay coil pull in, they provide it with power, latching it on. They also supply the inverter from a 12-volt car battery.

The computer receives power from the inverter through FL 3, an EMI/RFI filter similar to the ones used in the outlet box for the rest of the system. The filtered output can be returned to one of the outlets in the outlet box through a wire, but it would probably be more practical to provide a separate set of backup outlets for the computer.

Since the computer is protected from a power failure, there is no way to turn it off except by unlatching the relay that controls power to the inverter. Turning the rest of the system off will not affect the computer powered by the inverter, and it shouldn't. Pushbutton PB 2 must be used for this purpose. It should be mounted in an accessible place because it will have to be pressed each time the computer must be turned off. It should not be mounted in such a way that it is easily bumped, however.

Heavy wiring is necessary to connect the battery, relay, and inverter. The relay contacts should also be able to carry sufficient current for the inverter. Make all connections to these components securely to prevent accidental disconnections.

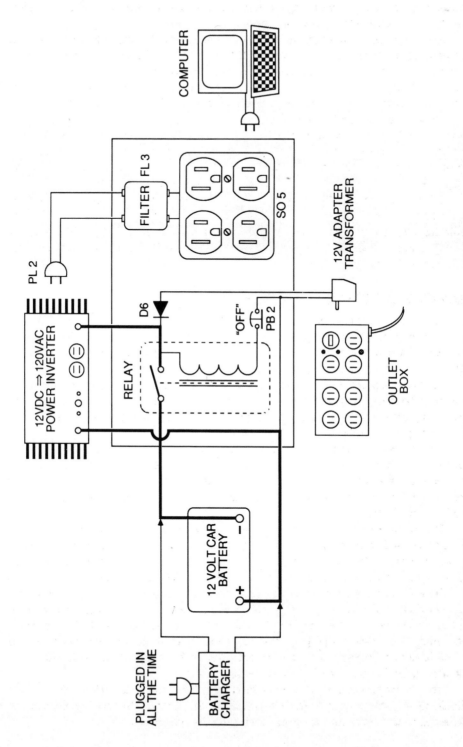

FIG. 9-8. *Use this diagram to connect an inverter to your computer system for emergency backup.*

Because the inverter draws power every time the computer is used, the battery that supplies it must be kept charged continuously. A car battery trickle charger could be used but costs money. It is easier to make a trickle charger by series-connecting a rectifier diode and a 40-watt light bulb in a circuit similar to the one in the Battery Charger section of Chapter 22.

OTHER USES OF THE OUTLET BOX

Of course the outlet box project described in this chapter isn't limited to serving only computers. Audio and video systems are also likely candidates because both have many components and are sensitive to power line interference. The receiver or preamp in an audio system typically assumes the role of power switch for the rest of the system. But with modern amplifiers that draw several hundred watts, the preamp or receiver's ability to switch an entire system's power is questionable. In this case, the auto-power switch becomes a useful feature, allowing one component to turn the rest on indirectly, without knowing what it's doing.

PARTS LIST:

Protected Power Outlet

(Not all parts needed for the simpler versions.)

C1, C3	.01μF, 200V bypass capacitor, value not critical
C2	3000μF, 6V or better, electrolytic
C4	1000μF, 6V or better, electrolytic
C5, C6	.1μF, 200V bypass capacitors, value not critical
R1, R4	390Ω, ¼W
R2	2.5KΩ, 2W
R3	150Ω, ¼W
R5	2.2KΩ, 2W
F1	3AG 10A
F2	(Optional) 3AG, 10A
NE1, NE2	Neon panel indicator with built-in dropping resistor
FL1 through FL3	5A, 125VAC or better EMI/RFI filters
MOV1 through MOV3	S10V-S14K130 or equivalent metal oxide varistors
Q	NPN with V_{CEO} and V_{CBO} greater than 85 volts (2N5655, 2N5656, 2N5657, MJE 340, TIP 31, TIP 48, or equiv.)
TRIAC1, TRIAC2	12A, 200V or better
D1 through D6	1A, 200V or better (rectifier diodes)
OPTO1, OPTO2	MOC3031 zero-crossing triac driver opto-isolators
S	SPST power switch (part of SO4)
PB1	N.O. pushbutton switch
PB2	N.C. pushbutton switch
RELAY	10A or better relay with 12VDC coil (R.S. #275-226 ''Automotive Lighting Relay'' or equiv.)
PL1	Three-wire 10A line cord and wall plug
PL2	Line cord and wall plug
SO1-SO3	Duplex wall outlets
SO4	Single wall outlet (part of S)
SO5	Power outlets for computer as needed
BATTERY CHARGER	Use a commercial charger with a trickle charge setting or see text about making one.

12V CAR BATTERY
12VDC to 120VAC INVERTER
12V ADAPTOR

PLUS, steel junction boxes, hardware, single sided PC board material or solder lugs (see text), fuseholder (internal or external mounting, depending on available space), suitable enclosure for inverter circuit, hook-up wire, and solder.

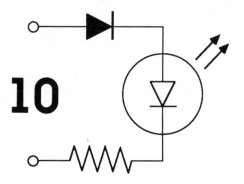

10

Telephone
Accessory

This project is a simple but useful telephone accessory that connects right to the phone line. It does two things. When someone is using a phone on the line, it lights the LINE IN USE LED. Its other function is a combination hold and on-hook dialing circuit. When the HOLD button is pressed, a corresponding LED comes on and lets you hang up the phone, move to another extension, and pick up the conversation again (see FIG. 10-1).

Another feature of this project is its appearance. Although it is easy to build, the finished project doesn't have a bulky home-built look. Instead it fits neatly into a modular telephone jack cover designed to blend in with the color of most phones. This type of box was chosen for its compact size and the modular phone jack it has built into it. The modular jack makes the project convenient to move from one phone to another without undoing any wiring.

THE PHONE LINE

When all the phones on a line are hung up, a potential of about 48 volts DC is present across the two wires. When someone picks up a telephone though, the phone's internal resistance shunts across the line, bringing that voltage down to about 6 volts. The phone company detects the lowered resistance and activates the line.

The circuit shown in FIG. 10-2 makes use of these facts to perform its functions. The hold circuit simulates a phone being picked up by applying a resistance similar to a phone's across the line until a real phone is picked up. The line in-use monitor works by detecting the lowered voltage that appears on the line when a phone is picked up.

FIG. 10-1. *The finished phone accessory shown here is a compact unit designed to be placed next to a regular phone.*

THE CIRCUIT

The complete circuit for this project is shown in FIG. 10-2. The part of it that provides the hold function is activated by hanging up the phone with the HOLD pushbutton depressed. When this is done, the voltage across LED1, SCR, D, and R1 rises from about six volts to 48 volts DC. The voltage increase is enough to trigger the SCR into conduction through the pushbutton. A circuit is then completed that lights LED1 and places a resistance of 1200 to 1500 ohms across the line, simulating a telephone. It is this lowered resistance that fools the line into thinking a real phone is still off the hook. The SCR remains conducting until an extension telephone is subsequently picked up. When this happens, the low resistance of the phone reduces the current available to the SCR, causing it to stop conducting and effectively disconnecting the hold circuit.

If the HOLD pushbutton is ever pressed accidentally during a phone conversation, nothing will happen because the six volts present on the line is too low to activate the SCR. But if it is pushed with the phone on the hook, it has the same effect as picking up the phone.

The LINE IN USE indicator is a low-voltage detector. It lights LED2 when the voltage across the line falls below the standard 48 volts that is present when no phone is being used. Resistors R3, R4, and R5 form a voltage divider to scale down the line voltage to a convenient size, reduce current draw, and to isolate the indicator circuit from the line. Resistors R3 and R5 are intended to add up to about 5.6 megohms together. It is possible to use a single 5.6 megohm resistor on either side, but it is a good practice to use two separate resistors if it is convenient so the circuit is more isolated from the phone line.

With 48 volts across the divider, Q1 is biased on by the voltage across R4. Current flows from the battery, through R6, and through the transistor. Because Q1's "on" resistance is so low, it diverts any current that would flow to the base of Q2, so Q2 remains off. When the line voltage drops below about 15 volts however, Q1 is no longer biased. Its impedance rises and current from R6 can flow through R7 to Q2, which then conducts. This turns the LED on signaling the line is in use.

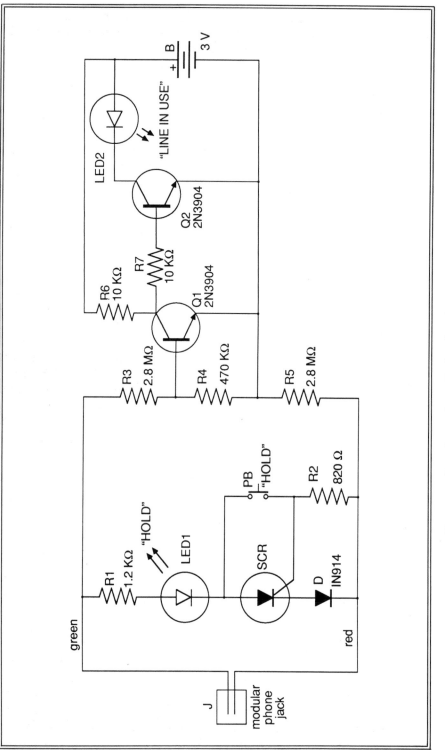

FIG. 10-2. *Complete schematic for the phone accessory.*

The circuit draws an insignificant amount of power from its battery supply when the phone is off the hook. Even when the phone is picked up, the current drain is only ten milliamps or so. Two AA batteries will last a long time in this circuit.

CONSTRUCTION

The circuit is simple, so building it shouldn't be difficult. Component values aren't especially critical, but most of them are polarized, so be sure to observe their correct orientation. The combination of R3 and R5 should add up to about 5.6 megohms, but any of several combinations that can be made up from standard values should work. The value of R4 might have to be varied slightly, depending on your local phone company's line voltage and the gain of the transistors. In the hold circuit, you might have to change the value of R1 depending on the sensitivity of the SCR. Once selected though, these component values should give no trouble; they might vary initially but won't change after that.

Because of the slight variations possible, it's best to test this circuit on a breadboard before building it into a case. Test each part of the circuit separately as you build it, connecting it to the phone line to ensure that it works with the line voltages present in your area. When you have both functions working satisfactorily, build the components into the enclosure.

Although other enclosures are possible and could even make construction simpler, the ideal enclosure for the project is a Radio Shack Quick-Connect Modular Phone Jack (#279-355) or an equivalent. To adapt it for this project, cut away the plastic reinforcement tabs at the corners inside the case with diagonal cutters and a hobby knife. Remove the yellow and black wires coming from the jack; they won't be used and will only get in the way. Leave only the red and green wires. To cover the bottom, cut a piece of plastic or cardboard to fit the shape of the case and drill a hole in it corresponding to the screw hole in the top piece. To hold it to the case, you need a nut and a longer bolt than the short stub originally provided.

With the case modified like this, two Radio Shack #270-401 AA battery holders will fit perfectly inside. Install them as shown in FIGS. 10-3 and 10-4, noting their polarity. Fasten them in place with epoxy, hot glue, or plastic model cement.

Apply lettering to the enclosure before the switch and LEDs are mounted in it. With the "hold" LED in close proximity to the HOLD pushbutton, a single word will explain both. The other LED should be labeled "in use" or whatever else it suggests.

Select a HOLD pushbutton that takes up as little internal spaces as possible. In the prototype, the "H" pushbutton salvaged from a surplus computer keyboard was glued to the outside of the case. Another alternative is a membrane switch or a calculator key. Mount this switch and the two LEDs approximately as shown in FIGS. 10-3 and 10-4 using glue to hold the LEDs in their holes.

You can build the circuitry without actually mounting most of the parts. The leads of the LEDs and pushbutton provide all the support that's needed. Add one component at a time, using needle-nose pliers or forceps to bend small loops into the ends of the leads—into which leads from other components can be inserted. This type of construction takes a little getting used to. It requires dexterity to do skillfully, or patience if the dexterity is lacking. But it is one way of building very compact circuits.

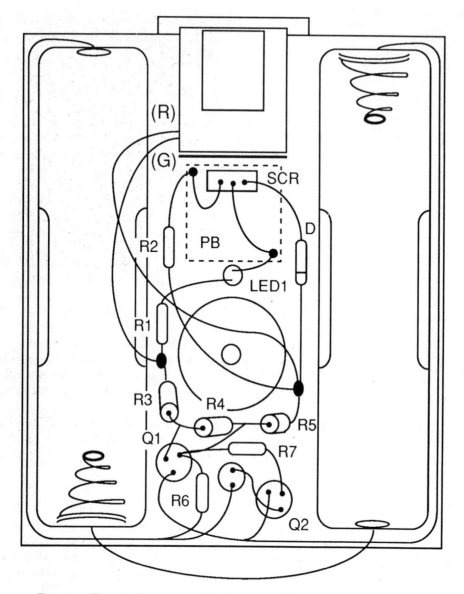

FIG. 10-3. *Use this diagram to plan the internal layout of the enclosure.*

It's best to build the hold circuit first. Start connecting components to the contacts of the pushbutton because they will be the hardest to reach afterwards. Many SCRs have a metal tab attached to them. If it gets in the way, the tab can be clipped off with diagonal cutters or removed with a hacksaw. Follow the diagram in FIG. 10-3 for the rest of the components, referring to the schematic for the correct polarity of each.

When building the line-in-use indicator, start with R3, R4, and R5. Connect Q1 across R4 and connect R6 and R7 to it. The other end of R6 goes to the anode of LED2 along

FIG. 10-4. *This photograph shows how the parts are built into the suggested enclosure following the diagram in FIG. 10-3.*

with the positive lead from the battery. Finally, Q2 attaches to the remaining component leads. The finished telephone accessory should look like the prototype in FIG. 10-4.

Once you have the project built, install a pair of AA batteries. With these installed and while it's not connected to the phone line, the ''line-in-use'' LED should light up since the device is not detecting a voltage—a condition that it interprets as a phone being used. Attaching the bottom plate to the cover with a nut completes construction of this project.

As soon as it is connected to a phone line that is not being used, the LED will go out. The project can connect to any phone jack by adding a modular cord and a splitter. While a wire and splitter are more expensive than directly connecting it to the line, they do make the device portable.

OTHER USES

The circuit for this project might easily be built into the case of an older phone to give it some modern features. Rather than buy one of the sleek modern phones that have many features, you might want to take a few hours to build the circuit for the hold/indicator into one of your older phones. This eliminates the need for a separate case and wire, and best of all lets you continue to use your old reliable favorite.

Telephone Accessory

R1	1.2KΩ, All resistors ¼W
R2	820Ω (might have to be changed, see text)
R3, R5	2.8 MΩ each, or any combination that add up to 5.6MΩ
R4	470KΩ (might have to be changed, see text)
R6, R7	10KΩ
B	2 AA cells
Q1, Q2	2N3904 or equivalent general-purpose NPN transistors
SCR	Almost any SCR
D	1N914 or equivalent
LED 1	Miniature yellow LED
LED 2	Red LED
PB	Small keyboard-style pushbutton
J	Modular phone jack (built into enclosure)

PLUS, AA battery holders (R.S. #270-401 or equiv.), suitable enclosure (R.S. #279-355 or equiv.), base plate for enclosure, rubber feet, hardware, modular line cord and duplex jack (for hookup to phone line), rub on letters, and solder.

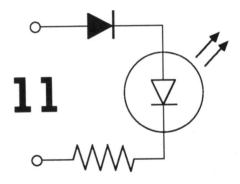

11

Tide
Clock

This project is a great idea for anyone who lives near the ocean or whose activities are affected by the tides. Fishermen in particular might find it quite convenient. It displays the current tide on a large, easy-to-read clock face. A synchronous motor salvaged from a standard clock drives a single hand, so it tracks the 12-hour, 25-minute tidal cycle. With the face divided into "high" and "low," it gives an instant visual indication of the current tide and the time remaining before it will change. Because its display is so easy to interpret, the tide clock is much more convenient than a printed tide table. See FIG. 11-1.

The project has two parts: the motor-driven clock and the electronic circuit that powers the motor. The clock motor, which normally completes one revolution every 12 hours when driven by 60 Hz AC, is driven at a slower rate by the drive circuit. By powering it at a slightly reduced frequency, the drive circuit electronically reduces the speed of the motor to one revolution per 12 hours and 25 minutes. The speed is adjustable over a narrow range to permit fine tuning or use in other applications. If other different clock faces are desired, the drive circuit can power more than one clock motor.

THE CIRCUIT

This project is only possible because of some unique characteristics of synchronous motors. Synchronous motors are used in almost all mechanical clocks and timers because their speed remains stable despite wear, uneven loading, and wide changes in line voltage. Although they are designed to work off a 120-volt AC sine wave, they can operate satisfactorily off the square wave of approximately 150 peak-to-peak volts that the drive circuit in FIG. 11-2 provides. Since the speed of a synchronous motor depends only on

111

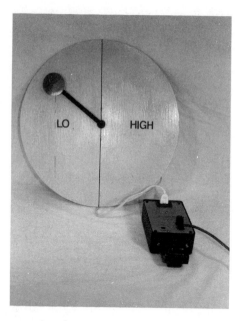

FIG. 11-1. *The tide clock has two parts—the drive circuitry and the clock.*

the frequency of the supply voltage, it is usually quite stable, but can be varied when driven by that circuit.

The drive circuit, which is built into the compact enclosure shown in FIGS. 11-1 and 11-3, has three sections: its power supply, a variable oscillator, and an electronic switch. The oscillator sets the frequency that ultimately determines the speed of the clock. It drives the electronic switch which rapidly switches the polarity of the DC supply, creating an AC voltage to drive the motor with.

The Power Supply

The power supply used in this project has two outputs—a 12-volt DC supply for the oscillator circuit and a 100-volt DC supply that eventually provides power for the clock. Neither of these voltages can be obtained directly from the power line without considerable loss, so at least one transformer must be used. It would be simple to build two separate transformer supplies for these voltages, but this project's design is complicated by the fact that it must be compact and inexpensive to make constructing it worthwhile.

The circuit illustrates how a single transformer can be made to do double duty, providing both voltage outputs. To obtain the higher of the two supply voltages, its 40-volt secondary of about 30 to 40 volts is connected in such a way as to subtract from the 120-volt AC power line. The 80 to 90 volts AC is the result and is rectified by D1 and filtered by C1 (a photoflash capacitor). In addition to their applications in camera equipment, photoflash capacitors are particularly suited to this and a number of other projects because of their availability, high voltage ratings, and compact size.

Without any loading, the DC voltage at the capacitor runs somewhat above 100 volts. With the current that the clock motor draws though, this voltage drops below 100 volts. This means the transistors in the switching part of the circuit must be rated at about 150 reverse-blocking volts or more.

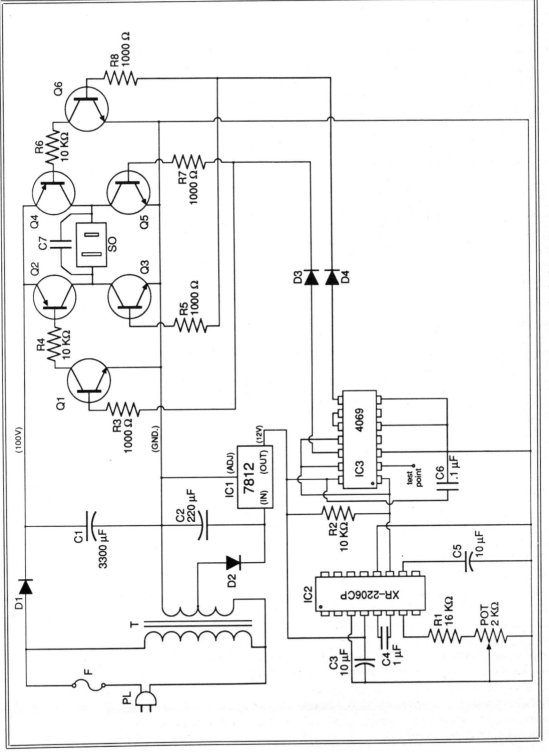

FIG. 11-2. *Complete schematic of the tide clock drive circuitry.*

The 12-volt supply for the oscillator uses the same ground as the high voltage supply. It takes its power from across the secondary of the same transformer used in the high voltage supply and rectifies it through D2. Capacitor C2 filters the pulsating voltage from D2 to 20 to 28 volts DC. This is too high for the ICs in the oscillator part of the circuit however, so a three-terminal voltage regulator IC is used to maintain a constant 12-volt output.

The 120-volt AC section of the project is as simple as possible. A 1.6 amp slo-blo fuse protects against overloads. No power switch is included in the schematic because this project is the type that is likely to be left on indefinitely. Of course, it's always possible to build one into the project if it would be useful for certain applications. No pilot light was intended either, since the drive circuitry will probably be tucked away in some inconspicuous spot anyway. But as with the power switch, adding one would be a simple task.

The Oscillator

A synchronous clock motor can be thought of as a stepper motor whose output shaft advances a small part of a revolution for every cycle in the AC supply it receives. To complete one revolution in 12 hours and 25 minutes instead of exactly 12 hours as it normally would, a synchronous motor must be driven at a slightly slower frequency. The new frequency would have to complete the same number of cycles in 12 hours 25 minutes as the standard 60 Hz frequency completes in only 12 hours. By simple multiplication, a frequency of 60 cycles per second completes 2,592,000 cycles in 12 hours. The frequency that completes the same number of cycles, but takes 12 hours and 25 minutes to do it in is 57.9865772 Hz. Driving the clock motor at this frequency will cause its output shaft to complete one revolution every 12 hours and 25 minutes.

There are many ways of building an oscillator that will produce the required frequency, but the most convenient and accurate way is to build a circuit around an IC oscillator chip. Of the ones available, the Exar XR-2206CP was chosen because it has the best thermal stability (20 parts per million per degree Celsius). This kind of stability is more than adequate for a clock with an analog display. The human error in reading the position of the hand alone is much greater than the oscillator would accumulate in weeks of worse-case usage.

Another advantage of the XR-2206CP is the small number of additional components it needs to form a square-wave oscillator. In this project, its frequency is determined solely by the capacitance of C4 and the combined resistance of R2 and the potentiometer. The frequency is specified by 1/RC. For 57.987 Hz and a capacitance of one microfarad, the resistance required is 17,245 ohms. Using ideal values, a 16,000 ohm resistor for R2 in series with a 2000 ohm potentiometer allows the frequency to be adjusted over a 55.5 to 62.5 Hz range. The small variation allows for tolerance errors in the capacitance of C4 and the IC's own one percent maximum deviation from the formula.

Along with its timing capacitor and resistor, the XR-2206CP makes up the heart of the circuit. The unconnected pins in the diagram are for its sine wave output and some of its other functions that are not necessary for the simple square wave output used to drive this project. Capacitors C3 and C5 are bypass capacitors whose values are not critical.

The square wave output of the XR-2206CP appears at its pin 11 where it is sent to IC3.

The 4069 IC acts mainly as a buffer between IC2 and the switching circuitry. It consists of six inverters, only four of which are used in this circuit. An inverter has an output that is either high or low. If its input is a low or negative voltage, its output is high. Conversely, if its input is up near its supply voltage, its output becomes low. The inverters can switch between their high and low states very rapidly and can follow the square wave output of IC2 with ease.

IC2 drives three inverters through pins 1, 10, and 12 of IC3. The output of one of these is provided as a test point at which the oscillator's frequency can be monitored with a counter. Another inverter's output goes on to drive the switching circuit through D3. The output of a third inverter is used to drive yet another inverter in IC3. The output of this fourth inverter, at pin 8, is also used to drive the switching circuit. Because one drive signal to the switching circuit passes through a single inverting stage while the other passes through two such stages, they are out of phase. While one is high the other is low, and vice versa.

The Switching Circuit

The two outputs from IC3 control the switching circuitry, causing current from the supply to flow through the clock motor in alternating directions. When the output from pin 12 on the IC is high, transistors Q1 and Q5 are biased by current flowing through D3. When transistor Q1 turns on, Q2 conducts and power flows from left to right through whatever is plugged into the socket. On the next half cycle of the oscillator, pin 12 of IC3 becomes low while pin 8 becomes high. This switches on transistors Q3, Q4, and Q6 while turning off Q1, Q2, and Q5. During this half cycle, current flows through the load in the opposite direction, from right to left.

Only one set of transistors is on at any time. The inverters ensure that both sets of transistors are never on simultaneously. If that happened, no current would flow through the clock and the supply would be shorted out.

This circuit has the effect of a DPDT switch that rapidly flips back and forth. It takes a DC supply and creates AC from it by sending it through the load first one way and then the other. Because the pulses that trigger the switching circuit depend on IC2, the frequency of the AC output is adjustable by the potentiometer in the oscillator circuit.

Other circuit components are important as well. Resistors R3, R5, R7, and R8 limit the current drawn from IC3 while diodes D3 and D4 prevent any current flowing back from the switching circuit. Other current-limiting resistors are R4 and R6. Across the socket is C7—a bypass capacitor that suppresses any transients developed by the clock motor or by switching.

CONSTRUCTION

There are two stages to this project's construction. Most of the work involves building the drive circuit that was just discussed and installing it in an enclosure. What remains after that is taking apart a clock to salvage the drive motor and constructing a new face and hand to indicate its new function. In the suggestions that follow, the drive circuitry is discussed first. The face and hand are less critical (and are the part of the project that most hobbyists probably have their own ideas about) so they are discussed later.

The Drive Circuitry

The prototype was built on three small circuit boards. None required etching and all were very easy to assemble. Except for the transformer, fuseholder, and outlet, all the parts are mounted on the boards.

Three boards were used instead of one for a number of reasons. Mainly, the separate boards made it easy to build and test the power supply, the oscillator, and the switching circuits independently. Three smaller boards were also easier to handle and mount inside the small project enclosure visible in FIG. 11-3. The circuit itself suggests using separate boards when building it because of the different types of parts it includes. The ICs of the oscillator section are suited to a different circuit board and construction method than are the larger components of the power supply and switching circuits.

For the oscillator circuit in the prototype, a section of a pre-etched experimenter board from Radio Shack (R.S. #276-168) was used. The simple circuit of two ICs and a few parts fit easily on the board with room to spare for a small 20-turn trimmer potentiometer for making frequency adjustments. Only four wires were needed to connect this board to the rest of the circuit, although a short fifth wire made it easy to connect a frequency counter to the test point for calibration.

No parts placement diagram is provided for the oscillator section because variations in component dimensions will probably be the largest factor influencing their placement. The only important considerations for building the oscillator circuit on a circuit board involve the placement of the power supply bypass capacitors and the treatment of the ICs.

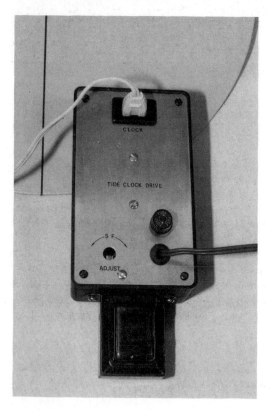

FIG. 11-3. *The drive circuitry is built into the enclosure shown here.*

To minimize the chance of stray oscillations, keep C3 and C6 reasonably close to IC2 and IC3 respectively. Avoid handling IC3 excessively and observe the procedure described in Chapter 21 for CMOS ICs when installing it. Otherwise, there is a chance it could be damaged by static electricity. Use sockets for the ICs to minimize handling and to make them easily removable. Too much handling is bad for IC3 because it is delicate. While IC2 is rugged, it costs a few dollars and should be treated with respect also.

The larger components that make up the power supply and switching sections of the circuit are more suited to surface mounting on one or two circuit boards. Two separate boards were used in the prototype because of the shape of the enclosure but a single board could be used if more room is available in the enclosure you use.

The power supply is a simple circuit that builds easily on the copper foil side of a piece of PC board stock. The method of cutting traces into the foil using a Dremel Moto Tool, that is described more fully in Chapter 2, was used in the prototype. It worked well and is strongly recommended. Using that method, the board was completed in about thirty minutes from initial layout to soldering the last component. The photoflash capacitor used for C1 was mounted on the board horizontally with short wires connecting its terminals to the foil. A nylon pull tie, piece of tape, or string is a good way to keep the capacitor flat on the board.

The same construction technique was used for the switching circuit. Foil-side mounting is especially suitable for power transistors, because it makes the finished board very flat and provides what little heatsinking these components need. The way the prototype board was cut is drawn in FIG. 11-4. The transistors bolt flat against the board with 6-32 hardware and without heatsinking compound or other hardware. This assures that a good connection is made to each transistor's mounting tab, which is also its collector.

When mounting the board, be sure to insulate the bolts used from the copper surface of the board. A fiber washer in each mounting hole will insulate the bolts or the Dremel tool could be used to remove the foil from around each hole so it won't make contact with the bolts.

Because the foil side is accessible, electrical connections can be made to the pads on the circuit boards wherever they are convenient. Because the entire circuit is accessible, wiring between circuit boards should present no problem. No holes are necessary; simply press a piece of wire to any place on the foil with a hot iron and apply solder to make a connection.

Although a rather small box was used to enclose the prototype, a larger one is recommended. As FIG. 11-5 reveals, the inside of the small box was crowded and the transformer had to be mounted on the outside. There is nothing fundamentally wrong with a crowded circuit layout, as long as it is well thought out. It is just more difficult to implement. The savings in size might not be worth the trouble it costs. Nor is mounting the transformer on the outside something to avoid at all times either. A remotely mounted transformer reduces the chance that stray magnetic fields will induce hum in sensitive circuitry. Audio devices frequently have external power supplies to keep the transformer as far from their circuitry as possible, because they are especially susceptible to hum.

Building the Clock

How the clock is built depends more on what materials and methods are available to you than what was done in the prototype. The decor you intend the tide clock to be

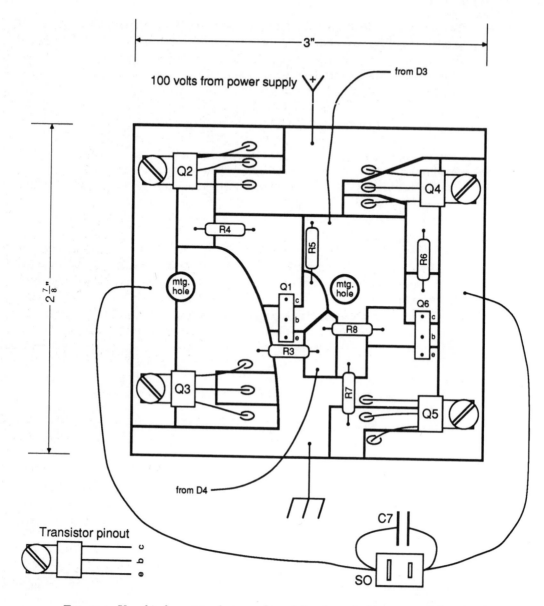

FIG. 11-4. *Use this layout to design a board for the switching part of the circuit.*

placed in will probably determine the materials and methods suitable for its construction. Because clocks are often made of the strangest things, it seems reasonable to suggest objects like a surfboard, a life buoy, the side of a large flat fish, a bulkhead from a small boat, an oar, a piece of driftwood, or the wheel of a boat as suitable for the face of a tide clock.

The tide clock's face should be marked to distinguish it from regular clocks. Instead of hour markings, it should be divided in two sections, one for high tide, the other for low. Given this one rather obvious requirement, there are many suitable faces possible.

FIG. 11-5. *The drive circuitry is visible with the cover removed from the finished project.*

The prototype used a circle cut from ⅛ inch plywood. The two sides were distinguished by two shades of blue paint and labeled HIGH and LOW. A very smooth circle was cut by clamping a square piece of the ⅛ inch plywood on top of a circular wooden cutting board that was already the right size. Then a router with a rolling bearing at its tip was guided around the circle. As the router's bit followed the existing circle, it cut out an identical circle in the plywood.

The best place to find a motor to drive the tide clock is in a used standard clock. With digital clocks so cheap now, many people get rid of their old analog clocks at garage sales and flea markets or just throw them out. As long as it works, almost any electric clock that has hands contains a suitable motor. If you already have the drive circuit built before making the clock face, see if it will drive the motor before wasting time taking the clock apart.

Removing the motor from one of these clocks is usually very simple. Mounting one to a new face is usually also quite easy. Small wood screws were used to mount the clock motor to the face in the prototype, although some additional holes had to be drilled through the motor's mounting plate.

The hands of the old clock can be discarded since the only one that would move at the correct speed is the small one. Making your own hand is usually necessary if you want it to be noticed. The new hand must be lightweight, especially because it will probably be much larger than the old one and will load down the motor more.

A control knob, especially one from a car stereo, is a good way to mount the new hand to the motor shaft. Another idea is to use a small cork with a hole of the correct diameter drilled in it. Although the motor shaft has two to four concentric shafts that different hands once attached to, use the one that formerly held the hour hand. Fortunately, the shaft for the hour hand is usually the largest and most accessible because it is the outermost one (besides the alarm shaft that some clocks have).

A thin balsa wood arm formed the hand of the prototype. The arm was painted flat black and a red cardboard disk was glued to the end. It was mounted to a small audio control knob that attached to the clock's output shaft with a setscrew. The hand, visible in FIG. 11-1, weighs only a few grams.

CALIBRATION

Accurate calibration of the drive circuit requires a frequency counter if it is to be done easily. Otherwise, trial and error over a long period will have to substitute for a quick setting. Frequency counters are more common nowadays than they used to be, thanks to new ICs that make them cheaper to build. Any college or technical school that teaches electronics has them. TV and stereo repair shops should also have at least one. Because you'll only need it for less than a minute, you should be able to arrange access to a frequency counter if you don't own one yourself.

Before calibration, be sure the circuit works by plugging a clock motor into the socket provided by the drive circuit. Let the circuit warm up for about five minutes with the motor running. If a frequency counter is available, connect it between ground (pins three, five, and seven on IC3) and pin two of IC3. But because the tide clock drive circuitry isn't isolated from the powerline, the counter used to calibrate it must be ungrounded before attaching it to the circuit. If it has a three-wire plug, use it only with an adaptor that allows the ground wire to be temporarily disconnected. Adjust the potentiometer to as close as 57.9865772 Hz as possible, although accuracy to two or three decimal places is quite sufficient. The powerline frequency which governs the timing of most clocks, including AC-powered digital ones, is typically accurate only to within a percent and will vary more than this oscillator.

Without a frequency counter, calibration is more difficult but still possible. Using an oscilloscope with both horizontal and vertical inputs, the output of the oscillator can be compared with the 60 Hz line frequency stepped down through a small transformer. With an ungrounded scope connected to pin 2 of IC3, adjust the oscillator's frequency to be equal to, then less than the 60 Hz. This completes only an initial calibration though. To get additional accuracy, the clock will have to be run for a day or two and timed over several tidal cycles. The potentiometer can then be fine-tuned until the clock turns one revolution for every 12 hours and 25 minutes.

Without a frequency counter or scope, just set the potentiometer near the middle of its rotation and hope for the best. Several corrections will probably be necessary over many days' time to calibrate the clock accurately. If you are calibrating it this way, it helps to mark the position of the potentiometer each time and write "s" or "f" next to the mark to indicate if the clock ran slow or fast at that setting. This gives an idea of how much rotation is necessary for a given change in speed. After a few resettings, you'll notice the marks zeroing in on a point that has slow settings on one side and fast settings on another.

USE

Once calibrated, the tide clock must be set to the current tidal conditions by consulting a chart. After its initial setting, the clock should dispense with the need for a tide chart except where exact times are needed. Once it has been calibrated and given a chance to prove its reliability, the drive circuit can be tucked away in some inconspicuous place, although it should have enough space around it to release the small amount of heat it generates.

OTHER USES OF THE CIRCUIT

Other synchronous motor-driven devices can be controlled by the drive circuit as long as they don't draw too much power. There is no clear-cut limit to this device's power output although its output voltage is sensitive to loading and motor performance is degraded when the voltage drops as a result of current drawn. But most synchronous motors are used in functions where their speed is more important than their power, so they don't draw much power; they don't need to because they are usually geared down considerably and don't have to produce much torque.

Tide Clock

C1	330μF, 100μF or better (Electrolytic photo-flash capacitors are a good source)
C2	220μF, 35V or better
C3, C5	10μF, 16V or better
C4	1μF non-electrolytic (mylar or film dielectric)
C6	.1μF bypass capacitor, value not critical
C7	.01μF bypass capacitor, value not critical
R1	16KΩ, all resistors ¼W unless otherwise indicated
R2, R4, R6	10KΩ
R3, R5, R7, R8	1000Ω
POT	2KΩ trimmer, preferably multi-turn
F	2A slo-blo
T	Step-down transformer with 40V center-tapped secondary
Q1, Q3, Q5, Q6	MPSU10 or equivalent NPN type power transistor
Q2, Q4	MPSU60 or equivalent PNP type power transistor
IC1	12V three-terminal regulator IC
IC2	Exar XR-2206CP function generator IC
IC3	4069 hex inverter IC
D1-D4	200PIV, 1A or better rectifier diodes
PL	Line cord and wall plug
SO	Outlet to plug clock into

PLUS, synchronous clock motor, materials for clock face (wood, paint, letters, etc.), clock hand, panel-mount fuseholder, PC board stock, pre-etched experimenter board, suitable enclosure, hardware, hook-up wire, rub-on letters, and solder.

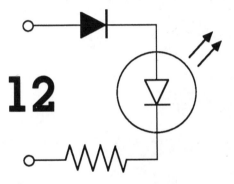

12

Fluorescent Bike Light

A bicycle light is a useful accessory if you do a lot of riding at night. By lighting up the road and making you more visible to cars, it reduces the chances of an accident. On rough roads, it lets you see what kind of surface you're riding on before it's too late. Although bike lights are popular accessories and are sold in just about every cycling store, there are good reasons for building your own. This project involves the construction of an unusual and useful bicycle light that isn't available commercially.

While generator-powered incandescent lights are the most common type used on bikes, there are a number of reasons why fluorescent lights are more suitable. For one thing, fluorescent lights shine with a brighter light that fully covers the road, the rider, and the bike and really gets the attention of car drivers. Because they are shaped in narrow tubes that can mount alongside a bike's frame, fluorescent lights offer less wind resistance than a comparable headlight would with its flat face. When used with a generator, a fluorescent light offers additional advantages over a conventional incandescent light—first of all because it is more efficient, giving more light for the same pedaling effort—and secondly, because it can't be burned out by the overvoltage that a generator can produce when speeding down hills. Fluorescent lights also last longer than incandescent bulbs do, especially on a bicycle where vibrations tend to weaken an incandescent bulb's filament. See FIG. 12-1.

Despite the considerable advantages of fluorescent lights, very few bikers seem to use them, probably because they are not available commercially. For a few years, a company called Electro Safety Products did manufacture a fluorescent bike light and generator combination and sold it under the name ''Mightylite.'' They seem to have stopped their activity in this area though, leaving no commercial source for a fluorescent bike light. With a little time however, you can make virtually the same thing yourself using parts

FIG. 12-1. *The fluorescent bike light mounts alongside the bike's tubing.*

you may already have or can easily buy. This chapter describes how to build a fluorescent bike light project similar to the "Mightylite."

THE CIRCUIT AND PARTS

The original "Mightylite" used a green Sylvania F14T8 tube that is still widely available in many colors (though not in green anymore). For this project, just about any tube 14 to 18 inches long with a diameter of 1 inch will work well. Suitable bulbs are sold in the electrical sections of most department stores in white and other colors. Their prices might seem somewhat high, but because the bulbs typically last several years, consider the initial price a good investment.

Fluorescent tubes usually have two terminals at each end. There is a filament connected between these terminals that is normally used to preheat the bulb for easier starting. In this project however, the filaments are used merely as electrodes. The two terminals at each end are wired together, shorting the filaments, and are treated as one.

A fluorescent tube glows when a sufficiently high AC voltage is present across its two ends. For a typical 15-watt bulb, this voltage is a few hundred volts. The circuit in FIG. 12-2 supplies this. It takes the output of an ordinary bike generator which is typically six to 18 volts AC and steps it up.

An audio output transformer connected backwards provides the correct step-up ratio. The transformer should have a primary impedance of around 1000 ohms and a secondary of 4 to 16 ohms. The smallest available size of these transformers is a little too small. Their cores saturate too easily when they are driven hard, but the slightly larger ones that are about 1½ inches on each side are most suitable. Essentially, that's all there is to the circuit.

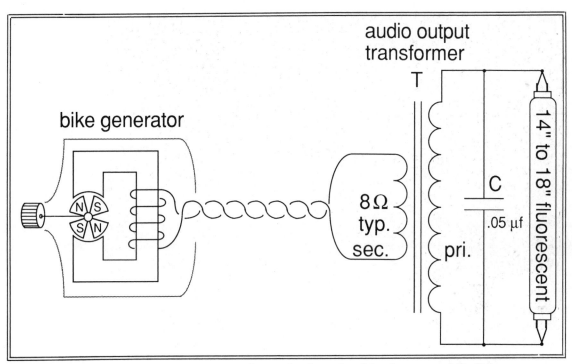

FIG. 12-2. *Here is the complete electrical schematic of the fluorescent bike light.*

The addition of the capacitor across the fluorescent tube is necessary for operation, although its function in the circuit might not be apparent at first. It's there to allow the transformer to draw more current from the generator than it otherwise could. The capacitor and transformer together form a tank circuit whose resonant frequency is ideally near the frequency of the generator's output. With each reversal of polarity, both the capacitor and the bulb load down the transformer, drawing more current from the generator than the bulb alone would. This extra current drawn by the capacitor is released into the light during the rest of the AC cycle. The use of a resonant circuit is merely a means of spreading out the current drain on the generator so as to utilize as much of its possible output as possible. The value of C is not critical; it can range from 0.05 to 0.1 microfarads.

CONSTRUCTION

Before installing the fluorescent light on a bike, build and test the circuit in your shop to make sure that the particular generator, transformer, and fluorescent tube you've chosen will work together. Temporarily connect the circuit with alligator clip test leads and hold the generator up to a moving V-belt or a rubber sanding drum with the sandpaper removed. The fluorescent tube should glow, although it probably won't be as bright as a standard fluorescent light fixture. Bike generators are typically rated at 3 to 6 watts of output and cannot drive a 15-watt tube to full brightness. If the tube doesn't light, try tapping it gently. If it still won't light, try a different audio transformer and vary the capacitance of C.

When you've tested the circuit, build the fluorescent light into a suitable enclosure for mounting on a bike. FIGURE 12-3 is an exploded diagram of the suggested way of

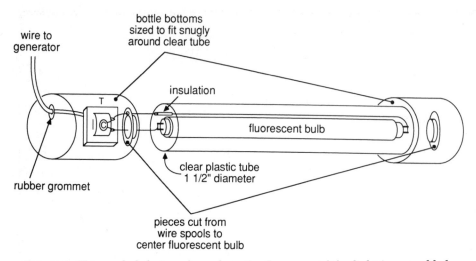

wire to generator

bottle bottoms sized to fit snugly around clear tube

insulation

T

fluorescent bulb

rubber grommet

clear plastic tube 1 1/2" diameter

pieces cut from wire spools to center fluorescent bulb

FIG. 12-3. *This exploded view shows how the fluorescent bike light is assembled.*

enclosing the light. It requires a clear plastic tube and some other pieces of plastic from household items. You might have to look around a bit for a suitable tube or go to a home improvement or plastic store, but the rest of the parts are common enough.

House the fluorescent bulb inside a clear plastic outer tube to protect it from flying gravel and to protect your legs if it breaks. The tube is also the best place to mount the transformer and capacitor to keep the high voltage section in one place, so make it about 3 inches longer than the bulb is. When selecting the length of the fluorescent bulb and plastic tube, consider how much room is available on your bike. Plan on mounting the light either below the top tube or in front of the seat tube and calculate the maximum length accordingly.

The rest of the parts indicated in FIG. 12-3 are fairly common household items. Pieces cut from a plastic wire spool are used to center the fluorescent bulb in the clear outer tube. The bottoms of straight-walled plastic bottles make suitable caps to cover the ends of the tube with. Use a longer cap piece from a plastic bottle over the end with the transformer in it. The covers on both ends should be trimmed so they are even with where the light-emitting part of the fluorescent bulb begins. Attach the bottle bottoms to the outer tube with electrical tape or duct tape to make the whole assembly waterproof.

Lead the wire from the secondary of the transformer out of the tube's end cap through a rubber grommet. Make it long enough to reach the generator. Mount the light assembly to your bike using tape or nylon ties. Neatly connect it to the generator so that no loops of wire stick out from the bike.

USE

In use, the fluorescent light is a real attention getter. The sight of a bright rod of light travelling swiftly down a dark road at night is quite eerie, especially when you use a bizarre color like green for the fluorescent tube. For an even stranger effect, a small circular fluorescent tube could possibly be hooked up to the generator or several smaller fluorescent lantern bulbs could be connected in parallel and arranged around the bike.

126

Fluorescent Bike Light

C	.05μF, 600V
T	Audio output transformer, 1000Ω primary, 8Ω secondary
FLUORESCENT TUBE	1″ diameter, 14″ to 18″ long (Sylvania F14T8 or equiv.)
BIKE GENERATOR	6 to 18V, 3 to 6W conventional bike light generator

PLUS, 2″ diameter clear plastic tubing, plastic end caps, plastic rings from wire spools, duct tape, two-conductor wire, and solder.

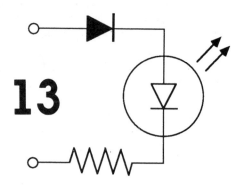

13

Straight Wire Without Gain

"A straight wire with gain" is an expression often used to describe the sonic qualities of an ideal amplifier or preamplifier. If it existed, such an audio component would impart no change except amplification to signals passing through it. But because all electronic circuitry and even wires and switches produce some distortion in an audio signal, this is an ideal rather than an attainable goal. That hasn't stopped equipment designers though, both amateur and professional, in their quest for an audio component with performance as close to a straight wire as possible.

All aspects of audio circuit design are subject to improvement, making the job of a professional designer very difficult. The amateur in search of improvement though, can simplify matters by eliminating the need for gain that current commercial equipment has. This is possible because there is often already enough gain in the rest of a stereo system.

An audio signal needs amplification, both current gain and voltage gain, on its way from the source (record player, tuner, CD player, or tape deck) to the speakers. In a typical system, the required amplification is split among a preamplifier and power amplifier. The preamplifier provides most of the voltage gain and controls the volume and switching. The power amplifier provides nearly all the current gain and some additional voltage gain.

The separation of preamplifiers and amplifiers became common when a phono cartridge was everyone's primary signal source. But many of the signal sources in use nowadays such as CD players, tuners, tape decks, VCRs, and turntables with built-in preamps don't need much voltage gain when used with typical modern power amplifiers. In fact, in a system without a phono cartridge requiring preamplification, a preamp might be an unnecessary piece of equipment. If it can be done without, it makes sense to eliminate the preamp entirely because it only adds distortion, no matter how good it is.

To test whether you can get along without a preamp, hook a line level signal source directly into your power amplifier's inputs. If the source doesn't have its own output level control, use a 100K potentiometer in between. If this setup can provide sufficient volume as it is, additional gain isn't really needed. This project provides the control functions of a preamp without the gain and would then be suitable.

But even if there's a chance that more gain is desired, it's still possible to build this project now and add an active stage at some later time to provide additional gain. There are many construction articles with instructions for building the gain stage of a preamplifier that can be used for this. Choosing a circuit from among the many published is something best left up to individual audiophiles, but this chapter concludes with how to build any of these circuits into this project to yield a very high quality preamp with gain.

The recommended procedure therefore is to first build this project without any amplification and then add active circuitry at some later time if increased volume is needed. Doing that will convert it to a true preamplifier. Either way, the project described in this chapter forms the heart of a high quality audio system that is simple to begin with and forms the basis for further improvements.

The advantages this project has over commercial preamplifiers are many. Most of them stem from the fact that the overall design considerations observed in planning this project differ from those followed for most commercial hi-fi products. The approaches used in this design yield the minimum in sonic degradation but in many cases contradict the way in which the audio industry typically does things. These methods, although they challenge those traditions, do represent valid improvements with measurable and audible results. In fact, some of the more esoteric manufacturers of audio equipment are, and have been, using some of the same approaches followed in this chapter. It seems likely that more and more manufacturers will change their designs to follow suit in the near future. Some of the design principles adhered to and discussed thoroughly in later sections of this chapter are: the use of minimal soldered or unsoldered contacts in the signal path; the use of a "star" grounding system with an effective electrostatic shield for input and output cables; the use of a precision stepped volume attenuator; and the use of high quality wiring and soldering methods throughout.

The whole approach taken in describing this project has assumed some knowledge of electronic project construction. Every detail has not been described, both because it would take too long and because many of them depend on the builder's choice between several options. Without any previous experience, hobbyists wishing to construct a project of this sort should review some books of basic electronics construction techniques or refer to one of the electronics magazines listed at the end of this chapter.

FUNCTIONS AND OPERATION

First of all, this project truly excels not in what it does, but in what it doesn't do—that is degrade the audio signals passing through it. A minimalist approach was followed in choosing what features to include. Starting with just the bare necessities, the circuit adds only those extra features that can't in any way extract a penalty in sound quality for the convenience they provide.

FIGURE 13-1 shows the schematic of the "straight wire without gain." Just one channel is drawn, but this is only to save paper; the other channel is independent of the one shown and is nearly identical. The only things that both channels share electrically are the common

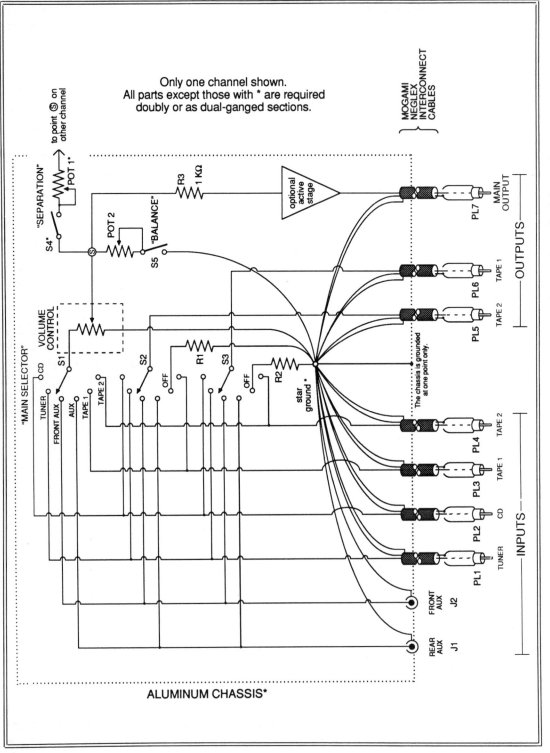

FIG. 13-1. *This schematic is complete but shows parts for only one channel of the project.*

star grounding point and the separation control that is composed of POT1 and S4 connected between the point marked "S" on each channel. Both channels are built into the same chassis and physically share S1, S2, S3, S5 and the volume control.

Input Wiring

Examining the schematic, you'll notice that instead of the usual jacks found on preamps for inputs and outputs, this project provides a number of audio cables terminating in plugs. These take the place of both the jacks on ordinary components and the interconnect cables that would have to be used to connect them to the rest of the system. There are quite a few reasons for this unorthodox approach. First of all, there is no reason that interconnect cables must detach at *both* of their ends to permit equipment to be removed; separation at one end is all that is necessary. Another good reason is the cost of audio plugs and jacks, particularly the high quality ones that are necessary for maximum fidelity. An additional two inches of wire costs considerably less than an audiophile-grade jack and plug. But the real reason why an additional connection is avoided is that it represents an additional electrical contact and can introduce a non-linear resistance to signals passing through it. More reasons for avoiding contacts will be discussed later, but as it stands, there seem to be only benefits derived by replacing the usual plug, jack, and interconnect cable with a single wire terminated in a plug.

The wire used for the input and output cables is of considerably higher quality than what is typically used in audio interconnect cables. It includes four twisted inner conductors surrounded by a shield. For audio use, the inner conductors are paired up and used to carry the signal; the outer conductive layer serves only as an electrostatic shield and not as a signal conductor. This is an improvement over the typical approach of using a single inner conductor to carry the signal, with the outer conductor used as both the signal return wire and the shield. Because some of an electrostatic shield's performance is sacrificed when it is made to carry current, the approach this project takes represents an improvement.

The parts list specifies Mogami Neglex wire for this use. However, many audiophiles have strong preferences for other brands and types of interconnect cable. If you have obtained good results with a particular brand of cable, if you later happen to, or if the perfect wire is someday invented, it is quite easy to adapt commercial interconnect cables for use in this project, involving only unsoldering the plug from one end and wiring the cable directly into the circuit.

In addition to wired inputs for four sources, there are two sets of RCA phono jacks provided as inputs. One pair mounts on the front of the project, the other in the rear. The front set is mainly for quick temporary connections to the system that would be convenient if you were testing a new or borrowed piece of equipment or plugging a musical instrument into your stereo. Although front panel jacks are uncommon, the gold-plated jacks used in this project look quite good on the front panel. The rear connectors are intended primarily for equipment that isn't always hooked up to your main system and can be left unused. Because your input requirements may differ, the recommended number of input plugs and jacks can always be changed.

Selector Switching

The design of this project differs from most preamps because it has three input selector switches but no tape monitor switches. Instead of conventional tape switching, a main selector switch selects what source will be sent to the output, while the two other selector switches choose what signals will go to the tape 1 and tape 2 outputs. While deceptively simple, this set-up provides all the tape monitoring, dubbing, and external loop functions that other preamps have and then some. More importantly, it inserts only a single contact in the signal path during normal listening.

After some getting used to, you'll find that the three-selector switch approach is by far the most convenient and versatile method of switching among inputs. It allows you to listen to one source while recording a second source to a tape deck and recording a third source to another tape deck all at the same time. With it, you can insert an equalizer or other type of processor in place of one of the tape decks and switch between equalized or flat listening, make equalized or flat recordings, and in different combinations at the same time. Instead of using one of the selector switches as a tape output, you could send its output through the remote volume control from Chapter 8 and listen to an entirely different source in another room. Although it is quite simple, this three-switch design allows for quite complicated switching arrangements.

Another advantage of separate selectors for each tape deck is that they allow the tape outputs to be turned off when you're not recording. This isolates the tape decks from the rest of the circuitry and prevents them from unnecessarily loading down the signal source. Most other preamp selector switches leave the tape outputs connected to the output of the preamp all the time. This is desirable when recording but degrades the performance of the rest of the circuit at other times.

There are two slight drawbacks of this type of switching but they are not serious. If you turn the Tape 1 selector to ''Tape 2'' while the Tape 2 selector is set to ''Tape 1'' (an unusual condition), a loop will be created that will cause feedback howling. This can be avoided by placing the potentially dangerous positions of each tape selector switch at the end of the switch's travel so that it doesn't have to be crossed over when switching between other inputs. Designed this way, the circuit requires a deliberate missetting to cause feedback.

A feature not present in this project but one that probably won't be missed is the ability to switch between TAPE and SOURCE instantaneously with a single switch. With the selector switches in this project, it might be necessary to move a knob two or more positions to accomplish this. But because tape decks commonly have tape/source switches anyway, there seems no reason to add one to a preamp, especially when it requires two additional sets of contacts.

Volume Control

A volume control is simply an adjustable voltage divider. Potentiometers are used in most receivers and are quite satisfactory there. But where uncompromising musical fidelity is desired, potentiometers fall short of stepped volume controls made up of multi-positioned rotary switches and precision resistors. These are typically found only on the highest quality commercial preamps and homemade equipment.

Three possible volume control options are discussed for this project. One is a simple potentiometer. The ones recommended are of good quality as far as potentiometers go, but fall short of the other two options in ultimate quality. A higher quality option is a stepped volume control using a 23-position rotary switch and precision metal film resistors.

Plans are given for this type of control and two Pascal computer programs are included to make it easier to select the resistor values. The other possibility is a stepped volume control kit available from Old Colony Sound Labs. These three alternatives differ in cost and convenience and are discussed individually in the construction section.

Other Controls

Despite standard practice, you don't really need a balance control. This project is intended for high fidelity systems and so it tacitly assumes proper speaker placement and an electrically balanced level between channels. In such a system, the only use a balance control gets is occasional, and then it is usually to test new hook-ups or perhaps to turn one speaker off temporarily. After dispensing with the balance control in their systems, most audiophiles find they don't miss it at all. But because it might have some usefulness, a balance control is included in this project anyway. It is completely disconnected when it is not being used, so quality is not sacrificed for convenience. When the switch S5 is off, POT2 is not connected to the circuit and cannot affect the sound. Only when it is needed and S5 is on, it becomes part of the circuit. There are actually two balance controls; two POT2s each separately control a channel. They subtract from whatever volume setting is selected by the main volume control. This way, they can take on a variety of uses. By turning them both down, they can be used to interpolate between the positions of a stepped volume control (though this is seldom necessary). Both channels can be turned down all the way to zero output together or independently if that is desired. If you anticipate using them independently very much, either for testing or other purposes, consider using two separate switches for S5.

Even if they're not used as balance controls, the two POT2s and S5 make an ideal muting switch. If the controls are set at their halfway points, S5 becomes a mute switch that enables the volume to be temporarily lowered for a phone call or ringing doorbell without changing the volume setting. You can "customize" the muting control with different settings for each channel, as you might want to do if one speaker in particular was next to a telephone.

Another control provided by the straight wire without gain is a separation control. Like the balance control, it is entirely out of the circuit when it's not being used. When it is switched on however, it connects POT1 across the two channels. This permits the stereo separation to be varied, which is sometimes desirable for listening on headphones or with speakers spread very far apart. When POT1 is turned all the way down, S4 becomes a mono/stereo switch. In any event, it is interesting and enlightening to experiment with while listening to different pieces of music. Like the balance control, it can be left out of the project if you don't want it.

The 1000-ohm resistor R3 connected in series with the signal output is there to prevent the volume or balance controls from shorting the input to the power amplifier when they are at their minimum settings. This is necessary because a few amplifiers behave poorly with their inputs shorted.

The triangle in the schematic shows where an active stage could be added to the "straight wire without gain." Adding one after you've already built this project without it is a simple matter, as long as there is room inside the chassis. It involves placing the active circuitry between R3 and the output interconnect cables and supplying it with power.

Tone Controls?

You might have noticed that tone controls are conspicuously absent from this design. That is because where and if they are needed, tone controls should be replaced by a separate equalizer. There is no way a single tone control, specified by a corner frequency and slope, can compensate for all the irregularities in system response it is likely to encounter. Often it does more harm than good. Many high-end audio manufacturers share my approach of keeping any frequency-shaping functions entirely separate rather than doing a poor job within a preamp design.

Many audiophiles will not consider using tone controls or equalizers at all even when they are available. These controls inevitably introduce distortion. They describe this distortion in many ways, but it invariably involves the phase relationships that provide the spatial cues in music. Audio purists are often content to sacrifice control of the frequency response only so that the other parts of the signal they hear will remain untouched. As with the balance controls, tone controls are seldom missed when one has gone without them for a little while.

Phase Reversal

There is another control that is absent from this project and though it is absent from most commercial preamps as well, I feel it needs some discussion. This is a "phase reversal" switch. It cannot be implemented in a strictly passive design, so it is not included in this project, but there is another way to incorporate a phase reversal switch in your system.

During a recording, the way the original microphones were hooked up in the studio establishes which polarity the electrical signal has in response to the compressions of air that make up sound. But in the many steps between live recording and playback through loudspeakers, a number of unavoidable reversals of this polarity occurs. Each gain stage in an amplifier introduces a phase reversal, and different amplifiers have different numbers of stages. Some audio components are advertised as "absolute phase" but they offer no significant advantage. Even if a single piece of audio gear maintained the same polarity at its input and output, it couldn't speak for the other components in the chain, some of which are at the recording studio and beyond the audiophile's control.

But because musical waveforms are highly asymmetrical, the correct phase is something to be concerned with. As the polarity of a signal is switched back and forth, reversing the phase by 180 degrees, I and other people can detect a difference. This is not to say that one way sounds better than another, or that we can detect which is more "real," only that a genuine difference exists. Given that there is a subtle difference, it is something worth experimenting with. There should be some way to switch the phase of your system back and forth.

Unfortunately this cannot be done passively in the preamp stage, because both channels use a common ground. Reversing the phase involves interchanging the "hot" and "neutral" leads of each channel. Because the neutrals are unavoidably connected together (this is called a *common ground*), a mono signal would result if they were used as the "hot" leads. The only places in a system where you could easily reverse the phase by switching polarities is where the signal is truly balanced (no distinction between hot and neutral). In a typical home system, the only places where this is possible are at the phono cartridge and speaker terminals. The better place to switch polarity is at the speaker terminals, because they are more accessible and are involved in producing all signal sources, which the cartridge is not.

It is also possible to reverse the phase by adding an additional active stage in the signal path. A switchable option that does this is rarely provided on commercial preamps though. This could be one reason for building active circuitry into this project when you have enough knowledge to modify circuits with an extra stage.

Summary of Features

The straight wire without gain provides the most useful features of standard preamps and more, while contributing the least possible sonic degradation. The versatile selector switches, volume control, balance (mute switch), and separation control (mono switch) introduce only a single contact and a volume control to the signal path during normal operation.

You can modify the circuit if you wish. More inputs can be added to the selector switches. However, six inputs were selected because they represent a commonly available size in rotary switches. You can add even more selector switches to provide outputs for another tape deck or signal processor. But keep in mind that driving all these outputs from just one unamplified input will load down the input too much. You will need an active buffer stage for each output unless the output devices have inherently high input impedance. It also helps if you switch off all unused outputs with the selector switches when they're not being used.

CONSTRUCTION

The minimalist approach that this project follows essentially states: use as few parts in the signal path as possible, and make those that you must use as good as possible. The following sections show how this was done to each area of the circuit and discusses the parts needed.

Contacts

Much has been written in audiophile journals about the detrimental effects of poor contacts on audio signals. Briefly, current at the level of audio signals can flow through a contact only where there is a direct metal-to-metal interface. Where the metal of the two conductors is separated by oxides, dirt, or air, the effective contact area is reduced and current flow is inhibited. This wouldn't be so bad if the only resistance introduced was linear—remaining the same at all voltages much like a resistor—but that isn't the case. Poor contacts often behave like semiconductors, introducing non-linear distortion to audio signals passing through them. Even the linear resistance of contacts introduces a slight amount of noise to the signal. In addition to their linear and non-linear resistance, poor contacts are more subject to intermittent failure and general unreliability. For these reasons, it is best to eliminate as many contacts as possible from audio systems and where contacts are necessary, make them as good as possible.

Unsoldered Contacts. Contacts that can't be soldered include the wipers of potentiometers, switch contacts, plugs, and jacks. These depend on pressure to maintain metal-to-metal contact. Unfortunately, oxides develop on the metal surfaces and inhibit conduction. A thin, hard insulating layer slowly forms that can only be removed by abrasion or chemical action.

Gold is the best material for contacts, particularly those that don't come together with a lot of wiping action. It is resistant to oxidation and is an excellent conductor of electricity, making good contacts possible. The phono plugs and jacks specified for this project are gold plated for this reason. Gold is not recommended for switches however, or for other contacts that employ wiping action, because it is quite malleable and would quickly wear away with use.

For those contacts that come together with a good amount of force, silver is the material of choice. The wiping action of the contacts breaks through the contamination that typically forms on the silver, making a good electrical contact possible. Silver is durable enough to withstand the frequent use that switches typically get and is therefore recommended for that use.

The performance of contacts can be dramatically improved by the use of a lubricant called Cramolin. A very light application of Cramolin coats metal surfaces with a layer a few molecules thick that seals out the atmospheric effects that cause oxidation. It is inexpensive, effective, long lasting, and apparently used by many manufacturers of expensive electronic equipment.

There are two Cramolin formulations: red for removing built-up oxides on contacts, and blue for preserving the contacts. The usual treatment procedure is to apply a small amount of red solution to a contact, wipe it off, and apply the blue. This treatment is recommended for the gold plugs and jacks, all switch contacts, and potentiometers in this project as well as the rest of your audio system. Audio equipment dealers sell an Electronic Maintenance Kit manufactured by Caig Laboratories which includes all that's needed to treat a stereo system with Cramolin.

Soldered Contacts. Soldered contacts don't present as much trouble to the audio signal as unsoldered contacts do, but there are more of them so they are of equal concern. There are two considerations to apply when making soldered connections. To begin with, the soldered joint must be as clean and contaminant-free as possible. Also, because the metals in solder are inferior electrical conductors, the two pieces to be joined should be in as close physical contact as possible.

For optimum solder joints, the iron tip should be kept clean by wiping it often on a sponge. Your hands, which hold the wire and solder, should also be clean. It's best to wash your hands often and avoid handling solder excessively anyway, because the lead in it can be absorbed through the skin and build up in the body. To ensure that the solder joints are clean and oxide free, it helps to clean them with red Cramolin before soldering. The Cramolin will not interfere with soldering and actually redistributes itself around the solder joint afterwards, preventing further contamination.

Solder is typically an alloy of lead and tin. Neither of these metals is a very good conductor, and alone or in an alloy they can only degrade sonic performance. But until a better means of attaching metals at low temperature becomes convenient, soldering is necessary. It can be improved if you use a solder with some silver content. This solder, sold by Kester in their 3S/60T/37L alloy, isn't much more expensive than regular solder and a roll should last long if it's only used on critical audio connections. Also, when soldering, let the two conductors be responsible for making the contact; wrap them tightly together or around lugs to minimize the amount of solder that the signal has to pass through. Following these suggestions also yields stronger and more reliable solder joints which can only increase the reliability of the circuit they are part of.

Wiring the Inputs

The input and output cables that emanate from this project are made up of Mogami Neglex 2534 microphone cable and Royce SCXT7 audio plugs (see parts sources at end of this chapter). The cable has four inner conductors surrounded by a shield. The twisted inner conductors, which are color-coded in two pairs, are composed of OFHC (oxygen free high conductivity) copper and insulated with polyethylene. The advantage of a twisted-pair construction is that it seems to pass phase information better then paralleled or coaxially configured conductors. The insulation material has a low dielectric absorption constant (DA) that is desirable when two conductors of an audio signal are in close proximity. It minimizes non-linear distortion due to capacitive coupling. The cable is jacketed in an attractive flat black covering. All in all, the Mogami wire is quite suitable for audio use and is recommended in several articles on cables. While it doesn't currently represent the cutting edge in interconnects, its excellent performance at a reasonable price make a strong case for it.

To use this wire for the input and output cables, connect the four inner conductors in two pairs, using one pair to carry the signal and the other for the neutral conductor. Connect the shield at only one end—the end inside the chassis; do not connect it to the shield of the phono plug.

The phono plugs recommended are hefty gold-plated gems machined out of brass. They're available from Old Colony Sound Labs for eight dollars a pair. This seems like a lot of money and it is, but the plugs will surely last a lifetime. As with the other parts used in this construction project, each builder will have to weigh cost with the expected returns. It's hard to predict how a component will sound without hearing it first, but all the parts recommended in this chapter represent some genuine sonic benefits to be had for their expense. There has been quite a bit of money spent on far more outlandish schemes for improving stereo sound than those described here. Spending eight dollars for a pair of plugs is by no means extravagant in comparison with the expenses some audiophiles incur for far more exotic materials.

Solder the precious plugs to the Mogami wire following the directions included with them, being careful to insulate the shield wire from the outer conductor of the plug. Cut the interconnects to whatever length you think is appropriate for your system, allowing for the length inside the chassis. If you are using commercial interconnects, unscrew the the phono plug from one end and unsolder the wire from it. If this is impossible, cut the wire near the plug and strip the ends. Solder the interconnects to the star ground and selector switch as described in the following sections.

Grounding

It was mentioned earlier that an electrostatic shield loses some of its effectiveness when current passes through it. For this reason and to avoid ground loops, a "star" grounding system is used in the straight wire without gain. All the shields for the interconnect wires are connected together at one end to a single point within the circuit. The chassis, which is also an electrostatic shield, is electrically in contact with system ground, but at this point only. In fact, all the grounds in the stereo system go to this one point, independently of other ground wires. The circuit resembles a star with arms radiating outward from the central ground to all parts of the stereo system that this project forms the heart of. The top view of the project's internal layout in FIG. 13-2 illustrates this.

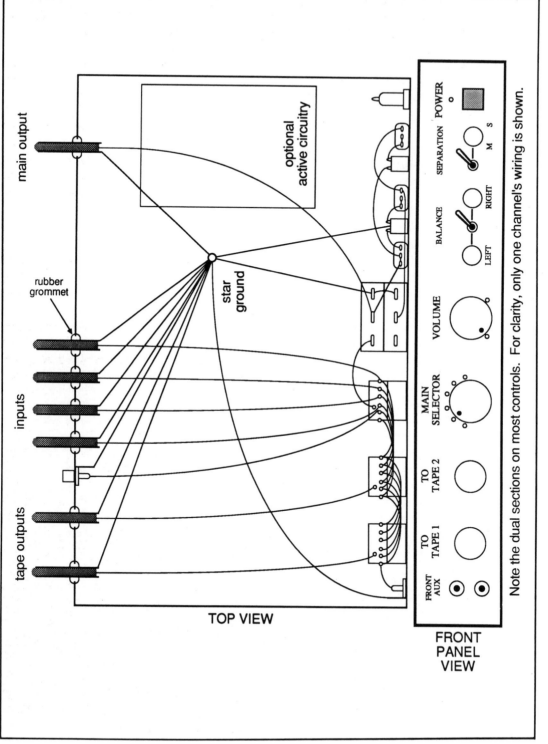

main output

optional
active circuitry

rubber
grommet

star
ground

inputs

tape outputs

TOP VIEW

FRONT
AUX

TO
TAPE 1

TO
TAPE 2

MAIN
SELECTOR

VOLUME

BALANCE

LEFT   RIGHT

SEPARATION   POWER

M   S

FRONT
PANEL
VIEW

Note the dual sections on most controls. For clarity, only one channel's wiring is shown.

FIG. 13-2. *Shown here is a suggested front panel layout and top view of the project's interior.*

This ground point will have quite a number of wires soldered to it, so it must be large. To create it, take a solder lug as in FIG. 13-3 and solder a length of twisted OFHC wire from the Mogami cable between two lugs. Make all other connections to it by wrapping around the wire and not by going to the lugs, because they are inferior conductors. Make sure the lugs used contact the chassis at their mounting point. If they don't, run a short wire from the star ground to a lug that does. This is the only place where the chassis should be in electrical contact with ground.

Wire the interconnect shields and neutral wires to this common ground point, leaving only their signal-carrying conductor to go to the selector switches. Because the front and rear RCA jacks shouldn't be in electrical contact with the chassis, you can't mount them directly in the front or rear panel unless they have plastic bushings to isolate them from the metal. Make the ground connection to J1 and J2 by the solder lugs supplied with them, and use OFHC wire to connect their grounds to the star ground. A single wire can be used for both channel grounds in this case.

The Selector Switches

The recommended selector switches are six-position, two-pole, shorting rotary switches, noted in the parts list. They have silver contacts, sealed bodies, are quite rugged, and have a precision feel to their switching action. There are suitable switches available from Grayhill, Janco, and Stackpole listed at the end of the chapter. The chief characteristics they should display are silver contacts and a sealed enclosure. Some of the manufacturers make their switches available with gold-plated contacts, but the additional expense is not worth the short-lived benefits. Gold is really necessary only in the case of extremely low level signals and where oxidation is a problem. But the selector switches used in this project will probably be rotated frequently enough that the gold would only become worn away after a short while.

FIG. 13-3. *The star ground is a wire strung between two solder lugs.*

An alternative to a rotary switch is a bank of toggle switches, but this is not recommended because of the additional expense and the confusion that 16 separate switches would cause. Toggle switches are sometimes used as selector switches on preamps, but only with a few inputs and no tape outputs.

Although there are three selector switches, the main one is the most important. Connect the input wires directly to it, and use separate wires to connect the other two selector switches to its contacts. Remember to keep your wiring faithful to the switch positions marked on the front panel. The order of the positions is arbitrary, but remember to keep the "Tape" positions of the tape selector switches at the end of their rotation to lessen the likelihood of a feedback-prone setting.

When ordering selector switches, give some thought to future expansion of your system. If you intend to use more than six inputs, purchase a two-deck switch that lets you use up to 12 inputs. The use of separate decks will also reduce the possibility of crosstalk between the two channels. Be sure to specify *shorting* (make before break) contacts. This will prevent loud pops from occurring when the switch is rotated. If there's a chance you might later want front-panel LEDs to indicate which input is selected, consider buying switches with a third pole to allow this.

The Volume Control

Ordinary potentiometers have at least four problems when they are used as volume controls. For one thing, they wear out with use—something a volume control gets quite a lot of. As they wear, and even when they are new, stereo potentiometers "mistrack;" this means they give different output levels for each channel. They also change their total resistance and their taper over time and with use. The resistive material they are composed of is electrically noisy, creating a slight distortion and hiss when current passes through it. Worse though, is the contact formed between the resistive element and the wiper arm. This contact only covers a small area under relatively low pressure. It is formed by two different substances, so it has a junction with some properties of a semiconductor. This introduces non-linear distortion to a signal passing through the volume control.

Standard Potentiometers. Regardless, potentiometers are inexpensive, give smooth control, and are conveniently available—so they are a viable alternative as a volume control. Manufacturers of high quality standard potentiometers include Allen-Bradley, Alps, Bourns, Noble, and Tech Labs. Things to look for in a potentiometer are: sealed construction, a metal body, "Cermet" resistive element, and at least a 1 watt power rating. Be sure to get an audio-taper, sometimes designated as an "A" taper.

Don't be fooled by potentiometers with detents. A detented potentiometer is merely one that clicks from position to position. It may have some of the feel of a stepped volume control, but electrically it is still a potentiometer. Still, if a potentiometer must be used, there's no reason why it shouldn't be detented. The detents do offer some measure of repeatability that is useful over short intervals but becomes less meaningful as the potentiometer ages.

Building a Stepped Volume Control. The advantages of genuine stepped volume controls are: precise tracking between channels, exact repeatability, the use of lower noise-resistive elements, metal-to-metal contacts, and the flexibility that comes from designing your own taper. However, stepped volume controls are difficult to make because they use hard-to-find switches, require tedious soldering between closely spaced terminals, and can involve laborious math to determine resistor values. The first two of these disadvantages cannot be overcome, but the math can be simplified with the two computer programs later in this chapter.

The volume control will be constructed in the most popular of the three ways in which stepped volume controls are made. Another way is the "ladder" type described by Leonard Hupp in "A Ladder Attenuator" (*Audio Amateur, 5/82*). I have avoided this type because of the additional resistors and extra set of switch contacts it requires. The two advantages the ladder type offers, namely fewer solder joints in the signal path and simpler calculations, are not enough to recommend it. A third way of making controls is to use a fixed resistance as the lower half of a voltage divider and to switch different resistors in for the upper half. This type of control is rendered impractical by its sensitivity to variations in source and load impedance and the inevitable loss incurred by its low total impedance.

The two programs are written in Pascal using Think Technology's Lightspeed for the Macintosh. With slight modifications, they will run on different machines or with different compilers. The programs are also available as stand-alone applications for the Macintosh computer. See the end of the chapter for details.

Program A lets you enter the parameters of the volume control and the particular circuit it will work in. It then computes and displays the resistor values.

Because it is virtually impossible to find standard value resistors that match the values the computer asks for, a slight discrepancy will result. In most cases, the closest standard resistor value can be substituted in place of an impossible-to-match ideal value and where necessary, two resistors can be connected in series or parallel.

The resistors that will be used can then be measured and their values fed back into Program B which computes the attenuation between steps and the total attenuation that will result with the given resistors. Running Program B isn't necessary, but it gives an indication of how closely the actual volume control will match the chosen taper. Program B lets you go back and change resistor values one at a time and indicates the overall result of such changes.

Using the Programs. FIGURE 13-4 is a schematic representation of a volume control connected between a signal source and a power amplifier. An ideal signal source would have zero source impedance, and an ideal load would present an infinite impedance to the volume control. But these conditions never occur. Typical impedance values for solid state equipment are under 10 kilohms for source impedance and more than 50 kilohms for load impedance. Tube equipment typically has much higher impedances.

Because of the load and source impedances connected in parallel with it, a volume control doesn't work in isolation and must be designed with those impedances in mind. The first two pieces of information that Program A asks when it is run are the source impedance and the load impedance. It needs these to accurately compute the values of the resistors used in it.

The load impedance of power amplifiers are usually specified in the owner's manual. The input impedance of an active gain stage should be given in the construction article its circuit is from. If you're not sure what the load impedance presented to the volume control will be, enter 75000 for load impedance. This will yield accurate results for almost all situations the volume control is likely to encounter.

The impedance of most signal sources is given in their specifications. If not, then 1000 is a fairly good example of source impedance. It is also possible to measure the output

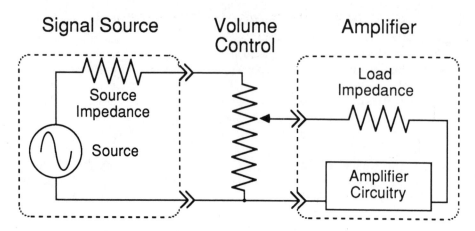

Signal Source   **Volume Control**   **Amplifier**

Source Impedance

Source

Load Impedance

Amplifier Circuitry

FIG. 13-4. *Practical signal sources and amplifiers have internal impedances that must be considered when designing the volume control.*

impedance by playing a steady tone from the equipment into an AC voltmeter with no load at first and then into a load resistance, noting the change in voltage. The output impedance of the device under test is given by the formula:

$$\text{Output Impedance} = (V_{unloaded}/V_{loaded} - 1) \times R_{load}$$

After the source and load impedances have been entered, Program A asks how many switch positions you plan to use. Rotary switches usually come in a maximum of 23 positions, so 23 will be the usual answer. Any less than 23 positions is not quite enough for smooth transitions between volume levels, but the number of switch positions is nevertheless left as an option.

The program automatically selects a total impedance for the control based on the source impedance entered. If the total impedance it chooses is too low, much of the input signal will be lost in the source. On the other hand, if the control impedance is made too high, the control's taper will be overly sensitive to variations in load impedance. The relationship used by the program

$$\text{Total Impedance} = 4 \times \text{Source Impedance} + 10000 \text{ ohms}$$

makes a good compromise between these two competing constraints. It can be altered by a simple change to the program. Among its other features, the Macintosh application allows you to change the total impedance while running the program.

Based on the source impedance and the total impedance, Program A will compute the minimum loss that the volume control will incur. With a source impedance of zero there would be no loss, but because real signal sources do in fact have some impedance, there is some voltage lost within the source. Program A displays the inevitable loss in decibels (dB) that will occur even when the volume control is turned all the way up. The only way to minimize this loss is by decreasing the source impedance or increasing the control's total impedance.

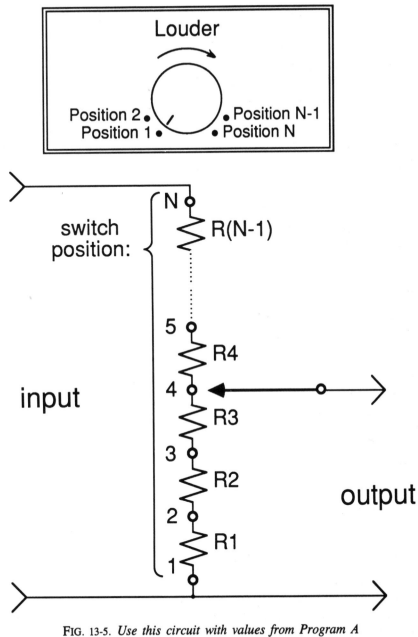

FIG. 13-5. *Use this circuit with values from Program A to construct a stepped volume control.*

Next the program asks if you want every volume step to be the same size or whether you'd rather specify the size of each step individually. If you choose uniform spacing, the volume control will have the usual audio taper where each position represents the same increase in loudness over the previous one. This is the most common choice for a volume

```
PROGRAM A (input, output);
{This program produces a list of resistor values for a stepped volume control.}
        USES
                Sane;
{The Sane library is necessary for the function XpwrY used at one point.}
        VAR
                ZI, ZO, ZT, IL, US, dBs, vr, rbp, prt : real;
                NP, NS, n1, n2, n4 : integer;
                b : STRING;
                r : Rect;
                gp, resistor : ARRAY[1..100] OF real;
BEGIN
        SetRect(r, 5, 40, 500, 340);
        SetTextRect(r);
        showtext;
        writeln('Enter:  source impedance, load impedance, # of switch positions');
        readln(ZI, ZO, NP);
        NS := NP - 1;
        ZT := ZI * 4 + 10000;
        IL := (20 / ln(10)) * ln((ZO * ZT) / (ZO * ZT + ZI * ZO + ZI * ZT));
        writeln('Inevitable loss: ', -1 * IL : 2 : 2, ' dB.');
        writeln('Enter <U> for uniform spacing.');
        writeln('Enter <E> to enter each separately.');
        readln(b);
        IF (b = 'U') THEN
                BEGIN
                        writeln('How many dB should each step represent?');
                        readln(US);
                        FOR n1 := NP DOWNTO 2 DO
                                gp[n1] := IL - (NP - n1) * US;
                END;
        IF (b = 'E') THEN
                BEGIN
                        gp[NP] := IL;
                        FOR n2 := NS DOWNTO 2 DO
                                BEGIN
                                        writeln('How many dB should step ', n2 : 1,
' change the volume?');
                                        readln(dBs);
                                        gp[n2] := gp[n2 + 1] - dBs;
                                END;
                END;
        writeln('The quietest volume control setting (position #2) will be ', gp[2] : 2 :
2, ' dB.');
        prt := 0;
        FOR n4 := 2 TO NP DO
                BEGIN
                        vr := XpwrY(10, gp[n4] / 20);
                        rbp := (ZT + ZI - ZO / vr + sqrt(sqr(ZO / vr - ZT - ZI) + 4 * ZO
* (ZT + ZI))) / 2;
                        resistor[n4] := rbp - prt;



                        writeln('R', n4 - 1 : 2, ' should be', resistor[n4] : 11 : 3,
' ohms');
                        prt := rbp;
                END;
END.
```

control. But some audiophiles prefer to start out with narrow steps, about 1dB or so, for the first few steps, then go to something like 2dB per step for most of the steps, with the highest steps 3dB apart. This and other possible tapers are possible by specifying each step separately.

For smooth operation, a volume control needs about a 40dB range, although this figure depends on your particular equipment. If the steps are uniform this means each one should represent about 2dB for a 23-position (22-step) switch. The computer will tell you the control's total range by displaying the attenuation in dB at position two of the switch. Position one is customarily off (infinite attenuation), so position two, the maximally attenuated switch position, is used to give an idea of the range of the control. The idea is to have position two sufficiently attenuated so that the jump from position one (no output) to position two (minimum output) is as smooth as possible. But at the same time, position two should not be attenuated too much or the control's lower positions will scarcely be used and resolution will be sacrificed.

Finally, the computer lists the values for each resistor in the control. The resistor numbers it lists correspond to those used in FIG. 13-5. For a switch with n positions, the computer produces $n-1$ resistor values, because the resistors go between positions.

For any likely parameters, Program A will give a realistic sequence of resistor values. Some odd choices of source and load impedance, number of positions, and possible tapers will produce resistor values of zero or close to it for the lower positions. This occurs because not every combination of source and load impedance and taper is possible to achieve in practice. All conditions that would realistically occur in a hi-fi system are possible, however, so you will probably never encounter resistor values of 0 ohms.

Program B lets you double check the values specified by Program A and lets you see how close a volume control with slightly different values will come to your selected taper. A computer program is helpful for these calculations because changing a single resistor value changes the attenuation of all the steps slightly and requires a complete recalculation.

```
PROGRAM B (input, output);
{This program checks a list of resistor values for the results it will produce.}
        LABEL
                1 ;
        VAR
                ZI, ZO, ZT, nrv : real;
                NP, NS, n1, n3, n5, n6 : integer;
                a, b : STRING;
                r : Rect;
                resistor, rbp, dBs, dBc : ARRAY[0..100] OF real;
BEGIN
        SetRect(r, 5, 40, 500, 340);
        SetTextRect(r);
        showtext;
        writeln('Enter:  source impedance, load impedance, # of switch positions');
        readln(ZI, ZO, NP);
        NS := NP - 1;
        ZT := 0;
        rbp[1] := 0;
        FOR n1 := 1 TO NS DO
                BEGIN
                        writeln('enter R', n1 : 1, ' (in ohms):');
                        readln(resistor[n1]);
                        IF n1 < NS THEN
                                writeln('');
                        ZT := ZT + resistor[n1];
                        rbp[n1 + 1] := resistor[n1] + rbp[n1];
                END;
        rbp[NP] := ZT;
1 :
        FOR n5 := 2 TO NP DO
                BEGIN
                        dBs[n5] := (20 / ln(10)) * ln((ZO * rbp[n5]) / ((ZT + ZI) *
```

(continued)

```
(rbp[n5] + ZO) - sqr(rbp[n5])));
                        dBc[n5] := dBs[n5] - dBs[n5 - 1];
        END;
    writeln('');
    writeln('switch position:' : 16, 'level:' : 12, 'resistor:' : 22, 'step:' : 23);
    writeln('');
    FOR n3 := NP DOWNTO 2 DO
        BEGIN
                writeln(n3 : 8, dBs[n3] : 18 : 3, ' dB');
                write('R' : 35, n3 - 1 : 3, '=' : 4, resistor[n3 - 1] : 11 : 3,
' ohms', 'step: ' : 11);
                IF n3 <= 2.5 THEN
                        writeln('-INF')
                ELSE
                        writeln(dBc[n3] : 3 : 3, ' dB');
        END;
    writeln(1 : 14, '-INF' : 12);
    writeln('Enter <R> to go back and change resistor values');
    readln(a);
    IF (a = 'R') THEN
        BEGIN
            ZT := 0;
            rbp[1] := 0;
            FOR n6 := 1 TO NS DO
                BEGIN
                        writeln('Is R', n6 : 1, ' (', resistor[n6] : 3 : 3,
' ohms) Okay?');
                        writeln('      press return if that value is okay,
or');
                        writeln('      enter <C> to change the value');
                        readln(b);
                        IF (b = 'C') THEN
                                BEGIN
                                        writeln('Change R', n6 : 1,
' (currently ', resistor[n6] : 3 : 3, ' ohms) to what (in ohms)?');
                                        readln(nrv);
                                        resistor[n6] := nrv;
                                END;
                        ZT := ZT + resistor[n6];
                        rbp[n6 + 1] := resistor[n6] + rbp[n6];
                END;
            rbp[NP] := ZT;
            GOTO 1;
        END;
END.
```

If typing in and running the programs is too much trouble, Table 13-1 lists three sets of resistor values obtained with a likely combination of parameters. For many hobbyists, this list will be all that's needed.

The resistors used should be ½-watt precision metal film with 1 percent tolerance. A 1 percent tolerance is indicated by a red band in the final place on the resistor body. Most of the mail order suppliers stock suitable resistors. There are more than one sequence of values available, so check with several suppliers if you have difficulty obtaining particular values.

The two-pole 23-position rotary switch required for the volume control is the most difficult part to locate. Ideally the switch should have enclosed contacts like the switches made by Stackpole, Grayhill, and Janco. Surplus dealers occasionally sell these or similar switches in used or new condition, but finding such a deal will take a lot of research and a little luck. Buying them new presents problems as well because 23-position sealed switches are special order parts and usually not available in small quantities except at high prices. Look for advertisements in audio magazines for this type of switch and consult other audiophiles and audiophile clubs in your area.

Source Impedance: 1000 ohms
Loan Impedance: 75000 ohms
Total Control Impedance: 14000 ohms
23 positions

Resistor values are given in ohms.

Resistor	all 2 dB steps	all 2.5 dB steps	five 1dB, eleven 2dB, & five 3dB steps
1	109.999	32.805	109.999
2	28.533	10.948	13.444
3	35.951	14.604	15.090
4	45.307	19.483	16.938
5	57.113	25.997	19.013
6	72.017	34.695	21.344
7	90.846	46.315	50.867
8	114.652	61.847	64.130
9	144.779	82.625	80.881
10	182.944	110.446	102.051
11	231.346	147.741	128.828
12	292.802	197.810	162.732
13	370.906	265.137	205.706
14	470.214	355.835	260.238
15	596.405	478.206	329.513
16	756.315	643.409	417.583
17	957.633	866.026	529.548
18	1207.760	1163.833	1072.226
19	1511.066	1555.007	1526.961
20	1863.616	2049.015	2149.497
21	2245.483	2626.501	2938.170
22	2614.312	3211.715	3785.242

**Table 13-1. Listing of Resistor Values
for a Standard Stepped Volume Control.**

A more commonly available type of 23-position switch is the kind with open contacts. The Centralab PA-4002 is an example of this type and is often used in stepped volume controls because of its availability and low cost. Because it doesn't have a sealed back and because it's contacts aren't silver, the Centralab and similar switches aren't quite as good as the sealed rotary switches listed earlier, but they are still far better than any potentiometer. When the controls are treated with Cramolin, most of the oxidation problems that open switches are typically prone to can be avoided. If sealed back switches are available, use them; they are the best. But the Centralab open back switch represents a good alternative. Whatever type of switch you buy, specify shorting contacts (make-before-break). Otherwise every rotation of the switch can produce a loud pop.

A Stepped Volume Control Kit. An alternative to designing and making your own stepped volume control is buying the stepped attenuator kit from Old Colony Sound Labs. For $36.75, it supplies all the parts to build a stereo attenuator. It includes the Centralab switch, two PC boards that make mounting the resistors easy, and metal film resistors that yield 23, 2-dB steps. While designing and building a stepped volume control yourself is cheaper and allows more flexibility, the Old Colony kit is certainly easier.

About Balance and Separation Components

Because the balance and separation controls are only in the circuit when they are being used, their switches and potentiometers don't have to be the highest quality. This only means that you don't need silver contact switches and stepped controls; you still should use quality components to ensure reliability. For the toggle switches, use sealed switches from Alco, C&K, or Mouser for long life and reliability. Use only high quality potentiometers for the separation and the two balance controls. This assures a long life and smooth operation to a component that will see frequent usage.

Chassis

Use an aluminum chassis to enclose the straight wire without gain. Aluminum is a good conductor and makes an effective electrostatic shield, keeping RF and other radiated electrical fields out of the audio signal. Avoid using a steel chassis and use as little steel hardware as possible. Ferrous materials with their high permeability and magnetic non-linearity introduce distortion in signal-carrying conductors running near them. Although a ferrous chassis provides magnetic shielding in preventing hum pickup, its detriments far outweigh its benefits. It's best to obtain magnetic isolation by separating magnetically sensitive components from those with large power transformers and motors.

Electronics stores and mail order companies sell aluminum enclosures of rack-mount width with front handles that would be suitable for this project, but they are more expensive than ordinary aluminum boxes. The best way to build this project is probably to buy an ordinary aluminum chassis of about $15 \times 11 \times 3$ inches and attach a faceplate separately.

The faceplate could be aluminum, but it need not be; acrylic plastic or even finished wood will do just as well. There are some suitable faceplates available from unlikely sources. Some aluminum mailbox nameplates, for example are just the right size for a faceplate. Whatever faceplate you choose, keep in mind that it will require lettering and should match the rest of your equipment in appearance and size. One small advantage of using a non-metallic front panel is that mounting the front panel RCA jacks is simplified, requiring only that clearance holes be drilled in the aluminum chassis to prevent contact.

GENERAL CONSTRUCTION SEQUENCE

The way to start constructing this project is by designing the front panel according to how the controls will be laid out. The layout depends on your preferences; FIG. 13-2 shows one suggestion. Then create a top-view diagram looking down through the chassis and draw where the controls will be as was done there. Draw in where the input wires will pass from the rear to the front and where the outputs will leave the back, and design the rear panel based on this layout. Notice the large open area in the rear of FIG. 13-2, behind the balance and separation controls. This leaves ample room for active circuitry that might be added later.

With the planning done, mount the front panel controls. Take care when doing this that everything is where you will be comfortable with it for years to come. Attach the faceplate to the chassis either with separate hardware or use the controls to hold it in place. Using separate hardware is slightly preferable because it allows the faceplate to stay attached without the controls installed.

Install the star grounding point in a location about equidistant from the points that will be connected to it. Then do the wiring between the front panel controls, the RCA jacks, and the ground, without yet installing the interconnects. Connect R1 through R4 by making loops in their leads in which to insert and wrap lengths of OFHC wire.

Install the interconnects last because they take up the most space. Pass each one through a rubber grommet where it enters the chassis. To make them neater, it is a good idea to bundle them with nylon ties or string. Tightly attach a nylon tie around the wires with a layer of insulation for padding at the entrance to the chassis. This is a better way to prevent the cables from being pulled loose than a strain relief or knotting them.

ADDING AN ACTIVE STAGE

Some audio systems need additional gain between the signal sources and the power amplifier. Driving multiple outputs from one signal source will probably also require an active amplification stage. Choosing an appropriate circuit for your needs is a matter of personal preference for certain types of sound, your skill as a builder, and the money at your disposal. Advice, circuits, and construction articles appear in the electronics magazines listed in the sources section at the end of this chapter. But regardless of the design you choose for the active stage, the switching and control functions remain the same. Whatever switching and control functions the construction article recommends for particular preamps represents only that designer's preference. It's doubtful this project could be improved on in these respects.

An active stage requires a power supply. This should be located in a separate box and its filtered DC output connected to this project with a cable. Placing a transformer and power line within the straight wire without gain would be disastrous. Magnetic and electrostatic radiation would get into the audio signal regardless of all the precautions taken to prevent it. Only the DC supply lines should enter the shielded enclosure.

A suitable external supply is given in FIG. 13-6. Specifications aren't given for transformer T1 because they must be determined by the supply voltage required by your circuit. It is important that the supply be filtered both at the external power supply and at the circuit board inside the preamp. Bypass the filter capacitors at the preamp according to the instructions in Chapter 22 and the suggestions in audiophile magazines. With power available in the preamp, it would be possible to add features like LED function indicators or externally activated relays for volume muting.

Because it is important to keep the AC powerline away from the sensitive signal-carrying wires, the preamp must be able to indirectly switch its power supply on and off. The circuit in FIG. 13-6 does this with a triac, controlled through the triac driver opto-isolator by a low DC voltage. Although a switch inside the preamp chassis controls the AC power for the system, it does so indirectly by passing only a few DC volts. All the AC is kept in the external power supply. The extra switched outlets SO1 through SO3 provided at the power supply are for other stereo components in your system.

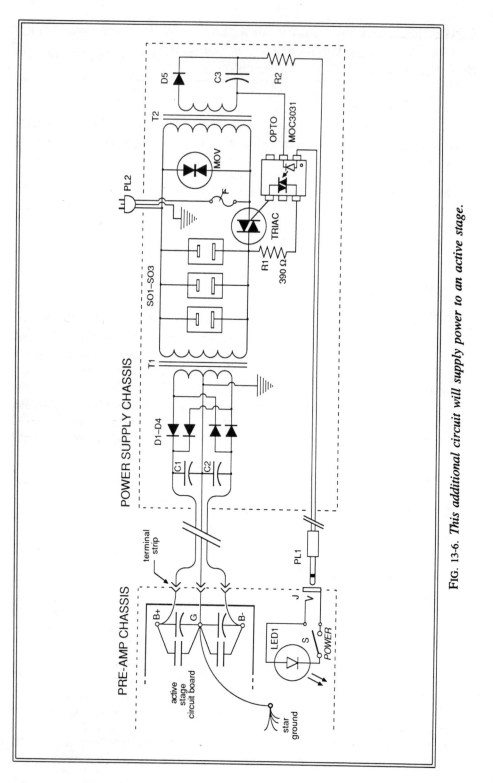

FIG. 13-6. *This additional circuit will supply power to an active stage.*

SOURCES

This section contains magazines for informative advice and various companies and their addresses for obtaining parts suggested for this project.

Separate Gain Stage

Construction articles for preamps are one source of circuits for a high quality gain stage. Articles for their construction and discussions of relevant design considerations appear in:

The Absolute Sound
Audio
IAR
The Audio Amateur
Modern Electronics
Radio and Electronics
Wireless World

In their construction articles and/or regular columns, these and some other limited circulation magazines offer considerable advice that would be useful to anyone building this project.

Addresses

Companies sometimes change their mailing address or post office box. It is always a good idea to check these and the addresses listed elsewhere in this book with the current Thomas Register of industrial parts and services in the reference section of most libraries.

Bi-Tronics Inc.
Box 125
Tuckahoe, NY 10707
1-800-522-7377

Caig Laboratories
1175—0 Industrial Ave. (P.O. Box J)
Escondido, CA 92025-0051

C&K Components, Inc.
15 Riverdale Ave.
Newton, MA 02158-1082

Centralab, Inc.
5757 North Green Bay Ave.
Milwaukee, WI 53201

Grayhill, Inc.
561 Hillgrove Ave.
La Grange, IL 60525

IAR (information about capacitors)
2449 Dwight Way
Berkeley, CA 94704

JANCO CORPORATION
3111 Winona Ave.
Burbank, CA 91504

MARSHALL ELECTRONICS, INC.
P.O. Box 2027
Culver City, CA 90230

MOUSER ELECTRONICS
Catalog Mailing Service
P.O. Box 699
Mansfield, TX 76063

OLD COLONY SOUND LABS
P.O. Box 243
Peterborough, NH 03458

PEERLESS RADIO CORPORATION
19 Wilbur Street
Lynbrook, L.I., NY 11563

THE STACKPOLE CORPORATION
P.O. Box 14466
Raleigh, NC 27620

T.R.T./WCO
P.O. Box 4271
Berkeley, CA 94704

The two programs featured in this chapter are available as stand-alone applications for the Macintosh computer. The applications offer a few options that the listed programs do not. Each program allows you to save its output as a textfile for later reference. They are more user-friendly with helpful prompts for input and output and offer a few other features as well. The price is $10 for both programs, from

Joseph O'Connell
134 Clarewill Ave.
Upper Montclair, NJ 07043

For this price you'll receive a Sony DS/DD disk (initialized as a 400K disk to be compatible with all machines) with the two programs as well as the Pascal source codes if you are a programmer and want to modify them for your own use.

PARTS LIST:

Straight Wire Without Gain

CRAMOLIN	Electronic Maintenance Kit available from Caig Laboratories, from Old Colony Sound Labs, or at most audio dealers.
SOLDER	Kester 3S/60T/37L Rosin Core Solder (.030″ diam.) or Wonder Solder, available from TRT.
INTERCONNECT WIRE	Use your own favorite interconnects or Mogami Neglex 2534 quad microphone cable, available from Old Colony or Bi-Tronics Inc. in small to medium quantities, or in larger quantities from Marshall Electronics Inc. Two of each required.
PL1 through PL7	Royce SCXT7 Audio Plugs sold by Old Colony. Similar plugs are available from Marshall Electronics.
GROUND LUG	Ordinary multi-lug terminal strip with its center lugs replaced by a piece of OFHC copper wire.
J1, J2	Gold-plated RCA phono jacks, available from Old Colony or Marshall Electronics. Two of each required.
S1 through S3	Six-position (or more), two-pole (or more), shorting rotary switch, preferably sealed and with silver contacts. Suitable ones include:

        Stackpole:
            73-1036 (stocked by Mouser)
            73-1076
        Janco Corporation:
            A-60 series
        Grayhill Incorporated:
            Series 44 (stocked by Peerless)
        C&K:
            A206-15-R-N-Z-G

S4	SPST high quality mini toggle switch available from many manufacturers and suppliers. Mouser is a good source.
S5	DPST (or two SPST switches) high quality mini toggle switch to match S4 cosmetically.

POT1	Good quality potentiometer; start with 100KΩ and experiment to find an ideal value.
POT2	Good quality potentiometer; start with 20KΩ and experiment to find an ideal value (two required).
ALUMINUM CHASSIS	Rack-mount chassis or ordinary aluminum box of approximately 15″ width, 3″ height, and 9″ depth
FACEPLATE	Finished aluminum, acrylic, or wood plate slightly higher and wider than the chassis. Must be able to accept lettering.
R1, R2	100Ω, type not critical, (two of each required)
R3	1000Ω, ½W, 1% metal film resistor two required)

VOLUME CONTROL OPTIONS:

POTENTIOMETERS: Allen-Bradley and Bourns are available from many parts suppliers, notably Hanifin Electronics. Alps available from Old Colony. Look around for other sources.

23-POSITION, TWO-POLE ROTARY SWITCHES: The type with enclosed backs and silver contacts are recommended. Suitable models of this type include:

    Stackpole: 73-6698
    Janco: A15-1-2 B 23 S L
    Grayhill: 53M15-2-1-23S-F

The alternative is the Centralab PA-4002 that is less expensive but not sealed. (available from Peerless Radio)

METAL FILM RESISTORS: are stocked by most mail order dealers. Some have different ranges of available values.

PLUS, nylon ties, lettering for front panel, rubber mounting feet, and hardware (preferably non-ferrous).

PARTS LIST:

Separate Power Supply

C1, C2	10,000μF, 100V or better electrolytics
C3	100μF, 30V or better electrolytic
R1	390Ω, ¼W
R2	Multiply voltage across C3 by 40 for answer in ohms.
F	Slo-Blo fuse to match equipment in SO1 through SO3
T1	Center-tapped step-down transformer to meet requirements of the active circuitry used.
T2	Low voltage step-down transformer, specifications not critical
MOV	S10V-S14K130 or equivalent metal oxide varistor
TRIAC	200V triac with higher current rating than system's expected rating
D1-D4	1A, 100V or better bridge rectifier
D5	1A, 100V or better rectifier diode
LED	Power indicator in preamp, size and color optional
OPTO	MOC3031 zero-crossing triac driver opto-isolator
S	SPST power switch in preamp
PL1	⅛" phone plug or similar
PL2	Three-wire line cord and wall plug
J	Jack to match PL1
SO1-SO3	Power outlets
TERMINAL STRIP	Three-position terminal strip or other connector for the power supply wire

PLUS, Additional filter and bypass capacitors mounted on gain stage board, suitable enclosure, three- and two-conductor interconnect wire, external fuseholder, hook-up wire, and solder.

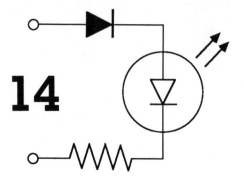

14

Portable Xenon Strobe

This project is a compact flashing beacon that gives off a bright burst of light about once per second. It's small enough to be carried easily by runners and bikers for exercising at night. See FIG. 14-1. The circuit is easy to build into a variety of cases that can suit all sorts of applications. In this chapter, a strobe that clips onto your belt and one that attaches to the back of a bicycle seat post are described. These are probably the most useful mounting arrangements, but some additional suggestions are also offered.

THE CIRCUIT

The circuit shown in FIG. 14-2 for the xenon strobe is quite similar to the circuit found in most camera flashes. It has two functional halves: a high voltage power supply section and a flasher circuit. The power supply is composed of Q, D1, and R1. Inverter transistor Q and transformer T1 form an oscillator that steps up the three volts DC from the batteries to about 115 VAC. Diode D2 rectifies the high voltage and charges C1. This forms the power supply to the flasher circuit.

The remainder of the circuit flashes the xenon flashtube V by discharging C1 through it about once per second. From the voltage present at C1, C3 charges through R3 while C2 charges through R3 and R4. By the time C2 has reached the 80-to-100-volt turn-on point of neon lamp NE, C3 is already fully charged. When the turn-on point is reached, the neon lamp conducts to the gate of the SCR, firing it. The SCR quickly discharges C3 through the primary of the trigger coil T2. The resulting high voltage spike at the trigger coil's secondary (about 4 kilovolts) ionizes the xenon gas inside the flashtube, creating a conductive discharge path for C1. The coil marked L is an inductor that spreads

FIG. 14-1. *One version of this project fits inside the bottom of a clear plastic bottle.*

out C1's discharge through the flashtube, producing a slightly longer flash. It is not essential and can be left out of the circuit. After V flashes, C1 begins recharging from the power supply again and with it C2 and C3 recharge as well. Since C1 is so large, the flash rate depends more upon the rate that it is recharged by the supply rather than the time constants of C2 or C3.

PARTS

If you tried to buy all the parts used in the strobe circuit new, you'd have considerable trouble locating some of them. The inverter transistor, inverter transformer, trigger transformer, and flashtube are not always available in parts catalogs or from stores. And when they are available, their prices are often too high to make building the project worthwhile.

Fortunately, there are other sources for these parts. One of these is camera flashes. If you can find a non-working camera flash at a garage sale or in a camera store, most of the parts this project requires can be obtained from it for less than they would cost new. Some electronics surplus companies sell non-working electronic flashes for parts quite cheaply. Some of these companies also sell separately the special parts that this project requires and sometimes even sell kits that do exactly what this project does. A kit, if you can find one, is naturally an excellent source of parts.

The high voltage supply circuit is shown in FIG. 14-2 within dotted lines because the one you use will vary depending on how the parts for it are obtained. If they are salvaged from a camera flash, it's best to duplicate the high voltage supply exactly as it is constructed in the flash. This makes certain that at least half of the circuit will have been tested beforehand. The circuit shown inside the dotted lines is merely a typical high voltage supply circuit constructed using the parts specified in the parts list.

The power supply capacitor C1 determines the rate at which the strobe flashes. A value of 40 microfarads gives a flash rate of about once per second. You probably have to buy this capacitor new because the photoflash capacitors included in camera flashes are usually too large. Be sure to get one rated for at least 170 volts.

Some of the other circuit components are also available from camera flashes. The trigger transformer, neon bulb, and xenon tube will probably all be included in the cam-

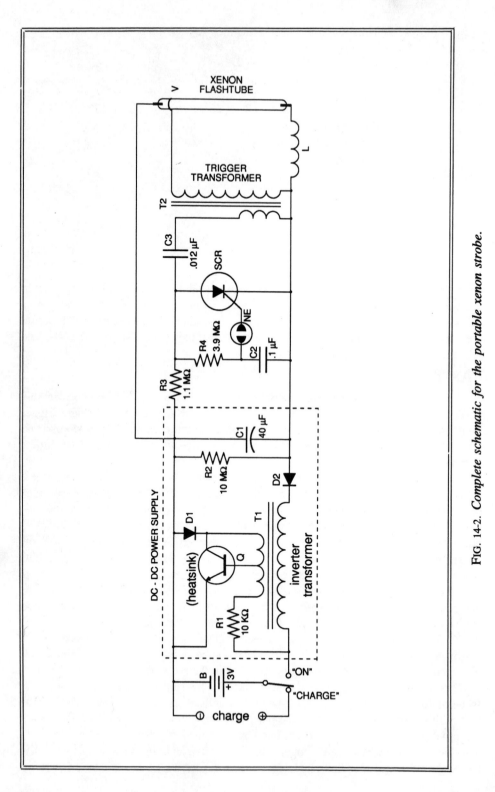

FIG. 14-2. *Complete schematic for the portable xenon strobe.*

era flash circuit. The xenon tube might have to be replaced though. Because this project works off batteries continuously, the power it can supply is limited and only a small tube can be used. If the tube in a flash is longer than about an inch, or if it won't work with the circuit for other reasons, buy a new tube from Mouser Electronics or one of the other suppliers listed in Chapter 23.

The inductor L can be left out, but for a slightly longer and brighter flash, it should be included. It is an air core coil, wound on a small plastic sewing machine bobbin or similar form. About 60 turns of AWG 24 magnet wire or wire wrap should just about fill the bobbin to complete the coil. Wrap a layer of tape around it or use a dot of glue to keep the coil from unwinding.

CONSTRUCTION

Before building this project, be sure you understand the danger of the high voltage supply it uses. When the circuit is on, the capacitor C1 typically holds enough energy to give anyone a dangerous shock. Even when S1 is turned off, this capacitor retains considerable energy until R2 bleeds it off. Another danger you might encounter making this project is when disassembling camera flashes. The photoflash capacitors used in them can retain a potentially dangerous charge. Eliminate any possible danger by insulating yourself and holding a 1000-ohm resistor across their terminals for a few seconds before handling them.

How you build the xenon strobe depends on the use you have in mind for it. If you intend to clip it to a belt, then build it into a small clear box and attach a bent strip of metal or a belt clip salvaged from a Walkman to it. Other possibilities are a box fastened to the back of a bike seat, a hand-held running weight, or inside a small container as a beacon for a boat. Look for clear plastic boxes in 5&10 stores that could make suitable enclosures. Also consider using the bottom of a clear plastic cosmetic bottle to house the xenon strobe.

Whatever your enclosure, the easiest way to build the project is on a perforated circuit board ("perfboard"). The enclosure determines the size and shape of the board you can use and to some extent the parts placement. For example, the flashtube must be mounted where it will be visible, and C1 and T1 should be mounted where there is enough room for them. Circuits are usually built on perfboard with "flea-clips"—tiny metal posts that fit tightly into the holes in the perfboard and provide tie points for component leads. The layout used in one of the prototypes is drawn in FIG. 14-3 and visible through the plastic cover in FIG. 14-1. Note how a small piece of acrylic mirror was used beneath the flash tube to reflect light that would otherwise be wasted.

The prototype shown in FIG. 14-1 uses a belt clip to attach to running shorts, to the back of a pack, or to any horizontal strap. This version would be useful to runners, bikers, and hikers who want to be visible to cars in the dark. Another useful arrangement is shown in FIG. 14-4 where a clear plastic box was used to mount a strobe to the back of a bike seat. The clip used to hold the strobe to the seat post is sold in hardware stores for holding tool handles to a wall. Other possible enclosures might be suggested by the various boxes and bottles sold by department stores.

Nicad batteries are the most suitable power source for strobes and most other portable electronic projects for that matter. They are lightweight, rechargeable, and not too

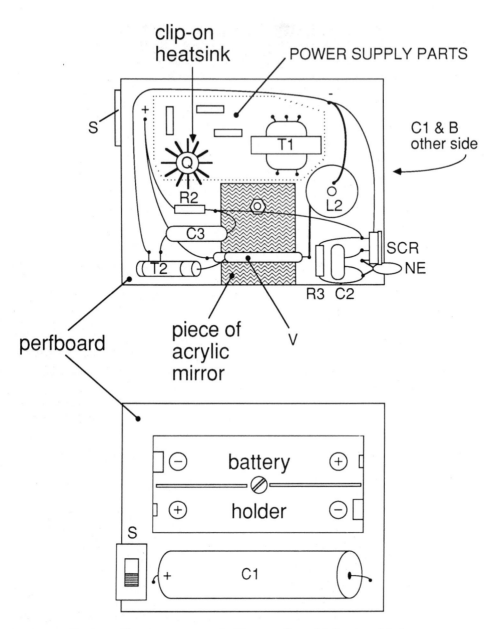

FIG. 14-3. *The prototype was built on perfboard following this layout.*

expensive. The xenon strobe uses power rapidly, so the cost of regular batteries would be prohibitive if they constantly had to be replaced.

It is convenient to be able to mount the nicads within the enclosure and have their charging terminals on the outside rather than have to remove and replace the batteries all the time. The prototype has two small screws protruding from its case that make

FIG. 14-4. *The project can also clip behind a bike seat, as shown here.*

convenient charging points for its internal AA nicads. The power switch S alternately connects the batteries to the strobe circuit in its ON position or to the charging posts when it is switched to OFF. A battery charger with alligator clip leads makes contact with the posts for recharging.

After only a few hours of use with the strobe, the small nicads used in the prototype need recharging. Of course, anyone running or biking vigorously for that long will probably require just as much time to recharge as the batteries.

The only logical alternative to nicads for this project are lithium batteries. While they are more expensive and can't be recharged, lithium batteries store more energy for their size and weight than any other common battery. They also have an extremely long shelf life. Three-volt lithium batteries suitable for the strobe circuit have recently become available and are considerably smaller and lighter than nicads or other batteries of the same capacity. They would be most suitable for applications where the strobe is used infrequently—where size and weight are important considerations, and cost is not—in an emergency beacon for example.

GOING FURTHER

The flash rate and intensity of the strobe vary according to the value of C1. Depending on how the strobe is used, you might want to raise or lower the value of this capacitor somewhat. If the strobe's purpose is to call attention to something in motion, a relatively rapid flash rate is most appropriate. For this, the 40-microfarad capacitor shown in the schematic yields an appropriate flash rate of about once per second. Lowering the capacitor's value increases the flash rate, but at the expense of its intensity. Conversely, raising the capacitance increases the intensity but at a slower flash rate. For stationary warning use (on a moored boat for example, or as a location bearing for a spotter located far away), a bright flash is generally preferable and a slow flash rate is acceptable because the strobe is always in the same place.

PARTS LIST:

Portable Xenon Strobe

(Parts with * may be replaced by a section from a camera flash.)

C1	40μF, 170V electrolytic (See text about different values.)
C2	.1μF, 100V
C3	.012μF, 200V
R1*	10KΩ, all resistors ¼W
R2	10MΩ
R3	1.1MΩ
R4	3.9MΩ
NE1	Neon bulb
L	60 turns of AWG 24 wire on a small plastic sewing machine bobbin
T1*	Inverter transformer (Peerless Radio or camera flash)
T2	Trigger transformer (Mouser Electronics or camera flash)
B	3V battery (see text)
Q*	NPN germanium inverter transistor (Texas Instruments W386 A7630 or equiv., Peerless Radio or camera flash)
SCR	400V, 3A or better SCR
D1*	100V, 1A or better rectifier diode
D2*	1000V, 1A (IN4007) or better rectifier diode
S	SPDT mini toggle or slide switch
V	Xenon flashtube about 1″ long (Mouser Electronics or camera flash)

PLUS, suitable enclosure, clip, piece of plastic mirror, battery holder, charging terminals, small heatsink, hook-up wire, and solder.

162

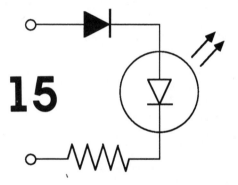

15

Electronic Incentive

Most exercises, especially those done indoors, involve repeating simple motions over and over. Stationary bicycles, rowing machines, running treadmills, cross-country skiing trainers, hand grips, and other exercise machines don't call for much mental involvement except to maintain a certain cadence. Since indoor exercise machines offer no change of scenery, and in fact no change at all, most people prefer to let their mind do other things when they use them.

To escape the inevitable boredom, some people watch TV, read, listen to music, or talk on the telephone while exercising. This works at first while they still have enough energy to do both, but then their attention wanders. And as more of it is taken up by what they really want to be doing, they find they've slowed down their exercise. No matter what the exercise, maintaining a sufficient cadence for proper training requires concentration, which is difficult to sustain while doing something else.

This project was designed to help exercisers maintain a cadence without having to monitor it themselves. It is directed mainly at those exercises that involve many repetitions over a long time period. It would not be suitable for weightlifting, for example, where the relatively small number of repetitions required must be done with intense effort. Rather it is a useful accessory for a stationary bicycle, rowing machine, or other machine that is used for endurance training.

Those machines involve repeated motions that an electrical sensor can detect. The sensor for this project is set up to send one pulse to the control unit for each revolution of a bicycle's cranks, each time a rowing machine is in the same position, each squeeze of a hand exerciser, or whatever action is appropriate to other machines. The control unit produces its own regular pulses whose timing rate is adjustable by a knob. As long as the pulses from the exerciser keep up with the rate set by the knob, the controller does nothing. But if the exerciser starts slacking off and the pulses from the sensor have longer and longer intervals between them, the controller emits a warning.

The warning can be as simple as a flashing LED. But so it is really noticed, a warning alarm can be selected by a switch to sound when the cadence drops below the preset level. For even more incentive, the controller could also be hooked up to a TV with a simple connection. When the cadence slows, it blanks out the TV picture as a warning. Obviously this would be a good incentive for those people who watch TV while working out. See FIG. 15-1.

To help you regain the correct cadence if you've slowed down, the warning that this project emits goes on and off in time with the preset target rate. The LED warning blinks, the bell rings, and the TV picture flashes on and off—all at the rate selected as the target cadence.

THE CIRCUIT

Although it offers quite a few features, the circuit in FIG. 15-2 is rather simple. Basically it is just an oscillator with a few modifications. Before building it, you should know that there are more sophisticated exercise computers commercially available. Along with many other functions, some of them monitor cadence and can sound a beeper if you slack off. They are more expensive than this project though and don't offer the unique TV hookup that this project does.

The 555 timer IC is the heart of the project. It is set up as a square wave oscillator

FIG. 15-1. *The finished control unit shown here is the heart of the project.*

164

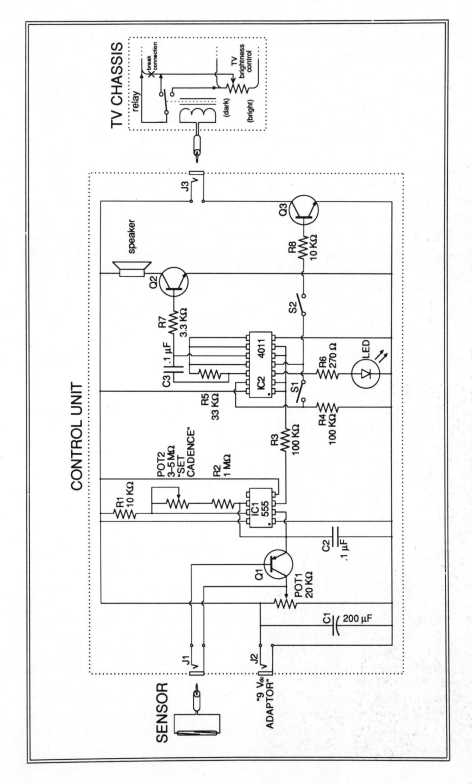

FIG. 15-2. *Complete schematic for the Electronic Incentive project.*

165

whose frequency depends on C2, R1, R2, and the potentiometer. The potentiometer allows the target cadence to be set over a sufficient range for most indoor exercises.

The timing of the 555's square wave output is determined by the charging and discharging times of its timing capacitor. The IC repeatedly charges and discharges the capacitor between two voltages set by the timing resistors and potentiometer. When the capacitor is charging from the lower voltage to the higher voltage, the output of IC1 is high. When it reaches the upper voltage though, the output becomes low and the capacitor begins discharging to the lower voltage. This cycle is repeated over and over again to produce a square wave output.

But if the capacitor was repeatedly prevented from charging up to the upper voltage, the output of IC1 would remain high. The project does this by discharging C2 through Q1 every time it receives a pulse from the exercise machine. When the base and collector of Q1 is shorted by the sensor, the capacitor is allowed to discharge down to the voltage set by POT1. Each time C2 is discharged, another timing cycle is begun and the capacitor patiently starts charging up again. As long as the interval between the exercise pulses is less than the time it takes the capacitor to charge, IC1's output is always high. But if the interval between the exerciser's pulses is ever long enough to allow the capacitor to reach the upper voltage point at which IC1's output becomes low, the warnings are triggered.

The second IC is a 4011 quad NAND gate. Two of the gates are configured as inverters by connecting their inputs together. Both inverters are driven by the output of IC1. Since IC1's output is usually high, the output of the inverters, at pins 3 and 4 of IC2, are usually low. But when the exerciser slows down, IC1's output momentarily goes low causing the inverters to go high.

The output of one inverter is taken at pin three of IC2 and is used to drive the LED through R6. With no input from the sensor, this LED flashes in time with the target cadence. But when the exercise is in progress, it only flashes to indicate if you're too slow.

With switches S1 and S2 turned off, nothing more than the flashing LED warns you of a slow speed. But with S1 closed, the output of IC2 at pin 4 is used to activate an alarm. The remaining two NAND gates of IC2 make up an alarm oscillator with C3, R5, and R7. The alarm is triggered into operation by a voltage at pin 13 and gives an output at pin 10. That output is amplified by Q2 to drive a small permanent magnet speaker. The alarm is no pipsqueak because it must be loud enough to command attention above a noisy exercise machine.

If additional incentive to keep going is needed, S2 can be closed—either by itself or in conjunction with S1. That allows the output from IC2 to activate a remote relay through transistor Q3. The relay is installed inside a TV and its contacts are connected across the brightness potentiometer where they have the same effect as turning it all the way down. When activated, the relay eliminates the picture. Because it does no more to the TV than what happens when someone turns a knob from outside it, the TV can't be damaged by it. Another set of relay contacts could be used to disable the TV's sound if even more reinforcement than a blacked-out picture is needed. The same principle is just as easily applicable to a stereo to eliminate its sound.

Although a battery could power the project, a 9 VDC adaptor is recommended because of the current drawn by the alarm and relay. The adaptor powers the project through J2. A filter capacitor is used to assure a smooth DC supply and suppress transients that occur when the adaptor is plugged and unplugged.

CONSTRUCTION

There are three different locations in which construction of this project must take place. One of these is the control unit that mounts within reach of the exercise machine. The prototype of this is shown in FIG. 15-1 on the handlebars of an exercise bicycle. The other two places where work on this project must be done are on the exercise machine itself where a sensor must be mounted, and inside the TV set where the relay is installed.

The Control Unit

The control circuitry is shown surrounded by dotted lines in FIG. 15-2. It is designed to be built into a small plastic project enclosure. All the parts except for the speaker, C1, the jacks, and POT2 mount on half of a Radio Shack Universal PC Board (R.S. #276-168) as shown in FIG. 15-3. Using only half the board saves space and saves the remaining half for other projects.

Following the pattern in FIG. 15-3, construction is a simple matter of plugging in parts and soldering them. The ICs should have sockets, particularly IC2, which is a CMOS.

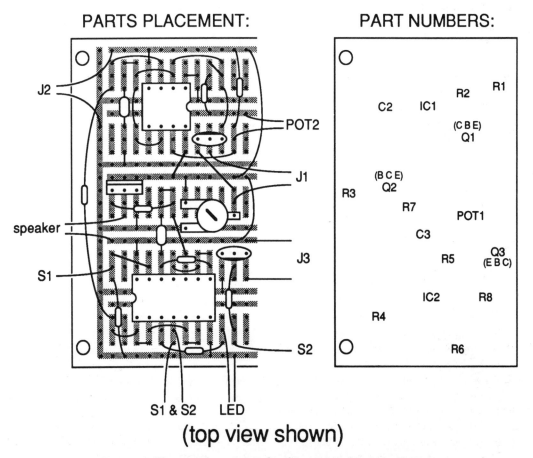

FIG. 15-3. *The complete circuit for this project fits on half of a Radio Shack #276-168 Universal PC Board following this diagram.*

Transistor Q2 can be any NPN transistor with a power tab case. A good source for a suitable transistor is a junked piece of stereo equipment or power supply. The filter capacitor C2 wasn't included on the veroboard because there wasn't enough room. It can be hooked across J2 or wherever there is space for it.

The jacks J1 through J3 could be either phone jacks or RCA jacks, depending on which is most available. It is conventional for low voltage DC power supplies and signal-carrying connections to use ⅛-inch phone plugs, but RCA jacks are an equally valid alternative. They are cheaper, more commonly available, and don't briefly short out the plug when it is inserted like the ⅛-inch jacks do. The only disadvantage to using RCA jacks is the possible confusion with stereo connectors that might result.

A necessary calibration must be performed to POT1. Connect an analog voltmeter, preferably one with a sensitive movement, across C2. With the circuit operating, the LED should blink on and off as the meter needle oscillates between two voltage values. Vary the setting of POT2 and note how the upper and lower limit of the voltage swing across C2 changes. When you have observed the lowest point that the meter indicates over the complete range of cadences, short out J1 and set POT1 so the meter indicates that voltage or slightly less. That completes the calibration of the control unit.

Wiring the Sensor to an Exercise Machine

On a machine like a stationary rower that has a simple back-and-forth motion, a small permanent magnet can be positioned to pass near a reed switch. Every stroke should activate the sensor once. Another possibility is a leaf switch mounted so it is depressed once per stroke.

A bicycle is a slightly more complicated machine to interface to. The ideal bicycle sensor should produce one pulse for every revolution of the pedals. And because most cyclists now train on real bicycles attached to windtrainer stands and might want to remove the bicycle frequently, the sensor should also detach quickly and easily.

The prototype met these requirements with the setup shown in FIG. 15-4. An inexpensive toy magnet from Radio Shack holds itself to the chain ring by attraction. It activates a reed switch that clips onto a nearby tube of the bike. Both the magnet and reed switch can be detached in seconds when the bike is removed from the stand.

The reed switch is held in a hole drilled through the end of a thin piece of wood. The wood is attached to a metal clip that fits around a tube on the bike. By moving the clip around on the bike tube, the reed switch can be brought as close to the magnet as needed.

Clips like the one used in the prototype are sold in hardware stores for holding tools on a wall. They cost very little and are a great way to temporarily attach things to metal tubes. A similar clip holds the control unit to the handlebars of the bike to allow quick removal. To keep the clips from scratching the paint on the bicycle, their inner surfaces are lined with a piece of electrical tape.

FIGURE 15-5 shows a hand exerciser fitted with a pushbutton to generate a pulse every time it is squeezed properly. It can be hooked to the control unit with a wire and suitable plug. A hole drilled in one of the handles held the pushbutton. It was designed so that the exerciser must be squeezed all the way for a count to register. Other possibilities suggest themselves by this example. Any exercise in which a high number of repetitions must be performed at a steady rate could be monitored by the control unit. The only requirement is a suitable sensor to generate input pulses.

FIG. 15-4. *This is how the prototype sensor was attached to a bicycle.*

Hooking It Up to a TV

Television sets contain parts that stay charged to potentially lethal voltages for some time after the set is unplugged. Therefore, leave the TV unplugged for several hours or overnight before opening it up to perform the following modification.

After it has had time to discharge, open the back of the TV set you intend to use with this project. Locate the brightness control and observe which way the potentiometer rotates to turn the brightness down. In most cases, the potentiometer is connected with

FIG. 15-5. *A grip exerciser was interfaced to the project by adding a pushbutton.*

two wires only. If this is the case, note whether it is an increase or decrease in the resistance of the potentiometer that darkens the screen.

If it is a minimum resistance that corresponds to a dark screen, connect the normally open contacts of the relay across the terminals. If a maximum resistance makes the screen dark, disconnect one wire to the potentiometer and place the relay's normally closed contacts in series with it. If all three connections to the potentiometer are used by the TV, follow the hookup in FIG. 15-2. Additionally, the TV's sound can be disabled by disconnecting its speaker with an extra set of relay contacts if they are available.

Mount the relay near the potentiometer and route the wires from its coil to a jack mounted in the TV's case. Close up the TV after wiring the relay to the jack. The TV will operate normally the way it always did as long as there is no input to the relay. But when the relay is energized, the picture should go black.

USE

It's best to start using this project with switches S1 and S2 off. That way only the LED blinks. Set the cadence with POT2 at a rate that corresponds to how fast you intend to go. The control unit will let you go a little slower than that before it does anything, so you might want to set the speed slightly fast. Begin exercising and build up to a pace where the LED remains off. At this point in the workout you should be concentrating on the exercise itself and not require any reminders to help maintain a cadence. But after settling into it, switch on S1 or S2 to give you notice if you begin slacking off. Then you can direct your attention away from the exercise.

PARTS LIST:

Electronic Incentive

C1	200μF, 10V or better
C2	.1μF, value not critical
R1	10KΩ, all resistors ¼W
R2	1MΩ
R3, R4	100KΩ
R5	33KΩ
R6	270Ω
R7	3300Ω
R8	10KΩ
POT1	20KΩ trimmer
POT2	3 to 5 MΩ linear taper, panel mount potentiometer
Q1	PNP general-purpose transistor
Q2, Q3	NPN general-purpose transistor
IC1	555 timer
IC2	4011 quad NAND gate
LED	Large red LED
S1, S2	SPST toggle switch
J1, J3	⅛″ two-conductor phone jack
SENSOR	Reed switch or other appropriate sensor
SPEAKER	2 to 3″ 8Ω PM speaker
RELAY	SPDT miniature relay with a 9-volt coil
9VDC ADAPTOR	

PLUS, suitable enclosure, knob, wire, mounting clips, piece of wood to hold
reed switch, hardware, other sensors, wire, rub-on letters, and solder.

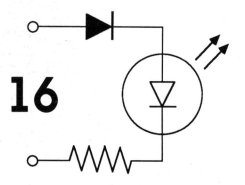

16

Tool Magnetizer
and Demagnetizer

Having a magnetized screwdriver or nutdriver around is often useful to help guide parts into tight spots. But at other times, tools that are permanently magnetized are a nuisance—always picking up loose hardware wherever they're laid down. The solution is not to give up on magnetized tools entirely, but to find a way to quickly and easily demagnetize as well as magnetize tools and other ferrous materials.

That's what this project does. In seconds, it can magnetize or demagnetize tools and other metal parts. A tool can be magnetized quickly, used for a single job, and be returned to its original state just as quickly. This project even doubles as a bulk eraser for magnetic tape and disks. See FIG. 16-1.

THE CIRCUIT

The circuit for this project is shown in FIG. 16-2. It is best understood in terms of the two separate functions it performs. The demagnetizing circuit is nothing more than an AC electromagnet made from a modified power transformer. When switch S1 is on, an alternating magnetic field is present on the top of L1. An object is demagnetized by switching S1 on while holding the object a few feet away. Then it is brought near the coil, moved around the top of the coil, and slowly removed before turning the switch off. Neon light NE1 is a pilot light for the demagnetizing circuit. It warns users not to bring any magnetically recorded tapes or disks nearby.

The atoms within the object are excited by the alternating magnetic field of the demagnetizing coil, but are left with a random orientation of their "spin" as the field slowly reduces in strength. The small magnetic force created by the spin of each atom's

FIG. 16-1. *The finished project is shown in use here.*

electrons tends to cancel the force of other oppositely oriented atoms. With the random orientation among the atoms that this demagnetizer leaves in a tool, no net magnetic force exists.

The magnetizing circuit is mostly separate and is controlled independently by S2, another power switch. Transformer T steps up the line voltage and charges the storage capacitor through D1 and D2 and through S3 when it is in the CHARGE position. Neon light NE2 is adjusted by the potentiometer to light just when the capacitor has charged to nearly its maximum value; the magnetizer is then ready to be used. The tool to be magnetized is place within L2 and S3 is pressed. This discharges the capacitor's considerable energy through the coil, creating a brief and intense magnetic pulse that lasts for a fraction of a second.

What actually happens is that L2 and C1 form a tank circuit that oscillates briefly after S3 is pressed. This creates a briefly oscillating but quickly damped magnetic field that persists after the initial strong pulse. The resulting changes in magnetic flux that occur after the first one aren't strong enough to seriously demagnetize the tool after it's initial jolt, so it comes away magnetized.

CONSTRUCTION

The circuit is simple and lets you use a variety of components that are usually salvageable from surplus equipment or stocked in a good junkbox. Component values here

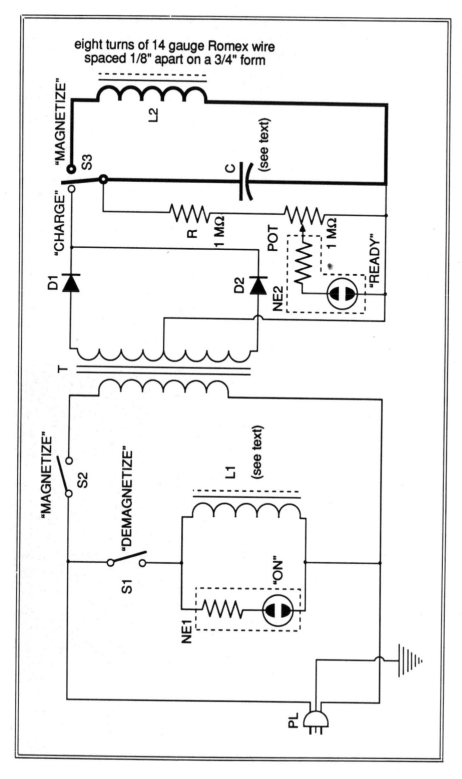

eight turns of 14 gauge Romex wire
spaced 1/8" apart on a 3/4" form

FIG. 16-2. *Complete schematic for the tool magnetizer and demagnetizer.*

are the least critical of any project in this book—basically because magnetizing and demagnetizing are simple processes. The photographs of the prototype might suggest a rather complicated project, but they represent only one way to build the project. Therefore, consider the following to be helpful suggestions rather than directions. They don't have to be followed explicitly, but can help you extract the best performance from the circuit.

The demagnetizing coil L1 is formed by modifying a power transformer with an "E I" core. Since only the primary is used, a transformer with burnt-out or otherwise unusable secondaries can be employed. To convert a transformer to L1, remove the "I" sections of its core leaving the "E" sections and the winding intact as the photograph of the prototype in FIG. 16-3 shows.

Although finding a transformer that uses an "E I" core won't be difficult, finding one that easily comes apart might be. In most "E I" core transformers, the laminations are alternated, making removal of the "I" sections impossible without taking the whole core apart. Finding a transformer constructed with separate "E I" sections takes some searching around. Doorbell transformers are often assembled in this way and are also just about the right size for this project, so look for them.

When you have found a suitable transformer, remove the outer shield, if there is any. The "I" section of the core is usually only held in place with varnish or thin tack welds. It is easy to remove with a few blows of a hammer and cold chisel. Use a bracket of angle aluminum or angle iron to mount the transformer core to the enclosure with the prongs of the "E" pointing up. Drill holes below it so the connections to it can pass into the chassis.

FIG. 16-3. *Notice how the top of the transformer has been removed.*

FIG. 16-4. *The heavy internal wiring is visible here in the completed prototype.*

There are other coils that can possibly be used for demagnetizing. The stator field coils of some motors are easily removed and develop powerful fields that can be used for demagnetizing. This type usually heats up rather quickly when used outside of a motor, so keep it on for short periods only if you do use one. Another possible source for L1 is the deflection coils in television sets. Larger sets have larger coils, of course, so look for them. Deflection coils are formed in a strange shape, but it is one that can be used with some imagination. The major problem with these and other coils that don't come from transformers is mounting them to a chassis.

Transformer T can be any step-up transformer with a secondary in the range of 200 to 400 volts. These transformers are common in surplus or junked tube equipment and finding one shouldn't pose much difficulty. The selection of the transformer depends mostly on the maximum voltage rating of the storage capacitors you find available.

Depending on the unrectified output voltage of the transformer and the maximum voltage of the capacitors you use, a bridge rectifier composed of four diodes might be a better alternative in place of the center-tapped full-wave rectifier shown in the schematic. Using a bridge rectifier, the filtered DC voltage across the capacitors is 1.414 times the transformer's secondary output voltage. Using a center-tapped full-wave rectifier as shown in the schematic gives half of that voltage.

The capacitor used for C should have a high enough voltage rating to handle the peak rectified output of the transformer. Photoflash capacitors commonly have ratings in the required range and are suitable for this project. Two or more will have to be used to achieve the required capacitance though. Another possible source for the storage capacitor is the filter capacitors used in the plate supplies of tube equipment. Because this type of capacitor is usually of low capacitance, quite a few of them will have to be paralleled. The prototype used 12 of these to reach a sufficient capacitance. As is the case with the transformer, the capacitors you use should depend more on what is cheaply available than the recommendations in the parts list. Just remember to use heavy wire when paralleling many capacitors to minimize the voltage loss that occurs during rapid discharging due to wiring resistance.

Switch S3 has somewhat special requirements. Its contacts have to withstand the arcing produced when it is switched to the MAGNETIZE position. Because it practically shorts out the capacitor, which is charged to several hundreds of volts, it must be able to handle an enormous current for a short duration. The flimsy contacts in most toggle or pushbutton switches would quickly arc away. However, a commercially available two-position knife switch is suitable for use as S3 or you could make one out of scrap aluminum and copper like the one in FIG. 16-5.

The coil L2 that creates the strong magnetizing field is made by wrapping eight turns of solid AWG 14 insulated house wiring around a ¾ inch form. The wire's insulation provides the correct spacing if the turns are wrapped right next to each other. The wire is stiff enough to allow the coil to be freestanding, provided the ends are firmly soldered. No mounting was used for L2 in the prototype. Its two leads made the necessary connections to S3 and the capacitors through two small holes drilled in the top of the chassis.

The construction and layout of this project is not very critical and should be determined mainly by what parts are available to you. It can be built in a metal enclosure, on a piece of wood, or into an gutted old tube chassis. An enclosure is not all that necessary because the project will probably be used in a work area anyway where its appearance

FIG. 16-5. *The heavy duty switch shown here was made from scrap aluminum and copper pieces.*

isn't as important as its function. With this in mind, consider building the magnetizer and demagnetizer on a piece of plywood or particle board. Or, because the transformer and storage capacitor may have come from surplus tube equipment, it might be convenient to build the rest of the project in the surplus enclosure that these components came from.

How ever you decide to build the project, the only important electrical considerations are safety and the use of short, heavy wiring between C, S3, and L2. Heavy wiring should be used wherever indicated on the schematic to minimize resistance that would decrease the current that flows through L2. To minimize resistance within the wiring, use the same type of wire that L2 is made of as indicated by thick lines in the schematic.

The only threats to safety are the exposed parts of S3. Knife switches and homemade switches have contacts that are difficult to enclose. They really don't have to be, though. As long as their handles are well insulated, they can be left exposed with little threat. For work area usage, the contacts are an acceptable danger because they only carry voltage when S2 is on. They're no more potentially dangerous than many other situations that exist in most work areas all the time. The bleeder resistor, R, drains any remaining charge left on the capacitor after it hasn't been used for a few minutes.

USE

Calibrate the potentiometer to light the "ready" light when the capacitors have charged to nearly their maximum value. With C left charging for at least ten seconds, advance the potentiometer from its minimum position until NE2 just turns on. This completes the calibration. In actual operation, you can expect the capacitors to take two or three seconds to charge each time they are used.

Keep the magnetizer and demagnetizer handy wherever you work with small hand tools frequently. To magnetize a tool, turn S2 on, insert the tool into the magnetizing coil, wait for the "ready" light, and press S3. There will be a spark at S3, and you'll actually feel a slight jolt in the tool as it is held rigid for an instant within the intense magnetizing field. Weak bar magnets suitable for children's games and experiments can be made by magnetizing nails this way.

Metal is more easily magnetized when it is warm or even hot. The warmer the metal is, the more energy its atoms have and consequently the less energy the magnetizer has to add to get them moving to a new position. Therefore, to make stronger bar magnets, heat a nail or other piece of ferrous material in a flame before using L2 to magnetize it. For an even stronger magnet, give it two doses of magnetization from L2, one right after the other.

When it is time to demagnetize a tool, switch the demagnetizer on, holding the tool a few feet away from L1. Slowly bring the tool to touch the coil and move it around the top of the coil for a few seconds. Just as slowly, withdraw it to a distance of a few feet and then shut the demagnetizer off.

The same procedure demagnetizes magnetic tape or computer discs. For this use, it might be a good idea to cover the top of L1 with a thin piece of plastic to prevent it from scratching anything fragile. Bulk erasing using the magnetizer and demagnetizer is preferable to the erasing done by the recording machine because it is quicker, avoids unnecessary wear on tape from heads, and does a more thorough job. For these reasons, it might be a good idea to build only a demagnetizer into a separate box to keep near your audio, video, or computer system.

PARTS LIST:

Tool Magnetizer and Demagnetizer

C	700μF or higher electrolytic; voltage rating should exceed filtered voltage from transformer (Photoflash or surplus filter capacitors are suitable).
R	1MΩ, ¼W
POT	1MΩ
NE1, NE2	Neon panel indicator with built-in dropping resistor
L1	Demagnetizing coil from modified transformer (see text)
L2	Magnetizing coil, 8 turns AWG 14, solid copper wire taken from Romex cable, on ¾ inch form (see text)
T	Step-up transformer with 200V to 400V secondary
D1, D2	600V, 1A or better rectifier diodes, or use a bridge rectifier of the same rating without the centertap
S1, S2	SPST toggle switch
S3	Heavy duty SPDT (commercial knife switch or homemade from scrap metal, as in FIG. 16-5)
PL	Line cord and wall plug

PLUS, suitable enclosure, angle bracket for L1, AWG 14 solid copper wire, solder lugs, hardware, rub-on letters, and solder.

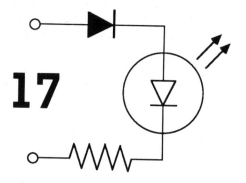

Multi-Sensor Digital Thermometer

Of all measuring devices, thermometers are particularly suited to digitization. Other analog readouts such as clock faces or meter needles can be made fairly clear without a digital display, but accurate analog thermometers are likely to remain difficult to read. Good accuracy at low cost is only possible in a mercury or dyed-water thermometer that inevitably has a tiny, difficult-to-read column for its display. Thermometers with dial readouts of reasonable cost have poor accuracy and are easily knocked out of alignment. A real need exists for accurate digital thermometers.

Probably the only reason why digital thermometers didn't become mass market items along with digital clocks and voltmeters is that they're not as easy to make. Measuring the temperature electronically and displaying it digitally is more complicated than the functions performed by a voltmeter or clock. A digital thermometer requires both a temperature transducer to convert temperature into an analog voltage and an analog-to-digital converter with display circuitry to provide a meaningful readout. Until recently, these were both difficult items to produce cheaply.

Nowadays however, accurate laser-trimmed temperature sensors are available in convenient packages at low cost and digital multimeters (DMMs) that contain the necessary analog to digital conversion circuitry are available for under $30. Complete digital indoor/outdoor thermometers, that essentially combine both these elements, are sold for less than $15.

These thermometers offer excellent accuracy and are a good buy. But commercial digital thermometers are usually limited in the number and type of sensors they can use. What they come supplied with is what their user is stuck with. For more versatility, this project allows its builder to include as many sensors as needed and add new ones at any time. Different types of sensors can be designed to monitor temperatures in a variety of ways and can be located hundreds of feet from the readout.

With an unlimited number of sensors possible, this project could be used to check on the temperature indoors, outdoors, in an aquarium tank, greenhouse, attic, swimming pool, hot tub, freezer, refrigerator, wine cellar, at a hand-held probe, and inside the cabinet of stereo or computer equipment. Many places can now have their own sensor where it would previously have been too troublesome to install a separate accurate thermometer. Although three to five sensors are all that most people probably ever need, it is reassuring to know that if you ever moved to an estate with all the features just listed, this multi-sensor digital thermometer project could easily expand to monitor them.

Besides the advantage of many sensors, this project makes very low cost a possibility as well. With DMMs as inexpensive as they are now, it is likely that most electronics hobbyists currently have one or will soon consider buying one. Both a DMM and a thermometer are the kind of thing that lies unused for most of the time. Consequently, some money can be saved by designing the thermometer to use the analog-to-digital converter and display circuitry that are built into a DMM. All that's required of the thermometer circuit then is to convert temperature to a voltage suitable for driving the DMM.

That's what this project does. It is designed to be used with either a 3- or 3½-digit DMM on its 1.000 or 2.000 volt scale. Its 10-millivolt-per-degree output gives the correct temperature reading on the DMM in degrees Fahrenheit or Celsius. When it's built to interface with a DMM this way, the thermometer circuit is very inexpensive. Total cost depends mainly on the number of sensors used, but could actually be lower than the comparable cost for the same number of mercury thermometers. See FIG. 17-1.

Although using the multi-sensor digital thermometer with a DMM is probably the option that most hobbyists will choose, a circuit is provided near the end of this chapter for a simple 3½-digit panel meter with a 2.000 volt input. For a continuous readout of temperature, the panel meter circuit interfaces successfully with the the circuit used to drive the DMM and forms a complete digital thermometer.

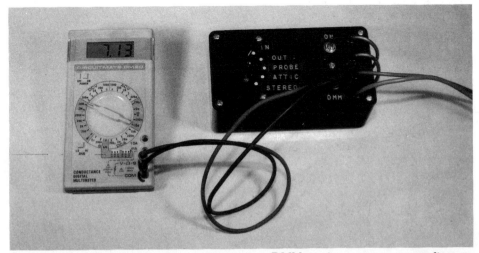

FIG. 17-1. *The finished project connects to a DMM to give temperature readings.*

THE SENSORS

There are a number of inexpensive temperature sensors presently available that are accurate enough to use in digital thermometers. But the Analog Devices AD590 temperature sensor IC used in this circuit has a number of features that distinguish it from the rest making its selection a clear choice. Among its other features, it was chosen because:

→ Different AD590s are interchangeable within a single measuring circuit. Unlike other sensors that are accurate only when each unit is trimmed individually, a single calibration is all that's necessary for all the AD590 sensors in a multi-sensor system.

→ Because it requires only two electrical connections, it can be used as a remote sensor over two-conductor wire.

→ Its output is in the form of a precise *current* that can be measured over long lengths of inexpensive wiring without the loss of accuracy that would result if a voltage output were used instead.

→ The current output varies linearly with temperature, making it possible to calibrate the thermometer's entire scale at a single known temperature.

→ Fast temperature changes are easily monitored because of the AD590's small metal can configuration. Because it offers low thermal resistance, it makes a good probe.

→ It consumes very little power, making it suitable for battery operation and eliminating the effects of self heating.

→ Pin reversals and supply irregularities will not damage the device, which is quite electrically durable.

The AD590 sensor is produced in five grades. The least accurate, the AD590I, is readily available from mail order electronics dealers. More accurate models are the AD590J, -K, -L, and -M. These are available too, but most suppliers don't stock them. Contact Analog Devices (at Two Technology Way; Norwood, MA 02062; (617) 329-4700) for their distributor in your area.

Although they differ in absolute accuracy, all AD590 sensors have less than 0.1-degree error when it comes to repeatability and long-term drift. This means that the more accurate grades aren't really necessary for most applications. Absolute temperature means less than most people think. What is truly significant and what carries more useful information are *changes* in temperature over time and *differences* between temperatures.

For example, when deciding how to dress in the morning, the amount the outdoor temperature has changed since yesterday at the same time is more important to consider than the absolute temperature. Likewise, deciding if a pool is warm enough to swim in depends more on how much the temperature has risen since you last poked your toe in than it does on the pool's absolute temperature.

In no temperature measuring system is absolute temperature measured as accurately as changes in temperature are. And even if an absolute temperature reading could be obtained accurately, it wouldn't be terribly significant anyway because it depends on many variables. Things like the sensor's placement and specific measuring conditions aren't always standardized between thermometers, making the relevance of absolute temperatures somewhat questionable.

So even though the temperature sensors used in this project can't indicate the temperature with 0.1–degree absolute accuracy, they still justify using a DMM with resolution that fine because of their repeatability and accuracy in measuring changes. Using any of the grades the AD590 is available in, a change on the DMM's display from 68.6 degrees to 68.2 degrees does indeed represent a 0.4-degree drop with great accuracy, even though the absolute temperature could be a degree or two off. Because of the absence of long-term drift, if the meter reports 68.6 degrees the next day or a year later, you can be sure that the sensor is at the same temperature it was when it gave that reading once before.

Temperature accuracy can be a confusing thing. There are different parameters that a sensor's accuracy can be specified by, resulting in potentially misleading claims. In one sense, the sensors used in this project can be said to be accurate to within 0.1 degree. In other ways, they are much less accurate, depending on the grade used. For the specifications of the different AD590 grades and an explanation of what they mean, write to Analog Devices for their data on the AD590 series. The data will make it clear just how good a thermometer built around the AD590 sensor can be when compared to commercial models.

THE CIRCUIT

The temperature sensors produce a current of one microamp per degree Kelvin. The circuit in FIG. 17-2 uses resistors to develop a voltage from that current and convert it to the Fahrenheit or Celsius scales to drive the connected DMM. The choice of three resistor values determines whether the output is in Fahrenheit or Celsius. Since most people use either one unit or the other exclusively, there is normally no need for both temperature scales. For occasional conversion, the formulas C=5(F−32)/9 and F=9C/5 + 32 only take a few seconds. But for those who prefer readouts in both units, two sets of resistors can be included with an additional DPDT switch built in to switch between them.

There are two parts to the circuit. On the right side is the temperature sensor IC in series with R4 and POT2. The voltage across their combined resistance is directly proportionate to the current through the sensor. If the resistor values are chosen for a Celsius scale, the voltage at the top of R4 is 10 millivolts per degree Kelvin—which equals 10 millivolts per degree Celsius plus 2.73 volts. The R4 and POT2 combination for the Fahrenheit scale develops a voltage of 10 millivolts per degree Rankine—which equals 10 millivolts per degree Fahrenheit plus 4.59 volts. If the output was simply taken from the top of R4, the resulting readouts would be in degrees Kelvin or Rankine. If you want the output to be in either of these scales, omit the left side of the circuit and take the output to the DMM directly across R4 and POT2.

But for the more useful Celsius and Fahrenheit scales, the left side of the circuit creates a steady voltage of 2.73 or 4.59 volts at PL1. This voltage provides the necessary offset required to convert Kelvin to Celsius and Rankine to Fahrenheit. The difference between PL1 and PL2 represents the temperature on the Fahrenheit or Celsius scales.

The offset voltage circuit is just a voltage divider. Integrated circuits IC1 and IC2 form a precision temperature-compensated 6.9-volt reference at the top of R2. The output at the wiper of POT1 can be adjusted to give a very stable 2.73 or 4.59 volts, depending on the values chosen for R2 and R3.

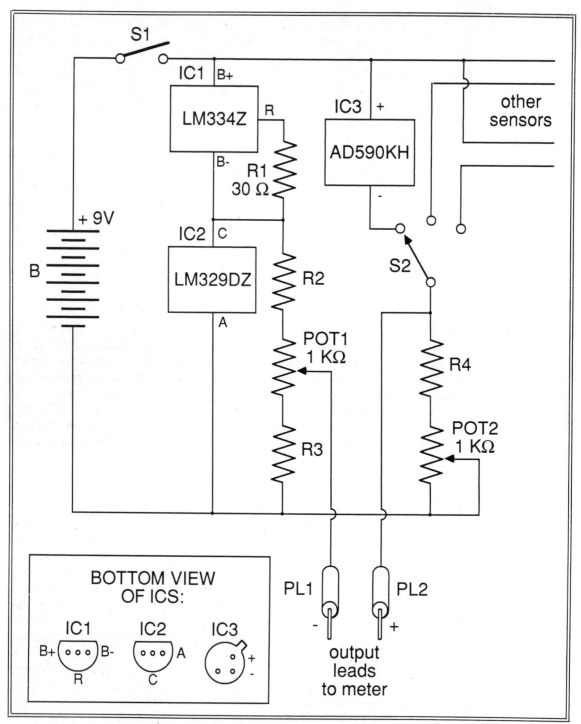

FIG. 17-2. *This is the schematic for the multi-sensor
digital thermometer. More sensors can be added by extending S2.*

The complete circuit is a variation on the standard resistive bridge. Bridge circuits like it are often used in measuring instruments with temperature sensors and other transducers because they make it possible to build a scale and offset factor into a circuit by selecting appropriate resistors. With the right resistors, the output of a bridge circuit can be in almost any units desired. In fact, if you are stubbornly independent, it is quite easy to create your own temperature scale. As long as it's for your own use and doesn't have to be compared to weather reports or tables, there's no reason why the scale factor and offset the thermometer uses can't be of your own choosing.

Although most people commonly use only one temperature scale to compare relative levels, sometimes it's necessary to know the temperature in both Celsius and Fahrenheit. This is especially apparent when correlating measured temperatures with published data. The recommended temperatures for most electronic components are usually only specified in one type of units. Weather and energy-related tables are another source of published temperatures that commonly use just one unit to save space. It is difficult to work with a thermometer whose output is in different units than those the data was published in.

To get both Celsius and Fahrenheit operation in the same unit, a DPDT switch can be incorporated to select between two sets of resistors. An additional three resistors and two potentiometers are required. To add the second scale, create a second R2/POT1/R3 voltage divider with the additional set of values given in the parts list and connect it in parallel with the first R2, POT1, R3 combination. Use one pole of the units switch to connect PL1 alternately to one or the other voltage divider, depending on its position. Leave PL2 connected to the wiper of S2 and use the other pole of the units switch to select a second R4/POT2 combination. This is all that adding another scale involves, except for having to calibrate the thermometer twice.

The 9-volt battery should last a long time because the circuit draws under 3 milliamps. Switch S1 prevents it from going dead when the thermometer isn't in use. A 9-volt battery eliminator or simple transformer power supply would make continuous operation possible.

CONSTRUCTION

The circuit is very simple and can be built and enclosed in a variety of ways. The size of the enclosure depends mainly on the number of remote sensors used. Enough space must be provided on the panel to clearly label each switch position and there must be sufficient room inside for all the wires. The circuit itself takes up very little room.

The prototype circuit was constructed on a Radio Shack #276-168 Universal PC Board that comes pre-drilled and pre-etched. The layout given in FIG. 17-3 is the parts placement diagram for this particular board. Following it could save you the trouble of planning your own layout. The universal PC board simplified construction of the circuit, was quite easy to use, and is strongly recommended. All parts except the switches, the battery, and the external sensors mount on the board, which is visible in the photograph in FIG. 17-4.

The indoor temperature sensor is included on the circuit board, but using an external sensor in its place is suggested if you anticipate locating the thermometer where it cannot get a good representation of average indoor temperature. For example, if you planned on mounting the thermometer above a radiator or electric heater, another place for the sensor would have to be found to give meaningful readings. Another thing that could cause misleading indoor temperatures is if a power supply circuit is built into the same enclosure

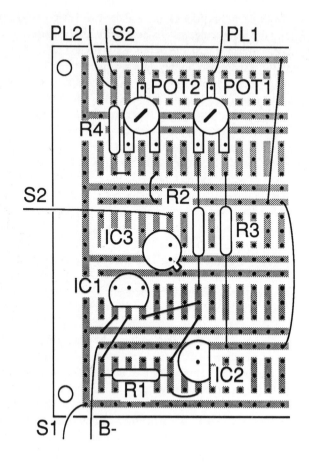

TOP VIEW SHOWN

FIG. 17-3. *The complete circuit for this project fits on half of a Radio Shack #276-168 Universal PC Board following this diagram.*

as the sensor. The heat from the transformer and voltage regulator will increase the temperature inside the box by several degrees.

The various temperature probes can be connected to the thermometer by ordinary two-conductor wire, but in many cases shielded cable is neater. If shielded cable is used, make the shield the positive conductor and leave the inner conductor as the return wire from the AD590. Runs several hundred feet long are possible with ordinary wire, but the manufacturer recommends that twisted wire be used over extremely long distances.

Connecting the wire to the sensor is easier if the unused case lead of the AD590 is cut off so it doesn't get in the way. At the other end of the probe wires, where they attach to the thermometer, one conductor of each wire connects to S2. For the other conductor of each wire, locate a tie point near the switch to attach them to, and connect the tie point to the circuit board with a short wire.

FIG. 17-4. *This is the internal view of the completed prototype.*

Different ways of making sensor probes depend on how they are to be used. To measure ambient temperature, the AD590 should be placed where air will circulate around it. For meaningful readings outdoors, temperature is always measured in the shade and at least a foot from buildings, light fixtures, dryer vents, buried pipes and anything else that radiates heat. Heat sources that wouldn't otherwise be obvious are revealed in the wintertime by the patterns that snow melts in. For outdoor use and to measure the temperature of liquids, the sensor and its connection to the wire should be encased in silicon sealant or epoxy. To use an AD590 as a hand-held probe, mount it at the end of a short plastic tube or pen body and fill the tube with epoxy. For specific situations, other sensor ideas shouldn't be hard to develop, given the sensor's small size and simple electrical requirements.

CALIBRATION

For best results, use the same voltmeter during calibration that will ordinarily be used with the thermometer. The first step is setting the voltage offset at PL1. Connect the zeroed voltmeter from PL1 to circuit ground. Adjust POT1 for a reading of 2.73 volts if you've built the Celsius version or 4.60 volts for the Fahrenheit version. If you've incorporated a switch to make both scales possible, set POT1 in each resistive divider at the correct voltage.

In a multi-sensor system, the thermometer only has to be calibrated with a single AD590, because ideally all the sensors are interchangeable. This greatly simplifies the rest of the calibration procedure. Another thing that makes calibration easy is the fact that the output current of the sensor is linearly dependent on temperature. This means that the entire temperature range can be calibrated by a setting made at a single known temperature.

The source of the required temperature standard can be a highly accurate laboratory thermometer in close thermal contact with the AD590, or it can be the boiling or freezing points of water. The freezing point of water is more suitable as a temperature standard than its boiling point, which must be compensated for altitude and barometric pressure. The freezing point is also the only convenient natural standard that can be used to calibrate a Fahrenheit scale, because the boiling point of 212 degrees is outside the range of most digital voltmeters. The freezing point is the obvious choice among simple temperature references.

A mixture of 50 percent distilled water and 50 percent crushed ice made from distilled water will drop to 0 degrees Celsius (or 32 degrees Fahrenheit) within 30 minutes. Because it should be allowed this much time to reach equilibrium, the mixture must be contained in a styrofoam or other insulated container to minimize heat entry. An ordinary household thermometer can be used to monitor the falling temperature of the mixture. When its temperature hasn't fallen for five minutes or more, it is within 0.5 degrees Celsius of freezing and can be used to calibrate the digital thermometer.

For the final calibration, connect PL1 and PL2 to the DMM as if for normal usage. Perform the calibration by adjusting POT2 for a 0.000- to 0.005-volt reading on the DMM if a Celsius scale is used or 0.320 to 0.329 volts for a Fahrenheit scale. If both scales are accessible with the switch discussed earlier, calibrate them both. But keep in mind that the temperatures displayed on one scale are no more accurate than figures obtained by applying the conversion formula to readings from the other scale.

BUILDING A DIGITAL PANEL METER

To continuously display the temperature, a DMM has to be dedicated for exclusive use with the thermometer. Digital multimeter prices are quite low and still falling, but using a DMM for only its 2.000 volt scale is still a waste of money. It is cheaper to duplicate only the necessary parts of the digital voltmeter than to buy the whole thing.

The circuit in FIG. 17-5 is essentially a 2.000-volt digital multimeter without the selector switch and other parts that would be necessary for additional ranges. The Intersil ICL7106 is a 3½-digit A/D converter and is the same IC used in most inexpensive DMMs and panel meters. Constructing a circuit around it with just the necessary components for a 2.000-volt scale saves the cost of unused components.

The IC chosen is particularly suited for use with this project because it operates from a 9-volt supply. The IC accepts an input voltage that floats above its ground, making it possible for the meter circuit to use the same supply as the thermometer circuit. It's power consumption is quite low, so a single 9-volt battery can supply power for both the thermometer and the panel meter circuits.

The IC needs a minimum of external support components for its intended use here. The values chosen set it up to take three readings per second. With a maximum reading of 1.999 volts, the highest temperature it can display is 199.9 degrees Fahrenheit and beyond the 150-degree range of the AD590 on the Celsius scale.

All the parts for the digital panel meter, including the IC, passive components, and the digital display fit on a single pre-etched and pre-drilled PC board. Connecting the IC's display outputs to all the connections on the LCD is tedious and will probably require jumper wires on both sides of the circuit board. Mount the IC at least an inch away from the display to allow room for the necessary jumpers. The most convenient kind of LCD

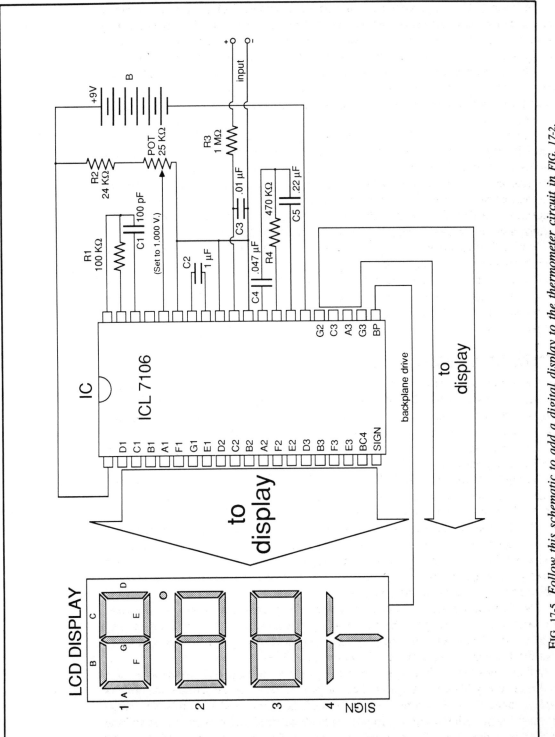

FIG. 17-5. *Follow this schematic to add a digital display to the thermometer circuit in FIG. 17-2.*

display to use is the type that slips into a socket, allowing you to do the wiring first and install the display as a last step. A socket is also strongly recommended for the IC as well to prevent possible damage while soldering and to permit easy removal.

A single calibration is required to set up the digital panel meter for use. To use as an accurate voltmeter without the thermometer circuit, adjust the 25,000-ohm potentiometer for 1.000 volts at its wiper. If it is to be used as the display for the thermometer though, adjust the potentiometer in conjunction with POT1 of the thermometer circuit to give the correct voltage offset. Then perform the temperature calibration with a laboratory thermometer or the ice/water mixture as described earlier.

Multi-Sensor Digital Thermometer

R1	30Ω, 2% metal film resistor, all other resistors 1% metal film
R2	4.02KΩ for Farenheit or 11.8KΩ for Celsius
R3	7.86KΩ
R4	17.4KΩ for Farenheit or 9.53KΩ for Celsius
POT 1, POT 2	1KΩ trimmer potentiometer
B	9-volt transistor battery
IC1	LM334Z constant-current source IC
IC2	LM329DZ precision temperature-compensated zener diode (IC)
IC3	Analog Devices AD590KH (more accurate) or AD590IH (more easily available). One required for each sensor.
S1	SPST mini toggle switch
S2	Single-pole rotary switch with number of positions to match number of expected sensors
PL1, PL2	Banana jacks to fit DMM (one red, one black)

PLUS, DMM, suitable enclosure, knob, battery clip, pre-etched experimenter board, shielded cable for remote sensors (unshielded wire can be used instead but may be less convenient), hook-up wire, rub-on letters, and solder.

PARTS LIST:

Digital Panel Meter

C1	100pF, 5% or better
C2	1μF, non-polarized tantalum or electrolytic
C3	.01μF bypass capacitor, value not critical
C4	.047μF
C5	.22μF, polypropylene preferred
R1	100KΩ, all resistors ¼W
R2	24KΩ
R3	1MΩ
R4	470KΩ
POT	25KΩ trimmer potentiometer
B	9-volt transistor battery or use the supply from the sensor circuit
IC	Intersil ICL7106 3½-digit single-chip A/D converter IC
LCD DISPLAY	3½-digit LCD display (non-multiplexed)

PLUS, suitable enclosure, pre-etched experimenter board, hook-up wire, and solder.

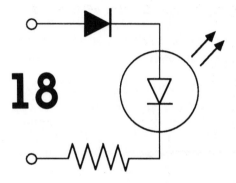

18

Active Minispeakers

Minispeakers, which became possible with advances in speaker materials and popular with mobile lifestyles, are characterized by their combination of good sound and compact size. Though their market was originally directed at home hi-fi systems, small aluminum minispeakers have found their way into automobiles, other vehicles, and attached to the sides of portable radios. This project takes a pair of popular minispeakers and makes them even more versatile by building amplifier circuits into them.

The amplifier built into each speaker lets it be used with low level sources. With built-in amplification the minispeakers modified in this project play loudly from the output of a Walkman type portable or anything else that is normally used only with headphones. In combination with a portable sound source, especially one of the new miniature CD players, these speakers make a great hand-held sound system. With their superior sound, greater power, and a high quality signal source, they produce better sound at higher volume than typical boom boxes do.

But active speakers are not limited to just one use; their real value is that they can be moved from one application to another. Another suitable use for them is a part of a high quality temporary stereo installation for a car or other vehicle. Because their amplifiers are built right into their enclosures, the active minispeakers eliminate the need to install a separate dash-mounted amp or power booster. They are also easy to remove from the car so they're not stolen or damaged and can be moved around whatever space they're in to experiment with acoustic placement.

Even when it's not playing music, the minispeakers can be quite useful. They can serve as test equipment—as a signal tracer on an electronics workbench, as a sensitive hum detector, or in setting up stereo equipment. Around the house, they can easily become telephone amplifiers or one-way intercoms with the appropriate inputs.

Because their power supply and input requirements are flexible, many more uses suggest themselves. Even when the minispeakers are modified, they can still be used as normal speakers with a stereo system in the way they were originally intended. It is quite possible to switch the same pair of speakers among several different situations: as part of a portable radio, in a car, with a home stereo system, and in other applications.

The first step in constructing this project is modifying the minispeakers. That involves building a pair of compact IC amplifier circuits, adjusting them, and installing them in the speaker enclosures. After that, suggestions are given for a carrying handle that forms the basis of a portable radio. It holds the two minispeakers, a portable stereo, and a 12-volt battery pack in a compact unit about the size of a typical portable radio. The prototype carrying handle is shown in FIG. 18-1. Finally, some other accessories that make speakers more useful are discussed.

THE AMPLIFIER CIRCUIT

Because ICs are used, a number of discrete components are avoided and the circuit is easier to build. The short parts list allows the amplifiers to be quite small, something that is always an important consideration for installation in small enclosures. A compact circuit also takes up less of the speakers' internal volume and changes their sonic characteristics less.

A single LM383 IC and a few passive components can form a simple amplifier circuit. In the circuit this project uses however, a pair of them are bridged. This means that the speaker output is taken across the outputs of two nearly identical amplifier circuits instead of between an output and ground. Bridging increases the maximum amount of power possible and eliminates the need for a bulky and distortion-producing output capacitor.

FIG. 18-1. *A pair of minispeakers modified by this project form the basis of a nice portable radio.*

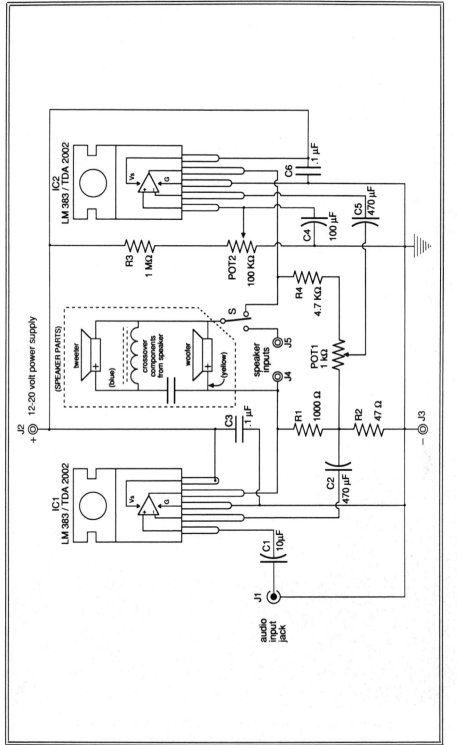

FIG. 18-2. *Complete schematic for modifying one minispeaker.*

The complete schematic for one channel of this project is drawn in FIG. 18-2. The two amplifier ICs are connected so that they are out of phase. While the output of one is positive, the other's output is negative and vice-versa. Placing a speaker or a test load between their outputs allows current to flow from one to the other. The speaker will receive almost the full supply voltage in either direction. This is an important design consideration in mobile applications where the available supply voltage is relatively low and must be carefully maximized in an amplifier circuit. With a 12-volt supply, the unloaded output of the circuit can theoretically be plus or minus 10 volts, for a total voltage swing of 20 volts. Bridged circuits like this one allow the maximum power to be obtained from a low supply voltage and are commonly used in car stereos and power boosters.

The signal the amplifier circuit receives from its input jack, J1, is fed to the non-inverting input of IC1 through C3, which blocks any DC voltage and passes only the musical signal. The input is amplified and appears at the output of IC1 where it is applied to the voltage divider made up of R1 and R2. The divider takes a portion of the output and feeds it back into the inverting input of the IC to set the gain by negative feedback. The voltage gain of IC1 is specified by $(R1 + R2)/R2$. Capacitor C2 is a DC-blocking capacitor that feeds back only the musical signal and not the DC component in IC1's output.

The divider also applies a portion of the output of IC1 to the inverting input of IC2 through POT1 and C5. Because the inverting input of IC2 is used, IC2's output is out of phase with that of IC1. The negative feedback that sets IC2's gain comes from the divider made up of R4, POT1, and R2. During calibration, the gain of IC2 will be adjusted by POT1 to precisely match the gain of IC1.

Resistor R3 and POT2 apply a small DC bias to the non-inverting input of IC2. The DC bias is greatly amplified and appears at the output of the IC. Potentiometer POT2 adjusts the amount of DC in IC2's output to allow the DC offset between the two ICs to be nulled to zero.

The amplifier's specifications make it suitable for portable use. With a 13.8-volt power supply, which is what a car's electrical system typically provides, the amplifier circuit will produce a maximum of 8 or 9 watts into 4 ohms. The limitation on output power depends primarily on the supply voltage and not on the ICs. They can accept supply voltages up to 20 volts and will produce considerably more output power at that voltage.

At 13.8 volts, playing a musical signal at maximum volume into a 4-ohm load, the amplifier draws an average of about 500 milliamps. Quiescent current is approximately 125 milliamps. The low current draw makes the amplifier suitable for portable use with rechargeable batteries as the power source.

BUILDING THE AMPLIFIER INTO THE SPEAKERS

First obtain a pair of Realistic Minimus-seven or similar minispeakers. The Minimus-seven was chosen for the prototype because it is widely available, sounds good, and is frequently discounted by Radio Shack. Other minispeakers will work just as well as long as they have an aluminum enclosure that will allow this project's circuit board to be placed inside it. The enclosure must also be aluminum to provide heatsinking for the ICs and to allow mounting holes to be drilled.

The following description of the modification sequence is based on the Minimus-seven. But that speaker is by no means unique. So many minispeakers from other manufacturers differ only in their dimensions, specific drivers, and crossover that the following description applies to them with only slight changes.

The first step after purchasing the minispeakers is opening them up. The back of the Minimus-seven is sealed, so all access to the inside of the enclosure must be through the holes that the drivers occupy. To reach these, remove the aluminum grill protecting the drivers with a flat-tipped screwdriver. The best place to pry the grill off is at one of the corners where the risk of deforming it is minimal. Small blobs of sticky clay are all that hold the grill to the front of the enclosures. They should allow it to be removed without much trouble.

With access to the drivers now, remove them one by one. As you remove them, note on a piece of paper their orientation and which color wire went to which terminal on which driver. This information will be necessary to successfully put the speakers back together again. Be careful around the drivers with screwdrivers and other ferrous tools. The drivers' powerful magnets can pull the screwdriver right through a speaker cone if you're careless. Set the drivers in a safe place along with the eight phillips screws that hold them to the enclosure.

Next remove the fiberglass batting that acts as acoustic damping inside the enclosures. It might be a good idea to wear gloves for this step, especially if your hands are particularly sensitive or have small cuts in them. The type of fiberglass used in speakers readily produces small splinters of glass that are painful and hard to remove. (If splinters do work their way into your hands, coat them with soap to help loosen them. Once they have acquired a coating of soap, the splinters will soon work their way out of the skin.)

Inside the speakers, against the back, is a black plastic plate on which the crossover components are mounted. This plate will be replaced by the amplifier circuit board, so remove it by loosening the three screws that hold it in place. Remove the capacitor and inductor that make up the crossover and set them aside. They will be mounted on a new PC board with the amplifier circuit that you will build shortly. It is also a good idea to save the wires from the crossover at this point because they are easily removed and have the right connectors for the drivers.

This would be an appropriate time to consider replacing the original crossover capacitor with a better one. For an audible improvement, replace the non-polarized electrolytic with a polypropylene or polystyrene capacitor of the same value. Audiophile publications are a forum for thorough studies of the relative merits of different types and brands of capacitors. They are the place to look if you're interested in extracting the best possible sound, but for a substantial improvement, almost any type of capacitor is better than the original ones.

FIGURE 18-3 shows how the amplifier circuit is built onto a PC board and a small piece of aluminum following the diagram in FIG. 18-4. The amplifier and crossover circuitry are mounted on the foil side of the PC board in the method described more fully in Chapter 2 and used in others. The input jack and the switch mount on the aluminum rectangle and protrude through the hole in the back of the enclosure that once held the input connectors. The only parts of the circuit not included on the PC board and aluminum are the two drivers and the binding posts J2 through J5. The binding posts are mounted in four holes drilled in the back of the enclosure underneath where the PC board is mounted.

The PC board and aluminum rectangle mount to the back of the speaker enclosure by the three screws that previously held the black plastic plate there. Notice how the ICs are held to the aluminum plate and to the enclosure itself by two screws. This allows them to conduct their excess heat to the large thermal mass of the speaker enclosure. No electrical isolation is needed in this case because mounting tabs on the ICs and the enclosure are all at ground potential.

Three of the four binding posts that mount in the back of the enclosure do need to be isolated from the enclosure, however. Two of them are inputs for driving the speakers directly by an external amplifier. They must be kept from ground potential by the use of a plastic bushing which is usually supplied with or molded into commercially available binding posts. The other two binding posts are for the DC power supply. The negative power supply connection can be in contact with the case, but the positive one must be isolated. Each pair of binding posts should have exactly ¾-inch spacing so it will accept stackable dual banana plugs which commonly have that spacing. Feel free to substitute alternatives to the four binding posts if they are not suitable for your intended use.

Begin construction of the amplifier circuit by cutting the PC board and aluminum rectangle to size and drilling mounting holes in them according to FIG. 18-4. You need two of each for stereo. After drilling holes for J1 and S in the piece of aluminum, temporarily bolt the ICs to it and solder them to the PC board in their final positions. Doing this assures that the two sections of the amplifier circuit will be in alignment. As indicated in FIG. 18-4, only four leads of each IC need to be soldered to the board. The center lead can be bent away from the board because it is internally connected to the mounting tab which makes a good contact to ground by itself. The center leads could just be ignored, but they provide a convenient point to attach the bridging capacitors C3 and C6, which incidentally have been omitted from FIG. 18-4 for clarity.

With the ICs mounted like so, use a cut-off wheel, chucked in a Dremel Moto-Tool or similar high speed drill, to cut the foil between their legs. Doing this after mounting the ICs rather than before greatly simplifies their alignment and eliminates the possibility of solder bridges occurring later.

Using the dimensions of the other parts in the circuit and following FIG. 18-4 as a guide, cut the rest of the circuit board into the appropriate pattern of foil islands. Check for

FIG. 18-3. *Each of the minispeakers has a board like this containing its amplifier and crossover circuitry.*

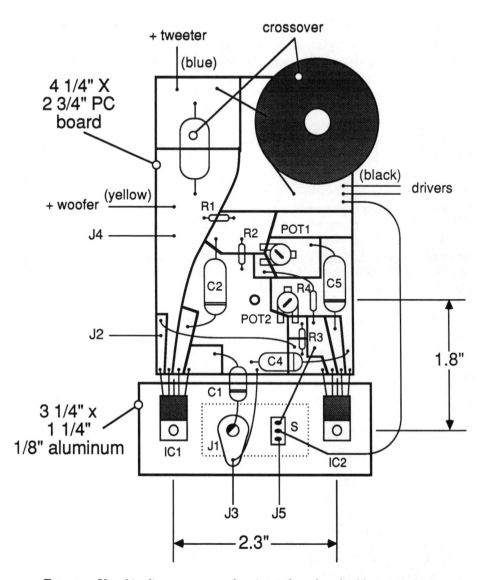

FIG. 18-4. *Use this diagram to cut the circuit board and add components.*

continuity between all adjacent foil sections that should be separated. Tiny foil bridges are easy to miss by eye, but the electrons will find them so this step is important. Holes have to be drilled for the trimmer potentiometers and the other small parts. Wires and larger parts can be attached to the board without a hole to hold their leads.

Mount the parts to the board using FIG. 18-4 as a rough guide, although your layout may differ slightly due to different component dimensions. The input jack and the switch should be installed and connected at this point. Attach connecting wires to the circuit board and components where they are indicated in FIG. 18-4, retaining the original wires from the speakers if possible.

ADJUSTMENT

Before installing the amplifier circuit boards in the enclosures, POT1 and POT2 must be adjusted. During this calibration, the ICs will require a bit more heatsinking than the aluminum rectangle alone can provide, so clamp the aluminum in a metal vise or work out another suitable arrangement.

Calibration requires an oscilloscope, signal generator, voltmeter, and a four- to eight-ohm resistor. The voltmeter and resistor should be easy to come by. If a signal generator is not available, a music source playing a slow piano piece will do. There is really no adequate substitute for an oscilloscope, however.

Set the signal generator frequency to 1000 Hz and adjust its output level to about 50 millivolts rms. Connect it to the input of the amplifier and place the load resistor across the amplifier's output. Use the oscilloscope to check the output of each IC separately. Setting it for AC input, attach its ground wire to the circuit ground and use the other input lead to verify that each amplifier has an output that resembles the input from the signal generator. Adjust POT1 so the outputs of the two ICs are roughly equal.

The next step is connecting the oscilloscope across the two outputs, but before doing that, you must disconnect the ground wire to the oscilloscope. Because neither output terminal of a bridged amplifier is tied to ground, it cannot be measured with a grounded device. Since the signal generator and oscilloscope probably both have three-conductor line cords and are almost certainly on the same power line, their grounds are identical. Connecting the oscilloscope across the amplifier outputs as the next step entails would short out whichever IC got the oscilloscope's ground wire. To prevent this from happening, temporarily unground your oscilloscope at its power outlet. Use a three-wire adaptor with its third terminal disconnected. This presents no safety hazard as long as you don't forget and leave the scope plugged in that way permanently.

Once that necessary step has been done, connect the oscilloscope across the output of the circuit (across J4 and pin four of IC2). Adjust POT1 for maximum undistorted output as seen on the scope. Increase the input from the signal generator until the output waveform just begins to clip. Return to POT1 and adjust it to get the maximum output level without clipping in either the positive or negative direction.

Finally, connect a DC voltmeter across the amplifier output and adjust POT2 for zero voltage. It might take a few seconds for the voltage level to settle after each change of the potentiometer because of C4. With patience though, the offset can be trimmed down to 10 millivolts or less. If a large offset adjustment must be performed, it might be necessary to go back and re-adjust POT1 for the maximum undistorted output level.

Once it has been calibrated, the amplifier circuit board is ready to be mounted in a speaker enclosure. First though, it must be wired to the binding posts, because they will be covered by the board when it is finally installed. Make the necessary connections, then remove the temporary bolts that held the aluminum rectangle to the PC board while the circuit was being constructed. Slip the board into the enclosure through the round hole that the woofer once occupied and mount it to the rear of the enclosure by the three screws that originally held the plastic plate there. FIGURE 18-5 shows the amplifier circuit mounted inside one of the minispeakers. No heatsinking compound is necessary for the ICs and would only become messy, so avoid it.

Minispeakers are mostly "acoustic suspension" type speakers that depend on an airtight enclosure of fixed volume. As much as possible, the original conditions should be

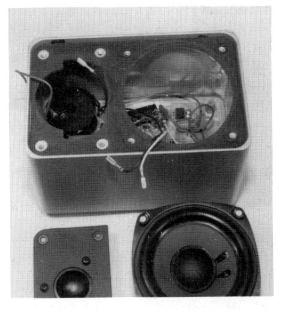

FIG. 18-5. *The circuit board from FIGS. 18-3 and FIGS. 18-4 can be seen through the holes in one of the minispeakers.*

maintained. The slight extra volume occupied by the amplifier components doesn't noticeably affect the sound of the Minimus-seven and can't be helped anyway. As for the airtight seal between the aluminum rectangle and the hole in the enclosure—line the hole with a small amount of Plasticine or other sticky clay to make it as good as it once was. To maintain the airtight enclosure, plug up J1 whenever it isn't being used as an input. A dummy RCA plug can be made up to serve this purpose.

With the board mounted to the back of the enclosure, the minispeakers can be put back together again. Start by replacing the fiberglass batting, observing the previously stated precautions for your hands. Leave the four speaker wires accessible through the fiberglass and connect the drivers to them, referring to the notes you made as you took the speakers apart. Although push-on connectors are convenient, many audiophiles believe they detract from sound quality. Accordingly, you might prefer to solder the speaker wires to the driver terminals rather than rely on the original connectors.

Observing the original orientation, replace the drivers in their mounting holes and screw them into place. Replace the protective aluminum grille with a few light slaps. The sticky clay that originally held the grille to the enclosure can be discarded since it isn't really necessary for securing the grille. Another possibility is not replacing the grille at all. The speakers look attractive enough without it and the grille certainly doesn't improve the sound. How much it detracts from it can be debated, but it is certain that a fairly rigid metal grille can produce such effects as interference, resonance, and re-radiation of distorted sound. For environments where the speaker cones might be damaged though, it is probably best to replace the grilles for protection.

CONSTRUCTING THE PORTABLE CARRIER

Probably the most useful accessory for getting the most out of the pair of active minispeakers is a carrying handle and battery supply. If you already own a Walkman or similar headphone stereo, you can effectively turn it into a high quality portable radio that will play quite loudly. Even counting the cost of a new Walkman, the total expense will be less than for many high quality portables with speakers. Since the minispeakers have additional flexibility though, a system based on them is far more valuable.

A suitable holder could be simply a piece of metal, plastic, or wood that attaches to the back of each speaker and provides a place in the middle for 12 volts worth of batteries and a Walkman. Or it could incorporate some of the features of the carrier pictured in FIG. 18-1 and drawn in FIG. 18-6. Although it doesn't represent the only way to build a carrier for the active minispeakers, the following description of the prototype makes some good points for speaker carriers in general.

It is usually desirable that the speakers in a portable radio be removable so they can be moved as far apart as possible for stereo separation. Another nice feature would let the speakers pivot as well. This would allow them to be arranged for good sound without having to be removed from the handle. The prototype has both these features because it uses a pair of swivel mount holders sold by Radio Shack specifically for use with the Minimus-seven (R.S. #40-2031). These brackets hold the speakers securely for traveling, yet make it easy to pivot them around or remove them entirely. They are a good investment in general, because they can be used to mount the speakers at home or in a car as well.

The prototype in FIGS. 18-1 and 18-6 uses ten rechargeable D cells to provide a 12-volt power supply for the speakers but there are other possibilities as well. Your specific battery requirements depend on how loud and for how long the speakers will be played. The

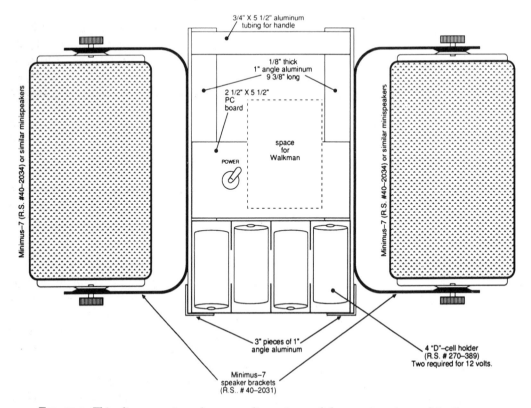

FIG. 18-6. *This diagram gives the exact dimensions of the carrier pictured in Fig. 18-1.*

maximum loudness depends on the power supply, which can be from 12 to 20 volts (naturally, louder sound results from higher supply voltages). Experience with the prototype has shown that a supply of more than 12 volts isn't really necessary, although it certainly can be used and will result in better performance.

Nickel-cadmium D cells are available with current capacities up to 4 amp/hours, although most are only rated at 1.2 amp/hours. Four amp/hours is enough to power the speakers at maximum volume for several hours—probably more than your ears can take. The lower capacity D cells are adequate for most casual use, which is a good thing because the higher rated D cells are quite expensive.

If a long playing time is necessary, it is more economical to buy a 12-volt battery pack rather than make one from separate cells. The advantages of battery packs are their more compact size, more effective price, higher possible current ratings, and fewer contacts to cause problems than with separate batteries in a holder. Common ratings are 1.8, 3, 5, 6, and 10 amp/hours. Good sources for suitable rechargeable battery packs are Mouser Electronics and some of the many surplus dealers.

Of course, using separate batteries is probably a better idea if you don't plan on using the minispeakers as a portable stereo very often. For occasional use, separate batteries make more sense because the cells can be removed from the holder to use them in other devices. Another advantage of separate batteries is they allow you to obtain a lower voltage tap (typically 3 or 6 volts) to supply the Walkman with. When using the batteries to supply the Walkman, take the tap from the batteries closest to the negative side in order to maintain the same ground for the Walkman that the minispeakers use.

The prototype was built from six pieces of aluminum. Two pieces of angle aluminum form the sides to which the speaker brackets attach to. Each side piece is supported by a smaller ''foot'' of angle aluminum attached to the bottom at a right angle. Owing to the dimensions of the carrier, the aluminum brackets at the bottom are the only points that provide support. They have small rubber feet to prevent them from scratching delicate surfaces.

The two four-cell holders are attached to the front and back of the side pieces as far down as they can go. If a battery pack had been used instead, the side pieces would have been moved closer together or farther apart accordingly. It is the size of the batteries that determines the width of the carrier.

In the middle of the carrier, a thin piece of PC board material is attached to provide a mounting surface for the power switch on the front and for two additional D cells on the back. The Walkman clips to the PC board by its belt clip but could have been attached more securely with a bolt if necessary. The back of the PC board is used to make the few necessary connections to the batteries, the switch, and the power supply wires leading to the speakers.

The handle at the top of the carrier is made from a piece of ¾-inch aluminum tubing surrounding a piece of aluminum bar stock. The bar is mounted by its ends to the side pieces and is just the right size so the tube can rotate freely around it. This is one very good method for making a handle but depends on having aluminum pieces of just the right dimensions. Alternatives that would work as well are an appropriately shaped piece of wood, a nylon or leather strap, or a door handle.

With the carrier built as described, only a signal wire between the Walkman and each speaker is needed for operation. Because it has an appropriate stereo plug and is of the correct length, a wire from a junked pair of miniature stereo headphones is used to send the signal from the Walkman to the speakers. The wire is split down the middle into a pair of shielded cables joined at a mini stereo plug that makes connection to the Walkman. An RCA jack is attached to each free end and plug into the speakers.

Although it was no challenge to build, the prototype just described has a number of advantages over commercial boom boxes. Because it is constructed almost entirely out of aluminum, it is certainly stronger, although slightly heavier. With the right signal source, it is sonically superior as well, in terms of low distortion, smoother frequency response, and greater power. Of course a big advantage that the minispeaker-based portable has over commercial models is that the minispeakers can be removed and used in a variety of other applications, some of which have been discussed and some of which follow.

OTHER ACCESSORIES

Additional input devices and accessories expand the usefulness of the active minispeakers. Around the house, they can be used to amplify sources that would ordinarily be too quiet. A telephone pickup coil with a suction cup mount will enable many people to hear phone conversations when it is plugged into one of the speakers. If a crystal microphone is used as its input device, an active minispeaker can be used to monitor a baby's room or as a one-way intercom in other monitoring applications.

With a probe and alligator clip on the end of a shielded cable, one of the speakers can become a signal tracer for audio circuits. A potentiometer is needed as a gain control, though. Turn down the gain to begin testing an unknown circuit and raise it if more volume is needed. Because they have capacitor inputs, the speakers are protected up to a certain point against DC voltages from the tested circuitry.

One of the speakers can be used to trace down sources of electromagnetically induced hum around an audio system if a coil is used as its input. A potentiometer might be necessary in this case, depending on the coil and the strength of the hum.

The speakers can also be used to amplify the audio outputs that many computers provide. They can temporarily serve in place of headphones in many experimental circuits for which it would be too much trouble to build a dedicated amplifier. Again though, it is always best to use a potentiometer for attenuation if it is uncertain what the inputs to the speakers will be. Other similar uses will probably present themselves once the speakers have been built and hooking them up becomes a simple matter.

All these applications require some kind of power supply. If you plan to use this project where AC power is available, then build a simple low voltage DC power supply to use with it. When operating off a power supply, there is no reason the active minispeakers must be limited to 12 volts. In fact, there is every incentive to provide a higher voltage for improved performance. Transformers are very commonly rated at 12.6 volts AC. When their outputs are rectified and filtered, they deliver 18 volts DC. One of these transformers, with four diodes and a filter capacitor, would fit neatly into a small chassis that could sit right below one of the speakers and can provide just about the ideal supply voltage. Because of the wide range of input voltages and the relatively low average current drain, regulation isn't necessary and would only lower the maximum available voltage from this supply.

PARTS LIST:

Active Minispeakers

(Parts for one channel given; the other channel is identical.)

C1	10μF, 25V, electrolytic
C2, C5	470μF, 25V, electrolytic
C3, C6	.1μF bypass capacitor, value not critical
C4	100μF, 25V, electrolytic
R1	1KΩ, All resistors ¼W
R2	41Ω
R3	1MΩ
R4	4.7KΩ
POT 1	1KΩ
POT 2	100KΩ
IC1, IC2	LM383 or TDA2002 audio amplifier IC (R.S. #276-703 or equiv.)
S	SPDT mini toggle switch
J1	RCA phono jack
J2-J5	Binding posts, or suitable equivalent

PLUS, pair of Minimus-seven minispeakers (see text), 4¼" × 2¾" single-sided PC board material, 3¼" × 1¼" piece of ⅛" thick aluminum, hardware, hook-up wire, and solder.

PARTS LIST:

Speaker-Carrying Handle

SPEAKER HOLDERS	Two Radio Shack #40-2031 brackets for Minimus-sevens
ANGLE ALUMINUM	⅛" thick, 1" sides, 9⅜" long
ANGLE ALUMINUM	Thickness unimportant, 1" sides, 3" long
ALUMINUM TUBING	¾" diameter, 5½" long (see text for alternatives.)
ALUMINUM BAR	To fit inside tubing, threaded at ends
PC BOARD	2½" x 5½" to hold sound source and power switch
BATTERY HOLDER	To hold four D cells (Radio Shack #270-389 or equiv.) Two required.
BATTERY HOLDER	For an additional two D cells (ten Nicads are needed because they each supply only 1.2 volts.)
POWER SWITCH	SPST toggle switch

PLUS, portable stereo sound source, RCA plugs, shielded signal wire and three-conductor plug to fit Walkman, hook-up wire, and solder.

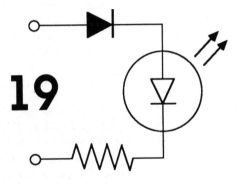

19

Plug-in Tester

When a newly completed electronic project is ready to be plugged in for the first time, the safest way to do it is to gradually bring the outlet it's plugged into up to the full line voltage. This project is useful in these cases where you've recently completed a project or just fixed a small appliance. It's offered as the intelligent alternative to gritting your teeth and tentatively poking plugs into an outlet while waiting for sparks and blowing a fuse. Instead of being surprised with an overload like that, this project provides presettable circuit breaker protection as you slowly turn up the voltage. It is also particularly useful as a workbench accessory for building and experimenting with circuits that use 120 volts AC. With it, you can switch circuits on and off frequently and change their connections safely by hand.

This project offers quite a number of features that are useful for building and testing 120-volt AC devices:

→ DPDT master power switch
→ Blown-fuse indicator light
→ House wiring tester
→ DPDT main power relay with pushbuttons for ON and OFF
→ Presettable circuit breaker (has the electrical effect of quickly pushing the OFF pushbutton when it is tripped)
→ Variable output voltage controller with bypass switch (utilizes a phase control circuit or an auto-transformer)
→ Switchable test points for inserting an external ammeter or other shunt
→ Beeping continuity tester with flashing probe

There are probably more features listed here than are really necessary, but the circuit is presented in modules so that unwanted features can be eliminated during construction. Even if they are not used in this project, certain parts of the circuit might find uses in some of your other projects.

THE CIRCUIT

The circuit is designed for maximum safety. As its schematic in FIG. 19-2 shows, at least three switches must be in the correct position for power to be delivered to the outlet. When the master switch S1 is initially turned on, the relay is off. If something later goes wrong with the internal circuitry or if a power failure occurs, the relay will return to its off position and the outlet will be shut off.

The master power switch is of the double-pole double-throw type (DPDT), so it interrupts both sides of the power line when it is switched off. That leaves only the ground wire connected to the load for safety. Most power switches turn off only one side of the supply. Although this is all that is necessary for on/off control, there remains the dangerous possibility that the "hot" side of the line could still be left connected. This situation could occur even when the switch is off if the house wiring was reversed or the switch was incorrectly installed. The master power relay is a DPDT switch as well and interrupts both sides of the line for the same reasons of safety. The circuit breaker operates through this relay, assuring a completely disconnected power source when it trips.

A neon light is connected across the main power fuse to indicate if it is blown. If the fuse is good, the neon is shorted out and doesn't light. But if the fuse blows, enough current can flow through to light it. Pushbutton switch PB1 and resistor R1 allow the fuse to be tested even with the power switch off. Note that an indicator for blown fuses is a feature of minor importance and one that is merely convenient, not absolutely necessary. It is included simply because I and many people sometimes forget to check the fuse when something goes wrong with a circuit. We wouldn't waste time looking for problems that don't exist if we had the blown fuse indicator right under our noses.

As an improvement over a standard pilot light, the plug-in tester uses three neon indicators to form a household wiring tester. The three neon lights NE1 through NE3 are connected across the hot, neutral, and ground wires of the power cord. With the list that is visible in FIG. 19-1, these three lights indicate a variety of ways an outlet it is plugged into could be improperly wired. For another project, you could build the three neons into a plastic wall plug to make a pocket-sized wiring tester. Its portability would be a great advantage because it is always a good idea to check unknown outlets in other places, especially for their ground, before plugging in sensitive equipment.

The master relay that controls the power to the outlet has a 12- to 24-volt DC coil. It is driven from the 120 VAC line through R2, D1, R3, and D3 when the ON pushbutton is pressed. When the relay contacts pull in, the coil is then continuously powered through D2 so the contacts stay latched on.

A low voltage supply to the relay coil is essential because that allows it to be shorted out momentarily by the OFF pushbutton when it's time to turn the relay off. When PB3 is pressed for this purpose, current to the relay coil is diverted through R4, releasing the contacts and unlatching the relay by interrupting its supply.

The circuit breaker that this project provides senses current and can be set to trip when a certain level has been reached. The current drawn by the load plugged into the

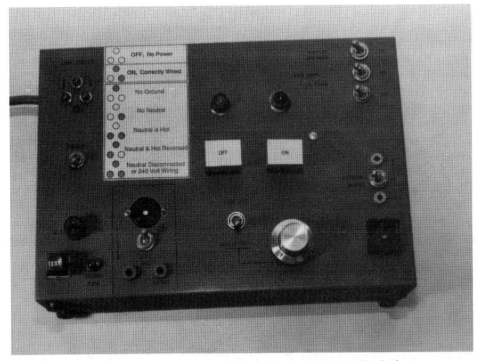

FIG. 19-1. *This is what the project looks like when it is finished.*
All of its controls are visible on the front panel.

outlet must flow through R6 and whatever other resistors R7 through R15 are selected by switches S3 through S5. By Ohm's Law, a voltage drop develops across these resistors equal to I/R. That voltage is applied across the base and emitter of transistor Q1 through POT2 and D4. If the voltage drop reaches a high enough value (signifying a current overload), the transistor is turned on, diverting current from the relay coil and switching it off in the same way that pushing the OFF button does.

The exact base-emitter voltage required to switch the relay off depends on the particular transistor and relay used, which is why POT2 is provided. Once set by the potentiometer, the voltage trip point remains the same, whereas the current it represents is variable depending on what resistors are switched in parallel with R6. During calibration, POT2 is adjusted so that the circuit breaker trips when 0.5 amps flows through R6, developing 1 volt. This setting effectively calibrates the rest of the current trip points.

With the 2-ohm resistor as the only current shunt, the circuit breaker trip point is 0.5 amps. Using S3 to switch a 1-ohm resistor in parallel with R6 effectively adds 1 amp to the trip point, because it then takes 1.5 amps to induce the same 1 volt across the resulting resistance of 0.66 ohms. Likewise, each additional 1-ohm resistor switched in parallel with the shunt adds another 1 amp to the trip point. With just three switches and the one, three, five grouping of 1-ohm resistors used in the prototype, trip points of 0.5 amps, 1.5 amps, 3.5 amps, 4.5 amps, 5.5 amps, 6.5 amps, 8.5 amps, and 9.5 amps are all selectable by different switch combinations. In your version of this project, different shunt resistors and combinations can be used to achieve whatever trip levels are desired.

This arrangement was chosen because 1-ohm, 5-watt resistors are fairly common. A 10 percent tolerance is specified in the parts list and was used in the prototype because it's all that is truly necessary. A 10 percent deviation from the current limit shouldn't matter all that much in the situations this project will be used in. The circuit under test either draws a lot of current under the limit in normal use, or way over it if something goes wrong. If more precision is really needed, using an ammeter is suggested. Just for comparison, fuses and commercial circuit breakers rarely trip within 10 percent of their rated value, either.

There are two commonplace means of varying AC voltage that are suitable for the plug-in tester. The more expensive and bulky of these alternatives is an autotransformer that provides a variable voltage output that is a true sine wave. An easier alternative is a triac phase-control circuit that varies output power like a light dimmer does.

The best control method for your project depends on how easily you can obtain a surplus autotransformer (sometimes called a Variac or Powerstat) and what loads you expect to control. For most appliances with motors, heaters, and transformer inputs, a phase-control circuit is adequate. But for powering certain electronic equipment, especially those that use triac or SCR switching, the autotransformer is best. The choice of which control circuit is used must be based on cost and your load requirements.

Both options are shown in the schematic of FIG. 19-2. They are interchangeable with each other, sharing only the points A, B, and C in the circuit. The switch S2 is provided to divert power around the controller for full output power and to avoid powering the autotransformer or phase controller when they're not being used.

Switch S6 can be used in case you want to place an ammeter or other shunt in series with the the load. The sockets J1 and J2, provided for an external ammeter, are the small type designed to accept meter test probes. The switch is wired so that when the sockets aren't being used, they are left safely disconnected from any hazardous voltages in the circuit. If this were not a concern, an SPST switch could be used instead, but the DPDT switch makes the project safer.

Although it's not electrically connected to the rest of the plug-in tester, a continuity tester circuit is also included. For all the parts it shares with the circuit just described, it might as well be built separately. However, it would probably come in handy in many of the same situations where the rest of the circuit is being used.

The tester circuit has two methods to indicate when it detects continuity between its test leads: an LED in the clear probe lights up and a piezoelement beeps. Both of these were designed so that the user wouldn't have to waste time looking up from the probes. Either a 9-volt battery or a simple transformer supply can power the continuity tester. Switch S7 is used to bypass the oscillator part of the circuit when the sound isn't needed, but the LED indicator always functions. Because the circuit draws only a miniscule amount of power when it is operating, a battery can be used instead of a power supply and should last nearly its shelf life.

CONSTRUCTION

Since this is a project with many panel-mounted components and only a few internal components, it lends itself to construction in a large flat box. When it is built in such a box, all the controls mount on the face, as in FIG. 19-1. The chassis can then be stood on end against the back of a workbench as a test instrument or laid flat for portable use.

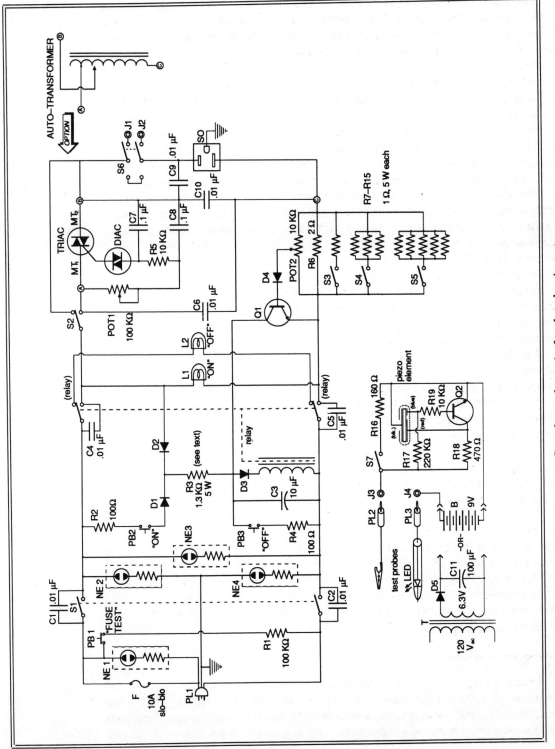

FIG. 19-2. *Complete schematic for the plug-in tester.*

Suitable boxes are sold new in stores, but a good alternative is the bottom half of an old piece of tube equipment. Quite a lot of older equipment was typically built on a metal plate mounted to a suitable chassis 3 or 4 inches high. If you can obtain one of these chassis, turn it over and cover the open side with a piece of aluminum, wood, or PC board material. The side that used to be the bottom now becomes the faceplate on which to mount most of the components.

Internal parts placement and wiring techniques are for the most part arbitrary and depend on how you lay out the front panel. See FIG. 19-3 or the photo in FIG. 19-1 for suggestions. The front panels of most pieces of electronic equipment are designed with their inputs on the left, their output to the right, and controls that affect the output in the middle. This project follows that convention.

After mounting the components in a logical way on the faceplate, use point-to-point wiring with a few solder lugs to connect them. (See FIG. 19-3.) If you are using a phase control circuit for the variable output, build it on a small piece of circuit board material cut into "islands" with a Dremel tool cut-off wheel. This method of construction is described more fully in Chapter 2 and yields a finished module like that shown in FIG. 2-9 of that chapter.

The continuity tester probe with the LED is constructed from the clear body of a cheap ball-point pen as FIG. 19-4 shows. Select the type of pen with a tiny hole in its tip for where the ball point protrudes and remove the ink cartridge, leaving only the body. Build a rectangular red LED into the pen where it will be visible as an indicator. The LED's sides will have to be sanded down considerably before it can fit inside the pen body without sticking. Be careful when doing this not to sand its sides down so much that the electrodes are exposed. When the LED is free to slide in and out of the pen barrel, bend its short lead 180 degrees so it will protrude through the tip of the probe. Solder a red wire to the other lead and use it to push the LED into the pen body. When the LED has gone in as far as it will go and its free lead sticks out of the pen tip, squirt some hot-melt glue or epoxy cement into the pen body to secure the test lead. Attach a red banana plug to the other end of the test lead. Make the remaining test lead out of black wire, using a banana plug on one end and a probe or alligator clip on the other.

CALIBRATION

The adjustable circuit breaker can easily be calibrated by a 60-watt light bulb. By the power law, 60 watts is 0.5 amps at 120 volts, so the bulb is ideal for setting the 0.5-amp initial trip point of the circuit breaker. From this initial point, all other settings derive their accuracy. The actual calibration is a simple procedure: Plug a lamp with the 60-watt bulb into the outlet with POT1 at its minimum setting and S3 through S5 off. The bulb should remain lit when power is switched on via the relay. Adjust the potentiometer just until the relay clicks off. This sets the base trip point at 0.5 amps and completes the calibration.

USE

As an appliance checker, this project is quite easy to use. Plug the tester in and use its outlet to supply power to the device in question. Preset the circuit breaker's trip point just above the appliance's rated value and slowly turn up the power control. With your

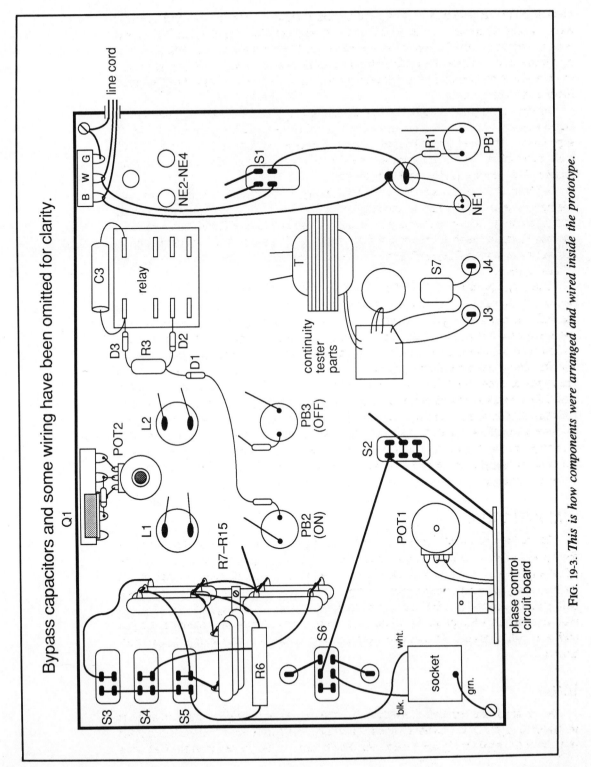

Bypass capacitors and some wiring have been omitted for clarity.

FIG. 19-3. *This is how components were arranged and wired inside the prototype.*

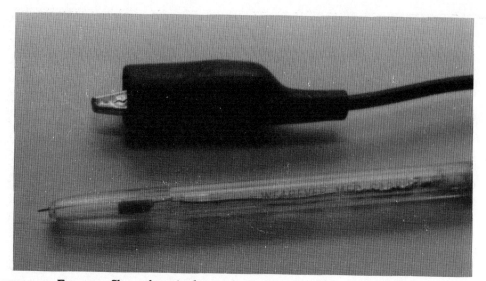

FIG. 19-4. *Shown here is the continuity tester probe with the LED in it.*

hand poised above the OFF switch, keep your eyes on the appliance to be ready if it starts acting strangely. If all goes well, you should reach full output power without the circuit breaker tripping. But if something is wrong with the appliance, the circuit breaker will catch it before real damage is done.

One possible problem with this method is that motor-driven devices take more than their normal running current when they start up. If the circuit breaker keeps tripping when driving a motorized appliance, increase the current of the circuit breaker to allow for the increased need of the motor. Before doing this though, check to make sure that the motor's shaft is free to turn and that it isn't drawing excess current because of too great a load.

As a workbench accessory for experimenting with AC circuits, plug a pair of alligator clips into the outlet of the appliance tester. Use the ON and OFF switches when you make changes and check their results. Keep the circuit breaker setting slightly above what you expect the circuit will draw to protect it against overload. The exact circuit breaker setting isn't terribly critical. It should provide adequate protection against short circuits at all its settings. The choice of current levels is largely a matter of setting it high enough so it doesn't trip frequently in response to routine current demands.

The continuity tester is particularly useful for testing foil traces on a circuit board and in other situations where many tests have to be made in a dense area. It's easier to use than an ohmmeter because it doesn't require lifting your eyes from what you're working on for each test. Because it is polarized, you can use it to test LEDs and other diodes. It is so useful that even if you don't build the plug-in tester, the continuity tester alone is a good project.

PARTS LIST:

Plug-in Tester

C1, C2, C4, C5 C6, C9, C10	.01μF, 200V bypass capacitors, value not critical
C3	10μF, 25V, electrolytic
C7, C8	.1μF, 200V
C11	100μF, 12V or better electrolytic
R1	100KΩ, all resistors ¼W unless indicated
R2, R4	100Ω
R3	1.3KΩ, 5W
R5, R18	10KΩ
R6	2Ω, 5W
R7-R15	1Ω, 5W, 10% tolerance
R16	160Ω
R17	220KΩ
R18	470Ω
POT 1	100KΩ linear taper potentiometer
POT 2	10KΩ potentiometer
F	10A slo-blo fuse
NE1-NE4	Neon panel indicator with built-in dropping resistor
L1	120VAC pilot light (red)
L2	120VAC pilot light (green)
T	Transformer with 6.3V secondary
B	9V battery (alternative to T, D5, and C11)
Q1	NPN general-purpose transistor with Vceo at least 50 volts
Q2	General-purpose NPN (2N3904 or equiv.)
TRIAC	12A, 200V or better TRIAC
DIAC	D-30 or equivalent DIAC
D1-D5	1A, 200V or better rectifier diodes
LED	Rectangular red LED
S1, S6	10A DPDT toggle switch
S2	10A SPDT toggle switch
S3-S5	10A SPST toggle switch

PB1-PB3	N.O. pushbuttons
RELAY	DPDT 10A relay with 12-24 VDC coil
PL1	Three-wire line cord and wall plug
PL2, PL3	Banana plugs
J1, J2	Test prod jacks
J3, J4	Banana jacks
SO	Grounded power outlet
PIEZO ELEMENT	Three-wire piezoelectric element (R.S. #273-064 or equiv.)
AUTO-TRANSFORMER	10A, 0 to 140V autotransformer (Variac or equiv.)

PLUS, suitable enclosure, hardware, pushbutton caps, solder lugs, alligator clip, external fuseholder, label for wiring tester lights, knob, clear pen body, battery clip, TO-220 mounting hardware, heatsink, hook-up wire, rub-on letters, and solder.

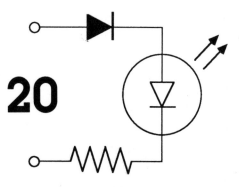

20

Electric
Hand Dryer

A project that could find itself more uses around the house than you might currently anticipate is this hot-air dryer, similar to the ones installed in restrooms. See FIG. 20-1. This project would be good to have outdoors or in other places where it's difficult to keep a towel. It could be installed near a faucet for cleaning up after yard work or near a pool. There it would always be ready and doesn't become soggy the way a towel does. Besides being an effective hand dryer, this project is useful around the shop for warming or softening plastics, making paint dry faster, and lint-free drying of small parts.

Building this hot-air hand dryer involves less real construction than you might think. The actual drying is done by parts salvaged from a hair dryer. This greatly simplifies construction and saves money; you can buy a hair dryer in department stores for about $5 on sale. It is a simple matter to obtain the heating elements and fan this way rather than fabricating your own. In fact, the bulk of the work this project requires is constructing the circuit that activates the dryer. Two possible circuits for doing this are presented.

DESIGN CONSIDERATIONS

It is quite easy to activate the hand dryer with a pushbutton and time delay circuit in the way that the commercially installed models do. For most applications, that is the way to go. The simple and reliable circuit in FIG. 20-2 is all that is needed for the hand dryer and can be adapted to control similar devices in other projects as well.

In addition to this conventional method of activating the dryer, an optional circuit is included near the end of the chapter that optically senses when a pair of hands or other object is placed under the dryer nozzle. It keeps the dryer on for just as long as they are

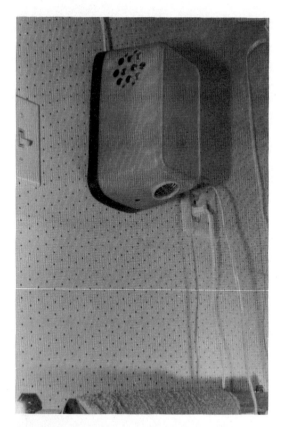

FIG. 20-1. *This is the prototype mounted on a bathroom wall.*

held there. This second activating circuit is naturally more complicated, and for most applications unnecessary. It is still an option worthy of some consideration though, and uses a circuit that is easily adaptable to other projects as well.

Included in the construction directions that follow are suggestions for building either of the two possible versions of the hair dryer. However, either way the dryer is activated, the same construction method applies for the first step: mounting and enclosing the hair dryer parts.

MODIFYING THE HAIR DRYER

The hair dryer should be the common pistol-grip kind with a centrifugal rather than an axial fan. The number of speeds and heat settings it has doesn't matter; it will be permanently wired in the highest setting anyway. When you've found a suitable dryer, open it up and take it apart. Save the line cord (to use in this project) and the switches for other projects. Study the switch positions before removing them however, so you know how to wire the fan motor and heating elements to give their maximum setting. Look at the baffle enclosing the fan and note what parts of the dryer can be removed without cutting into this airtight part of the enclosure.

Before cutting away any of the hair dryer, decide on an enclosure for the project. A good suggestion is to follow the example of the prototype and build the dryer and its activating circuit on a piece of wood with a detachable plastic cover. The plastic cover

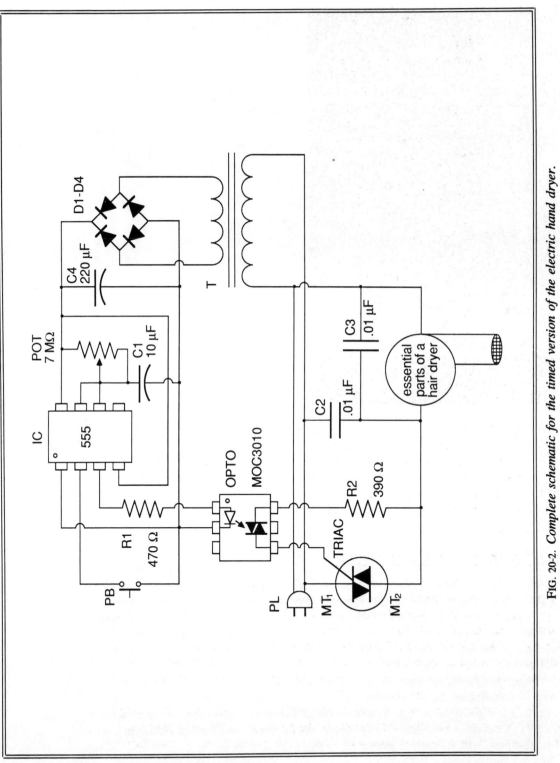

FIG. 20-2. *Complete schematic for the timed version of the electric hand dryer.*

FIG. 20-3. *Notice how parts of the hair dryer have been cut away in this side view of the project.*

could be the bottom of a wastebasket as in the prototype, or you could obtain a food storage box, typically available in the housewares section of department stores. If you build the dryer this way, use a wood base at least ⅜" thick and cut and smooth its edges so it will fit the cross section of the cover you intend to use with it.

Using a power or hand saw, remove the handle and excess plastic from the hair dryer. All of the parts of the plastic housing that don't enclose the fan can be cut away to make more room inside the enclosure. This is an easy task for a radial-arm saw if each half of the enclosure is done separately. When cut away to a minimum, the dryer should look like the one in FIG. 20-3; only the fan and the tube with the heating elements should remain. Before mounting it, wire the dryer in the highest heat and fan settings and leave the two wires protruding from the case. Wrap duct tape around the fan baffle to cover up any leaks in it, being careful not to tape over the air inlets.

While cutting away the excess of the dryer, keep in mind how it will fit into the case. Mounting is easiest if you cut a flat surface on the dryer where it can rest on the wood base. It's a good idea to mount the dryer so it points outward slightly when attached to a wall. This means its nozzle should point up slightly when it's mounted to the wood base.

Use a wooden bracket as in FIG. 20-3 to hold the dryer securely in the desired position. A friction fit around the heating element tube should be sufficient to secure it. Hold down the rear of the dryer using a small right angle bracket and one of the screws that hold the two plastic halves together.

With the dryer mounted this way, cut holes in the cover so it will fit over it and the base it's mounted on. You'll need to cut a hole in one end of the cover for the dryer nozzle to protrude slightly. In the sides, cut many holes for air to flow into the dryer's intake. Leaving about an inch for clearance at the top, cut the plastic cover off at a uniform level and test-fit it over the base and dryer.

The triac that switches the dryer on when the circuit is activated dissipates a lot of heat. Minimize the heatsinking it requires by mounting it where it will be cooled by the air flowing into the dryer. Mount the triac, opto, R2, C1, and C3 on a small PC board attached to the wood base next to one of the dryer's intake ports as shown in FIG. 20-4. No etching is necessary for such a simple circuit. Cut traces into the foil with a Dremel Moto-Tool or similar drill as described in Chapter 2. Attach the line cord to this board and leave places to attach wires for obtaining 120 VAC for the activating circuit.

THE ACTIVATING CIRCUIT

The activating circuit is a timer, based on the popular and widely used 555 timer IC. The transformer, D1 through D4, and C4 form a power supply for it. The IC in the circuit can operate over a 9- to 16-volt range, so values for the supply components aren't critical. Together with the potentiometer and C1, the 555 forms an adjustable time delay circuit. When it is triggered by pressing the pushbutton PB, its output at pin 3 goes high for a time period varying from about 5 seconds with the potentiometer at its minimum setting to over a minute at its highest.

The three-component timer circuit is right out of the manufacturer's applications data for the 555 and is quite accurate and stable. It is simpler than even a one-transistor time delay circuit and because 555 ICs are sold for as little as 29 cents from some mail order

FIG. 20-4. *The triac doesn't require much heatsinking because it is mounted in the hair dryer's intake airflow.*

companies, it is cost competitive as well. The circuit is adaptable to a wide range of similar applications with possible delays ranging from milliseconds to hours with suitable values for the potentiometer and C2.

The output from the IC goes through current limiting resistor R1 to turn on the triac via the opto-isolator connected to it. The triac controls the modified hair dryer. Any electrical hash that the dryer generates is kept from the triac by the bypass capacitors C2 and C3.

Note that the timing electronics are completely isolated from the AC power line, so there is no shock hazard possible from the contacts of the pushbutton switch. This suggests the possibility of a remote switch. If desired, the pushbutton could be mounted near a faucet so that the air from the dryer has time to warm up before you reach it after washing your hands.

CONSTRUCTING THE ACTIVATING CIRCUIT

The timer circuit builds easily on a small piece of veroboard or perf board. The only components that need to be circuit-board mounted are the IC, C1, C4, D1 through D4, and R1. The transformer mounts to the wood base and the triac driver opto-isolator, triac, R2, C2, and C3 mount on the single-sided PC board discussed earlier. The circuit is simple enough that it can be constructed one component at a time on a pre-etched experimenter board or perf board without planning a layout beforehand.

The potentiometer should be out of sight but still remain accessible through a hole in the cover because it will probably have to be set after some experimentation with the dryer. A small piece of aluminum bent at a right angle makes a good bracket for the potentiometer. Another possibility is to mount the potentiometer in a hole in the circuit board and mount the circuit board to the base with right-angle brackets. FIGURE 20-5 shows the prototype board mounted this way.

The pushbutton should be mounted in the cover and connected to the timer circuit with a piece of two-conductor wire long enough to allow the cover to be removed. A small pushbutton salvaged from a computer keyboard was used on the prototype, but an extra large button was glued onto it. Particularly good pushbuttons for this project are those that don't take up much room behind the panel they are mounted in. This is because space

FIG. 20-5. *The timer circuitry is visible on the circuit board mounted under the hair dryer's nozzle.*

inside the cover is limited. Calculator keys and other flush-mount buttons are good, low-cost alternatives for this reason.

The circuit is simple and doesn't leave much room for errors. It should be tested prior to installation in the dryer though, using a regular LED in place of the opto-isolator to determine it works and that the range of time intervals is sufficient. If it is not, change the value of the potentiometer or add fixed resistors in series with it. The time interval bears a direct but non-linear relationship to the resistance of the potentiometer. Increasing the resistance increases the time interval but not by the same ratio.

USE

A device this simple doesn't demand much explanation. If a large enough pushbutton is prominently mounted in the cover, people will press it even without being asked. Operation is automatic. For additional drying time after one cycle has ended, the button can be pressed again, yielding another equal interval.

AN ALTERNATE ACTIVATING CIRCUIT

There are a few drawbacks to using a timer circuit for the hand dryer. Despite the fact that commercial machines use them, a pushbutton with a timer is not the best way to let the dryer know when you want it to operate. For one thing, your hands are usually wet and clean after you've washed them, while the button probably carries germs. Another drawback is that the timing interval is arbitrary and usually turns the dryer off before you're done or else keeps going, wasting energy. Also, if you're not drying your hands but using the dryer to heat some electronic assembly, the button may not be that easy to reach.

Although these disadvantages are scarcely noticed in a commercial machine, the nice thing about making one yourself is that you can make it better. The best way to activate the dryer would be to just put your hands under it and have it turn on and stay on for as long as you held them there. That way it would stay on for only as long as you needed it to and shut off as soon as you didn't. What this requires is a circuit that senses objects placed under the dryer's nozzle without physical contact and switches on for as long as that object is there.

This would be a complicated task and probably not worth the effort, except for the existence of a relatively new IC designed primarily for burglar alarms. The "Motion Detector IC," available by mail order for $7.95, is a clear, encapsulated 14-pin chip. Its unique clear packaging enables it to optically sense motion in its field of view. Only a few external components are needed to adapt this IC to our purpose and interface it with the dryer. FIGURE 20-6 shows the the alternative schematic for activating the dryer with the Motion Detector IC.

But just as there are advantages to this circuit, there are also disadvantages. For one thing, the IC chip, which was originally designed as a burglar alarm, is very sensitive. Turning on a light near it triggers the dryer into operation for a few seconds. Walking below its field of view will do the same. Depending on the number of false alarms like these that you expect from your dryer's intended location and your estimate of the annoyance they will cause, the previous pushbutton/timer version might be the best alternative. Sometimes it's better to put up with the limitations of a dumb machine rather than have one that thinks it knows what's going on all the time.

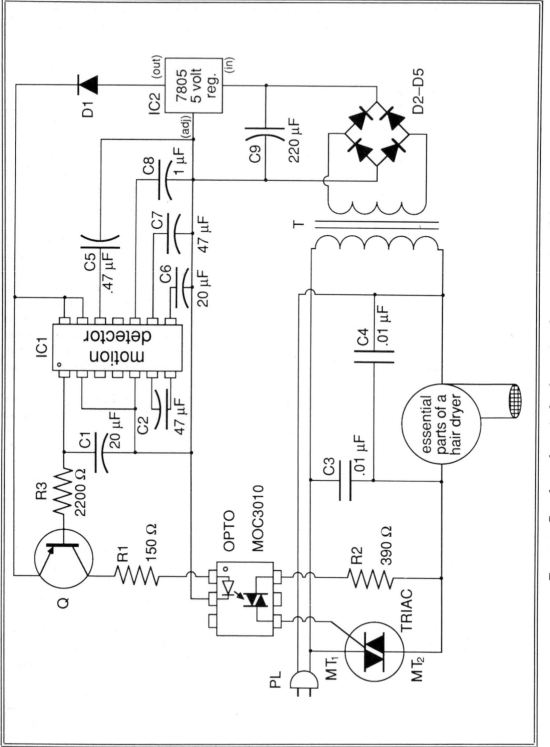

FIG. 20-6. *Complete schematic for the motion detector version of the project.*

But if you wish to activate the hand dryer with the motion detector circuit or adapt the circuit to some other application, the construction is relatively simple, similar for the most part to the previous timer circuit.

The Circuit

The Motion Detector IC requires 2.5 to 4.5 volts DC. The schematic in FIG. 20-6 shows one way of building a power supply for a voltage this low. An inexpensive 5-volt, three-terminal regulator is used to limit the rectified and filtered voltage from the transformer to 5 volts. A silicon diode connected in series with the supply drops it another 0.7 volts, making the output ideally 4.3 volts. If the regulator IC you use runs a little over 5 volts, connect two diodes in series to bring the supply lower. There are other possibilities as well for the power supply. One of these is using an LM317 adjustable voltage regulator in the circuit given in Chapter 23 with a trimmer potentiometer to set the output voltage within the desired range. Another possibility is using a zener diode and dropping resistor to obtain a voltage between 2.5 and 4.5 volts. Use whatever circuit is most convenient.

The circuit is simple because the IC is highly specialized for applications like this. The capacitors connected to it set its operating parameters. The interval that the IC waits after sensing motion before re-sampling light is set by C8. Experimenting with its value might be necessary to fine-tune the circuit to a particular application. Capacitor C6 lowers the IC's sensitivity to high frequency light changes like fluorescent light flicker. Capacitor C5 isn't vital to this circuit; it determines the pitch of the alarm output at pin 1. Capacitors C2 and C7 are used by the IC to block steady voltage levels and pass only the changing voltages that indicate motion.

When the IC senses motion, its output at pin 1 becomes a current sink. This means current can flow through R3 from the transistor, turning it on. Because the output is an alarm, it pulsates. Capacitor C1 smooths the pulsations into a steady DC voltage. When the transistor turns on in response to the IC's output, current flows through it and R1 to turn on the opto-isolator. The opto-isolator activates the dryer in the same way the previous timer circuit does.

Construction

Build this circuit on a piece of veroboard or perf board just like the timer circuit. The IC must be able to "look" down through a hole in the cover to see the area under the dryer nozzle, so plan the internal layout accordingly. FIGURE 20-1 shows the little peephole that the prototype looks through. The circuit board containing the IC was mounted directly behind this hole in the same way as the timer circuit was in FIG. 20-5.

A socket was used to hold the IC in the prototype and is strongly recommended. The IC is expensive enough to justify the extra protection a socket affords from heat damage; plus, a socket will raise it above the other components to give it an unobstructed view. It will also be possible to remove the IC for use in other projects.

Before installation in the dryer, the motion detector circuit should be adequately tested with a regular LED in place of the opto-isolator to ensure it is working correctly. Be careful not to hold the test LED too close to the IC, because the light it produces as it blinks on and off might be perceived as motion.

Use

Install the hand dryer in a place that is convenient but also where not much action occurs directly under it to avoid triggering the Motion Detector IC inadvertently. Another thing to avoid is rapidly changing light levels that can also trigger the dryer falsely.

Other Uses of the Motion Detector IC

Although the Motion Detector IC is intended as a burglar alarm, it can be used as a switch and is quite useful to the experimenter. With it, you can give your projects "eyes" with which to look out and monitor the world in a limited fashion. It can be interfaced to a number of other devices. In surveillance or nature photography for example, it could be set to trip a camera when something moves into its field of view.

PARTS LIST:

Electric Hand Dryer

(Timed Version)

C1	10μF, 16V, electrolytic
C2, C3	.01μF, 200V bypass capacitors, value not critical
C4	220μF, 16V or better electrolytic
R1	470Ω, ¼W
R2	390Ω, ¼W
POT	7MΩ linear taper (value not critical; fixed resistors can be placed in series with a lower resistance potentiometer)
T	Step-down transformer with 9V secondary
IC	555 timer IC
TRIAC	16A, 200V or better TRIAC
D1-D4	1A, 200V or better bridge rectifier
OPTO	MOC3010 or similar triac driver opto-isolator
PB	Large N.O. pushbutton
PL	10A line cord and wall plug (taken from hair dryer)
HAIR DRYER PARTS	

PLUS, piece of wood for base, suitable cover, wood to support dryer, hardware, piece of single-sided PC board material, pre-etched experimenter board, pushbutton cap, TO-220 mounting hardware, heatsink, hook-up wire, and solder.

PARTS LIST:

Electric Hand Dryer

(Motion Detector Version)

C1, C6	20μF, 6V, electrolytic
C2, C7	47μF, 6V, electrolytic
C3, C4	.01μF, 200V bypass capacitors, value not critical
C5	.47μF, 6V
C8	1μF, 6V
C9	220μF, 6V or better electrolytic
R1	150Ω, all resistors ¼W
R2	390Ω
R3	2200Ω
T	Step-down transformer with 6 to 12V secondary
IC 1	Motion Detector IC, circuit assembly part number SMD-01 ($7.95 including P+H) from:
	MICOR
	P.O. Box 1540
	Haverhill, MA-01830
IC 2	5V regulator IC
TRIAC	16A, 200V or better triac
D1	Silicon rectifier diode
D2 D5	Bridge rectifier
Q	PNP general-purpose transistor (2N3906 or equiv.)
OPTO	MOC3010 or similar triac driver opto-isolator
PL	10A line cord and wall plug (take from hair dryer)
HAIR DRYER PARTS	

PLUS, piece of wood for base, suitable cover, wood to support dryer, hardware, piece of single-sided PC board material, pre-etched experimenter board, TO-220 mounting hardware, heatsink, hook-up wire, and solder.

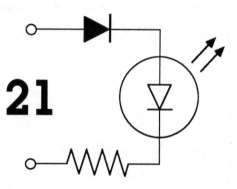

21

Construction Hints

This chapter offers some suggestions to use when building the projects in this book and other projects. More general advice on building electronics projects is published in books devoted to that task alone. The following advice is mostly what is not found in those books.

ADHESIVES

Every electronics experimenter should be prepared with a few good adhesives for bonding wood and plastic. Probably the most useful adhesive is *hot-melt glue*. It is sold in packages of hard sticks that can be melted in a hand-held gun and applied as a liquid. The melted glue is especially versatile, because it forms a waterproof bond to most materials, fills small gaps, and hardens within a minute. For stronger joints in wood or to provide more working time, *alphatic resin glue* (sold as Titebond and under other trade names) is very good. It is similar to, but stronger than, ordinary white glue. To bond other materials or for encapsulating small parts, *epoxy* in either the 5-, 15-, or 60-minute formulations is recommended. Acrylic plastic is a peculiar case, requiring its own special cement, sold in plastic stores. *Acrylic cement* is a highly volatile liquid that welds the plastic in the joints together by dissolving the surfaces slightly. "Miracle" adhesives have their occasional uses as well, but most of the time require conditions which are rarely present in the real world.

BREADBOARDS

Among electronics hobbyists, *breadboarding* means building a circuit in a temporary way before committing it to a circuit board or a final layout. By using a breadboard, components can be tested and circuit changes tried out easily before the final version is built. There are several different ways of doing this, and most experimenters have their favorite. FIGURE 21-1 shows these three different methods of breadboarding.

Solderless Breadboards

One preferred method of breadboarding uses commercially available *solderless breadboards*. These are white plastic grids of tiny sockets, each of which accepts a single component pin. The sockets are electrically connected together in rows. For low voltage circuits with many small parts, especially ICs, these boards are indispensable and justify their popularity.

Perhaps the major advantage of using a solderless breadboard is that the pins are arranged in a pattern that can easily be transferred to a pre-etched circuit board. Translating an experimental design into a finished circuit is often just a matter of taking components out of one board and soldering them into another.

Solderless breadboards usually don't accept wire smaller than AWG 22. If you decide to get one of these boards, it's a good idea to start a collection of short wires stripped on both ends to go with it. The wire sold for wire-wrapping is especially suitable for making up these little wires because it is strong, flexible, comes in colors, and is usually silver-plated to make better contacts.

A Bed of Nails

A different type of breadboard is usually used for projects with large components of higher power that will eventually be point-to-point wired. A number of small wire nails with flat heads are driven into a piece of wood and component leads are soldered to their tops. To make one of these, drive some nails spaced an inch or two apart into a flat board. Keep in mind that you can always add more nails later if a particular circuit needs them.

FIG. 21-1. *These are good examples of the three types of breadboards discussed.*

To make connections to them possible, rub a wire brush across the heads of the nails and tin each one lightly with solder. A board set up this way can accommodate all sizes of components and permit alligator clips to be attached to the nails for temporary hook-ups.

Small Circuit Boards

If frequent connections must be made to the leads of a particular type of component like ICs or TO-220 packages, consider making up small custom circuit boards by cutting traces into the foil with a Dremel Moto-Tool or similar high speed drill. Shown on the right of FIG. 21-1 is a board made in this way to accept triacs, SCRs, and other three-legged parts. The component leads fan out to three foil pads to which other components can be easily soldered. For ICs, Radio Shack and other parts sources sell PC boards with pads for 6- to 20-pin dual in-line packages (DIPs). These are very useful for breadboarding IC circuits, particularly when you solder a socket into the board to make it easy to change ICs. Small PC boards can be used alone in simple circuits or connected to other breadboards by short wires.

CMOS HANDLING

Complimentary metal oxide semiconductor (CMOS) and other ICs that use MOS gates such as computer circuits and some large-scale integrated circuits (LSICs) can be damaged by the static electricity the human body normally picks up. Avoid the possibility of ruined ICs in your projects by grounding yourself and the circuit you're working on. Ground yourself with a loop of wire around your wrist or by attaching an alligator clip to a metal watchband. Don't make the mistake of connecting yourself directly to ground though. If you're directly grounded and happen to touch a live wire, you could receive a lethal shock. Use at least a 200 kilohm resistor between yourself and earth ground for safety. Static electricity can still drain off this way, but if 120 VAC passes through the resistor, it won't be harmful to you.

If you're working on an existing piece of equipment, hook its circuit ground to the same ground you're attached to. When soldering to it, use an iron with a grounded tip. There are special irons available with three-prong plugs, but a regular iron can be temporarily grounded by wrapping a wire under one of the screws in its element or by applying an alligator clip to its metal parts. When desoldering, don't use the spring-loaded vacuums made of plastic; they generate a powerful static charge every time they are used. Use an aluminum solder vacuum instead.

To minimize unnecessary handling of ICs, use sockets whenever possible. Before installing them, briefly ground the conductive foam the ICs were shipped in, making sure your body is grounded as well. This puts you and all the IC pins at the same voltage potential. Touch all the foil traces that the IC will be connected to, putting each of them at the same potential. Realize that it is only voltage *differences* between the pins of an IC that can damage it. Earth ground is a convenient common point with which to set the pins, the circuit, and yourself equal to.

CONSTRUCTION METHODS

The projects in this book and those described in other sources can be built using the techniques described in the previous chapters of this book. There are other books fully devoted to advice on building electronic projects that can give more thorough advice on each method if you need it.

→ Point-to-point wiring: Chapter 1, 2, 3, 16, 19
→ Using pre-etched experimenter boards: Chapter 6, 8, 11, 15, 17
→ Foil-side circuit board construction: Chapter 9, 11, 18
→ Wiring without tie points: Chapter 10
→ Flea-clips and perf board: Chapter 14

ENCLOSURES

The price of commercial project enclosures seems disproportionate to what the electrical components that make up the actual project cost. Keep in mind, though, that not all suitable enclosures are sold with the name "project enclosure" attached to them. Department stores, 5 & 10 stores, and supermarkets sell many plastic and metal boxes that can house electronic projects effectively. There are also some other satisfactory alternatives to buying project enclosures new.

One of these is buying enclosures at surplus stores or reusing the enclosures that once housed other projects or devices. It's a good idea to buy inexpensive, used enclosures where and when you find them because they won't always be available. If they have unnecessary holes and markings (and they probably will), there are a few ways to make them look new. For one thing, your project's panel-mounted devices could be arranged to match the holes in the old panel. This seldom works completely but there are metal plugs called "goof plugs" sold by electronics stores that snap into the extra holes in the panel. If there are too many holes for this, it might be necessary to cover a whole side of the surplus enclosure with a new panel of aluminum, plastic, or wood.

One way to avoid paying for new enclosures is by not using an enclosure at all. Some projects can be built onto a flat piece of wood, particularly if they don't have to be very attractive. This method leaves the circuit accessible, creates no ventilation problems, and is easiest to build. All the parts mount to the board with wood screws. Because the components are very accessible when built on a board, this type of construction is suitable for experimental circuits but not good for those with high voltages. A project built on a flat piece of wood can later be protected with a metal or even cardboard box over it if safety is a concern.

Another possibility is building projects into existing enclosures. Some of the projects in this book can be built that way. The regulated supply of Chapter 3 can be built into a car dashboard as a low voltage outlet. The remote volume control in Chapter 8 can be built inside the audio amplifier it's used with and can use the same power supply to save even more money. Both of the phone accessories are suitable for building into telephones or other devices. For the other projects and those of your own design, you might be lucky enough to see ways in which they can be built into existing enclosures.

FUSEHOLDERS

Fuseholders can be mounted in two ways—internally or externally. Internal fuseholders are cheaper and easier to install but make it difficult to reach the fuses. On the other hand, changing fuses in an external fuseholder is quite easy. If either type can be built into a project, it's best to use an external holder if the fuse protects external circuitry but an internal holder for fuses that protect internal circuitry. Amplifiers with speaker outputs and projects with fused outlets should use external fuseholders because it's more likely that their fuses need to be changed through no fault of the device they're installed in. But if a fuse is designed to protect the device itself, mount it internally. If it blows, you'll probably have to open the case anyway to find out what went wrong. An internal fuseholder removes the temptation to install a bigger fuse in the hope that the problem will just go away.

LABELING PROJECT ENCLOSURES

Most of the labeling shown on the prototypes in this book was done with a few sets of rub-on letters. The variety these sets come in is overwhelming. Several colors are available and some sets are sold with words already spelled out that could apply to almost any conceivable project. Most sets also include a quantity of spare letters and numbers for unique designs. Sets with a variety of lines, circles, arcs, and shapes are also available. Rub-on lettering sets do dry out and become less sticky when their original packages have been opened for a few months, so don't buy a large set initially and hope to get years of use out of it. Buy small ones only as you need them and store them in a clean place when not in use.

Applying rub-on letters is tedious and painstaking. The only way to make it easier is to light your work area well and use tweezers to handle the individual words and letters. A piece of scotch tape, lightly applied to the faceplate, makes a good guide for aligning letters and words.

Lettering should always be applied to a panel after it has been painted and before the knobs and switches are mounted. However, it does help to have the knobs and switches handy to make sure they won't cover the lettering when they are in their final positions. When a project has been lettered, protect it with a few light coats of clear lacquer spray paint. The clear spray paint manufactured especially for rub-on letters and sold under their brand names is particularly good for this.

Computers offer another possibility for producing nicely labeled projects. Most of the prototypes were built before excellent computer graphics were a real possibility, which is unfortunate because better results would have been achieved with less effort. Only the projects in Chapters 15 and 19 show labels made from computer printouts.

In the last few years, computers that can produce sharp, detailed graphics have become available for sale and are generally more accessible for occasional use. Before Apple's Macintosh, the only computers that could produce suitable results were dedicated computer-aided-design (CAD) machines and engineering workstations. Printouts were usually made by flatbed plotters. But now a Macintosh with the appropriate graphics software and an Apple Laserwriter printer or a good dot matrix printer can produce comparable results for less cost. Apple isn't the only player in the game, though. Software and hardware is becoming available that allows the large number of IBM PCs and compatibles to do graphics as well as a Macintosh.

Although the cost of a suitable computer system and printer is still high, many computer stores offer use of their equipment for a small fee based either on time or the number of copies printed. A computer offers a much better way to do labeling than by hand. The two main advantages are the time saved and the ability to rearrange symbols on the CRT, trying out several designs before committing a final one to the project.

Although there are and soon will be other ways to do it, one successful method is to create a panel using a computer, print it out on paper with either a plotter or good dot-matrix or laser printer, and stick the paper to the project. To make accurate alignment possible, the piece of paper should include the hole-drilling guide for all the parts on the front panel in addition to the lettering and graphics. One copy of the paper can be used to mark the location of the holes with a centerpunch and a second copy of the paper can serve as the final faceplate. That way the parts will automatically be aligned with the panel labeling.

Sticking the paper securely to the enclosure is easy with a spray-on artists' adhesive like 3M's catalog number 6065. The best way to produce clean edges is by cutting the faceplate to the exact size before sticking it to the enclosure. If the panel isn't expected to get heavy use, the paper can be protected with a clear spray-on lacquer like Krylon. Use clear plastic Contact or a similar adhesive-backed plastic for more durability if more wear is anticipated. If the panel is small enough though, cover it with the somewhat thinner plastic laminate intended mainly for protecting photographs.

Whatever lettering method is used, the quality of the results usually bears a direct relation to the amount of effort put into the job. The efforts expended and consequent results obtained by electronics hobbyists cover a wide range. Some experimenters are content to hand-letter just the essential knob functions and positions and whatever else represents the bare minimum of information required to operate their projects. Others put as much effort into the appearance of a project as they devote to its electronics, producing beautiful showpieces that look better than most commercial designs.

I fall somewhere in between. My projects, and those of most hobbyists, are attractive and well laid-out only to the point where they are easy to understand and use. Their appearance is just good enough so that their user isn't distracted by their ugliness. Of course how good a project should look also depends to a large degree on the surroundings it is designed to work in. A project that will be placed in a living room has to look better than one that will never leave the workbench.

METALS

Aluminum is the most convenient metal to work with. It drills and cuts easier than steel but is still strong enough for project enclosures and supports. Most commercial project boxes are made of aluminum for this reason. Hardware stores sell many sizes of sheets, rods, and angles. In larger quantities, aluminum stores are good sources for sheets and extrusions of various thicknesses and alloys. They also do an excellent job of cutting aluminum to size using their large shearing presses.

Like other metals, aluminum is troublesome to work with using standard handyman's tools that were really designed for wood. Holes up to $3/8$-inch diameter can be satisfactorily drilled with standard high speed twist drills if the holes are center-punched first. The rough edges that form around drilled holes can be smoothed with a tapered reamer. But for larger holes, a chassis punch is recommended. These are sold singly and in sets, but either way they are relatively expensive. Chassis punches generally produce smooth holes that don't need further treatment.

An alternative to drilling or punching sheet aluminum is a Unibit, which drills smooth holes up to 1 inch in diameter. A Unibit is a fluted taper with a series of graduated steps of increasing diameter. The depth it is drilled to determines the size of the hole it cuts.

One of its advantages is that it doesn't get dull and require resharpening, something twist drills do.

Straight cuts can be made with a hacksaw or with a special power saw blade. The rough edges that inevitably form can be smoothed with a file. If the aluminum is thin enough, metal shears can cut it. But such thin aluminum isn't often used in electronics work.

Aluminum takes on a pleasing finish when it is brushed in parallel strokes with a wire brush or very fine sandpaper. The smooth metal surface that results can be preserved with clear lacquer spray paint or color can be applied. When applying a color, it's best to start with a primer coat or by etching the aluminum in lye. The paint goes on best when it's applied in several coats of flat color and finally covered with a clear shiny coat. Lettering is usually applied between the flat paint and the clear coat. After all the dials and switches are mounted on a project, another thin layer of clear spray paint applied over everything will give the panel and controls a uniform lustre.

ODD COMPONENT VALUES

The component values of resistors and the other passive circuit elements given in schematics are often arrived at mathematically or by another experimenter's success with a particular value. The specified value might not correspond exactly to available component values. But fortunately, components in the real world vary widely about their rated values as well.

Most passive components are described by both a value and a tolerance. It is very likely that their actual value differs from the specified value and is close to the tolerance limit. This is because components are available in different tolerance ranges (typically 20, 10, 5, and 1 percent), derived from the same production run. Manufacturers don't deliberately set out to produce 10 percent resistors; they just sort them that way. It's likely that those that end up in the 10 percent bin are just those that couldn't be sold as better resistors, and so will be between 5 and 10 percent off.

Take advantage of this situation by buying quantities of 10 percent resistors for when you want odd values. Almost any actual value will fall within 10 percent of a commonly available value. So resistors and other components with poor tolerances have their uses after all. The ones with tighter tolerances aren't essentially any better; their chief advantage is that they have been presorted.

The grab-bags of assorted resistors and capacitors offered by surplus dealers are a good source of odd values. They typically contain resistors of poor tolerance from which odd values can be selected by using the color code as an initial ball-park guide and an ohmmeter to measure the actual value.

Capacitors are another story entirely, because capacitance meters are not as common as ohmmeters. Capacitance meters are going down in price though and might be a good investment, because one would enable you to buy cheaper or unmarked capacitors and let you double check the expensive ones.

PLASTIC

Plastic, especially acrylic, is useful to have around in sheets and scraps. Sheets are available at plastics stores; they make good faceplates for projects because they require no paint and accept rub-on letters directly. Besides plastics stores, department stores are good sources for plastic. Many of the things they sell like serving trays and flat-sided garbage pails are useful for the pieces of plastic they contain.

Cut plastic the same way as wood but with less haste and more caution. Plastic can also be sanded and drilled like wood. When drilling with a twist drill though, back the plastic with a piece of wood so the hole doesn't splinter when the bit breaks through the other side. If the plastic is thin enough, a Unibit, mentioned in the section on metal, does an excellent job. As with metal, it is necessary to center-punch holes before drilling them to keep the drill bit from wandering around the shiny surface.

SOLDERING IRONS

Electronics magazines and books often advise hobbyists to use low wattage soldering irons when working on ICs, transistors, and other sensitive parts. Don't believe them. A low wattage iron doesn't appreciably reduce the heat that these frail components receive and only slows down work on larger components. A better practice is to avoid the risk of heat damage altogether by using sockets for the ICs and temporary heatsinks on the leads of the transistors. This makes more sense than reducing the amount of heat applied and risking bad solder joints.

With this in mind, get the soldering iron with the highest wattage you can find at a reasonable price. Anything below 40 watts is merely adequate; 42 watts is good, 47 watts better, and 56-watt irons are quite nice. In a tool as important as a soldering iron, you should get the best possible. The higher wattages won't slow you down when heating large component leads and actually reduces the time that heat has to be applied to solder the smaller contacts.

An iron that is too small is not entirely useless, though. It can be improved with one of the booster circuits in Chapter 22. Use one of the circuits shown under "Voltage Boosters and Cutters" to raise the iron's output to something more useful for real work.

Get as good a tip for the iron as you can. Iron-plated tips are a little more expensive but last much longer than the solid copper ones. They are worth it. For both heavy and light work, a screwdriver tip has the best geometry. Its fine edge allows precise heating of delicate connections. And for large solder joints, where maximum heat transfer is essential, its flat face is the optimum shape. The screwdriver shape is also good for the prying that is sometimes necessary to desolder complicated joints.

SOLDERING TOOLS

Hand-held soldering tools, with their various points and slots, are useless in most cases. Far from providing any assistance, they only occupy your second hand and prevent it from using a more effective tool. Better tools to use on difficult soldering or desoldering jobs are small diagonal cutters and needle-nosed pliers. The diagonal cutters are primarily used for desoldering wires from solder lugs where it is often necessary to cut and unwrap a stubborn wire from the lug while the solder is melted.

Another useless desoldering tool is a solder wick. In theory, the thick copper braid is supposed to wick molten solder away from a heated connection. While this does actually happen, it requires so much heat that components and circuit boards are often damaged. The solder wick is also so wide that it is difficult to desolder one connection without getting the ones nearby it as well. Spools of solder wick do have one use though; they are a good source for the flat copper braid often used in high current grounding straps.

236

The tool that obsoletes solder wicks is the spring-loaded solder vacuum. It is simpler and quicker to use than a solder wick, requires less potentially damaging heat, and can be more precisely directed. Two styles are available—the low cost plastic variety and the more durable anti-static aluminum ones.

Some special irons have vacuums built into them, either with a squeeze bulb or a motorized pump. The ones with the squeeze bulb usually do not develop sufficient suction—certainly less than the hand-held solder vacuums. Irons with base units that provide motorized suction, called desoldering stations, are effective but cost too much for experimenters.

One very inexpensive tool necessary for soldering is a sponge. The tip of the iron should be wiped clean on the sponge with every few solder joints completed. Otherwise, burnt flux and oxidized solder builds up and contaminates the connections made with it. Although electronics stores sell cute little sponges for use with soldering irons, theirs are often not the best. A supermarket is a good source, both for price and size. Look for the type of sponge that has a fibrous texture rather than a foamy plastic one. A plastic tray of the right size makes a good holder for the sponge to prevent it from drying out or sliding around. To wet the sponge, keep a water bottle handy on your electronics workbench. Use it to keep the sponge damp enough so it isn't burned by the iron but not so wet that it can't clean effectively.

TEST EQUIPMENT

No matter how much money you spend on test equipment, the most sophisticated diagnostic tool you own is your mind. But like other test equipment, it must be maintained and used correctly or it's just being wasted. The mind's most powerful feature is its ability to develop a feel for what it's doing—an intuitive expectation of what circuit elements should be doing when they are working correctly. However, the right attitude can be destroyed by frustration. When things don't work, it's best to take periodic breaks from work before frustration swamps you in hate of the equipment. Good mechanics in all fields recognize that hateful feeling as a waste of time, and then slow down to avoid it even when in a hurry.

Another reason to take regular breaks from work on electronics is to clear your lungs as well as your mind. Many of the chemicals used in electronics are irritating and potentially harmful when they have built up over several hours. Solder in particular is bad; its lead content can enter the skin when it is handled and by the vapor it releases when it is heated. The smoking rosin makes it difficult to breathe, especially as soldering is usually done by bending over a piece of equipment where the smoke drifts right up into your face. Good ventilation and frequent breaks help avoid breathing trouble from too much soldering.

Despite the importance laid on the correct attitude for electronics work, numbers don't lie and have their uses too. Just a "feel" for what's happening in a circuit won't get it to work. For a better qualitative picture of electronic operation, an oscilloscope is the most useful piece of test equipment. It can give visual indication of voltage levels, wave shapes, and approximate frequency. Most importantly, it presents information in a way that is consistent with intuition and other hobbyists' qualitative descriptions of circuit operation.

For exact quantitative measurements to supplement oscilloscope traces, a DMM gives voltage, resistance, and current measurements. Other specialized test instruments are necessary if you do work requiring precise measurement of frequency, distortion, capacitance, or other electrical quantities.

When shopping for an oscilloscope, consider what features you really need, and you will probably end up with a simple 20 MHz DC input scope with perhaps dual-trace capability. A scope like that would cost from $300 to $500, but if you own a personal computer, there is an alternative. Interfaces that attach to home computers and do the job of oscilloscopes have become popular in the last few years. For the same cost as a simple scope, these interfaces form an extremely powerful instrument that offers a high resolution display, multi-channel capability, digital storage, waveform analysis, and quantitative measurements to several significant figures. Not everyone needs these features, but they don't significantly add to the cost. As competition drives their prices down and as their features become standardized, these interfaces will very likely replace standard oscilloscopes in most applications over the next few years.

TEST LEADS

Here is a small collection of test leads that are practically indispensable. The number suggests how many are needed on an electronics workbench as shown by experience.

- ➜ Alligator Clip to Alligator Clip—connected with about two feet of wire (10)
- ➜ Alligator Clip to Alligator Clip—joined with an inch or two of solid wire (6)
- ➜ AC Wall Plug to Alligator Clips (1)
- ➜ RCA Phono Plug to Alligator Clips—connected by shielded cable (2)
- ➜ Bannana Plug to Alligator Clips—for test equipment (4)
- ➜ Alligator Clips to 120 Volt Light Bulb—as a 120 VAC tester and current limiter (1)
- ➜ Special Leads—for particular test equipment

TOOLS

Beyond standard wood- and metal-working tools, there are a few tools needed strictly for electronics work. Here are some suggestions on tools used mainly for electronics.

Chemicals

Two aerosol spray chemicals are recommended: a Freon spray for cleaning and a cleaner/lubricant for volume controls. There are many kinds of cleaning sprays with specialized applications, but only the ones that contain 100 percent Freon TF are recommended for universal use because they are safe on all materials and evaporate quickly, leaving no residue. Potentiometers and switches need some additional lubrication, though. A cleaning spray with additives formulated specifically for controls is best for them.

Crimp-On Connectors

A crimped connector is the best way of attaching wires to screw terminals or to the quick disconnects often found on commercial equipment. Special tools are sold for crimping these connectors, but a satisfactory job can be done with ordinary pliers. A number of manufacturers sell boxed kits that contain a small quantity of different kinds of connectors. It's a good idea to get one of these kits for occasional use and purchase separate packages of the types you use most frequently.

Cutters

Either diagonal cutters, nail clippers, or scissor-type cutters are necessary to cut the thin leads on electronic components. Nail clippers are cheaper while diagonal cutters are the most convenient and popular. The type that cuts with a scissoring action, while not as easy to use, is recommended for cutting the leads of semiconductors. A cut made with a scissoring action doesn't send as much of a mechanical shock up the component leads as a flush-cut made with diagonal cutters or nail clippers would. Shocks from lead cutting can create tiny fractures in the semiconductor crystal inside the device that might not make it fail right away but will shorten its life.

Drill Bits

Circuit board holes require tiny drill bits of sizes 56 to 68. Mail order parts sources sell them in quantity, but good hardware stores might stock them as well. They break easily and are next to impossible to sharpen, so order quite a few. A drill press is really necessary for drilling circuit boards, but its chuck usually won't tighten enough to grip bits this small. If this is a problem, use a pin vise to hold the bit in the drill press or wrap the shaft with tape to make it thicker.

Lead Benders

There are a variety of devices that make neat, right-angle bends in component leads so they can easily be inserted in circuit boards. Most people just use pliers for this, but specialized tools speed up the process and give more accurate results. Suitable tools come in a wide range of abilities and prices. The simple triangular plastic jigs with graduated slots are usually sufficient though and justify their low cost.

Mirror

A small adjustable dentist's mirror makes it possible to examine the interior of crowded projects. It lets you check soldered joints from different angles, read component values, and check for shorts. A fairly good substitute for one of these mirrors can be made by sticking a small mirrored glass tile to a loop of heavy copper or aluminum wire that can then be bent to the necessary shape.

Needle-Nose Pliers or Medical Hemostats

Pliers or hemostats must have a very fine tip to be useful for electronics work. Beware of the many low quality needle-nose pliers and imitation hemostats sold as electronics tools; often their bearings have some side play and their jaws might not close precisely. Hemostats are particularly useful because they can be locked in the closed position, although they usually can only lock around the very thinnest objects.

Tap and Drill Set

When working with metal, it makes sense to drill and tap as many of the holes as possible. Not only does this avoid using so many nuts, but it is also more convenient when putting things together and taking them apart if there are no loose nuts to hold in place while the screws are turned. The most common screw threads for electronics work are 4-40, 6-32, 8-32, 10-24, 10-32, and 1/4-20.

Wire Stripper

The best wire strippers are the relatively large kind, shaped somewhat like the letter A. They are quicker than any other method, requiring just a single squeeze of the handle. Because they have different slots for each wire gauge, they don't have to be reset for a new size each time a different type of wire is used.

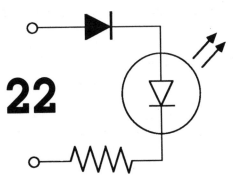

22

Electronic Hints and Simple Projects

As the title suggests, this chapter is filled with hints of an electronic nature—that is, those that deal with the design and modification of electronic circuits. Some of the suggestions that follow concern circuit elements that are valuable because they are not included in the large published encyclopedias of electronic circuits. Others are complete circuits that were too simple to be included in the book as full-fledged projects.

BATTERY CHARGER

You can get more life out of dry cell batteries than the manufacturers intended anyone to by recharging them with the simple circuit in FIG. 22-1. Despite what their labels say, carbon-zinc and alkaline batteries can be recharged if they haven't gone completely dead first. As long as they still have a little life in them before they are recharged, they are good for about ten charge/discharge cycles before they are finally done for.

The battery charger circuit in FIG. 22-1 is essentially a rectifier and current limiter. The diode rectifies the 120 VAC, changing it to DC. While also serving as a pilot lamp, the light bulb limits the charging current of the battery to under 20 milliamps. At this charging level, batteries should be left connected for about 12 hours, but they can remain that way for much longer without damage. Up to 25 volts worth of batteries connected in series can be charged with this circuit. Parts selection is not critical; the lamp can be an incandescent Christmas tree bulb and the diode can be any one with a reverse voltage rating of 200 volts or better.

Although their labels warn of explosion and other dire consequences if recharged, dry cell and alkaline batteries present little danger. If one does go bad while recharging,

BATTERY CHARGER

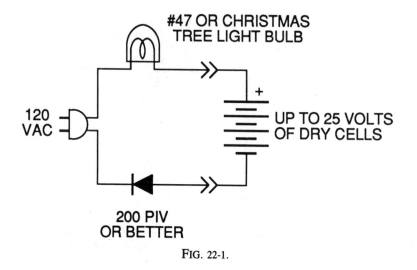

#47 OR CHRISTMAS
TREE LIGHT BULB

120
VAC

+

UP TO 25 VOLTS
OF DRY CELLS

200 PIV
OR BETTER

FIG. 22-1.

it will usually do so by leaking at the seams, not exploding. If you want to be safe though, cover the batteries with a box or heavy rag, just in case.

CAPACITOR BYPASSING

Across Switching Contacts

It's a good idea to connect small capacitors across switching contacts that handle any more than a small amount of power. The capacitors act as a short to the high frequency harmonics produced when the switch opens or closes, reducing noise and arcing at the contacts. They increase the switch's life and reduce the amount of radio frequency interference it radiates. Bypass capacitors should also be used across semiconductor switches to quench high frequency spikes that could cause damage or false triggering.

When you design your own circuits or build one from plans, try to include bypass capacitors across any circuit element that controls power. This includes switches, relays, triacs, SCRs, and power supply diodes. Use a 0.01 to 0.1 microfarad capacitor as shown in FIG. 22-2. Any type of nonpolarized capacitor will work well, as long as its voltage rating is high enough for its application. Dielectric quality is not important. Wherever possible, connect the capacitor close to the element it is bridging. Doing this reduces the inductance in series with the capacitor and consequently increases its effectiveness.

A possible pitfall to beware of when bypassing the power switch in some equipment is the neon power light could refuse to go off. This sometimes happens because with a capacitor across its power switch, the circuit is essentially "on" all the time. The capacitor lets a miniscule amount of current pass through it. While this current is too small for the rest of the circuit to notice, a sensitive neon light might stay lit or blink even with the switch off. If this happens, change the capacitor either to a smaller value, in the range

242

CAPACITOR BYPASSING

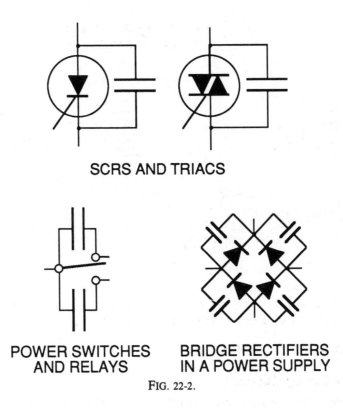

SCRS AND TRIACS

POWER SWITCHES
AND RELAYS

BRIDGE RECTIFIERS
IN A POWER SUPPLY

FIG. 22-2.

of 0.005 to 0.01 microfarads, or use a better capacitor—one with less leakage such as a polypropylene, polycarbonate, polystyrene, or mylar.

Across Larger Capacitors

Another place in circuits where small capacitors are useful for bypassing is across the large electrolytic filtering capacitors in power supplies. While electrolytics can store large amounts of energy, they have poor high frequency response. As the frequency at which power is drawn from them increases, so does their impedance. In an audio amplifier, where the filter capacitor is just as much a part of the circuit as any other component, this characteristic detracts from the high frequency performance.

The solution to the problem is to connect smaller, higher quality capacitors across the large power supply electrolytics. When DC and low frequency AC is drawn from the power supply, usually at high currents, the electrolytic capacitors supply all the power. But at high frequencies, where the current drawn is usually not that great, it is the smaller bypass capacitors in parallel with them that supply power.

This method of circuit design is one way in which the transient response of audio equipment can be improved. You can improve the power supply of commercial audio equipment using capacitor bridging as well as designing it into other circuits where good high frequency response is important.

It's usually best to bridge a power supply with a combination of several capacitors. Start by connecting a small electrolytic of about 10 microfarads and as high a voltage as is available across the main power supply filter capacitors. Parallel this with a 0.3 microfarad metallized polypropylene and a 0.1 microfarad polystyrene capacitor. Physically attach the power supply bypass capacitors as close as possible to the actual circuit they are used for and not necessarily across the filter capacitors themselves. Much of their excellent high frequency performance would be sacrificed if they were separated from the load by a wire and its inevitable inductance.

This is a brief look at some of the considerations involved in capacitor bypassing. For more information on current research, consult articles published in *The Absolute Sound, Audio, The Audio Amateur, Independent Audio Research*, and others.

COLOR ORGAN

Years ago, color organs were quite popular. Since then, they've become almost extinct as video systems became integrated with audio to give people more interesting things to watch when they listened to music. But if you ever get the urge to see what all the fuss was about, this simple color organ circuit in FIG. 22-3 flashes a lamp or string of lights in time to the music. It's a fun thing to set up for a party and has other uses besides.

The color organ circuit connects across one of the speaker outputs of your receiver, although two could be used for stereo. The audio-matching transformer is necessary to keep the AC powerline separate from the stereo. Its impedance is not critical; many possibilities will work. The voltage from the transformer fires the SCR into conduction on musical peaks, lighting the lamp. Sensitivity is set by the potentiometer and should be varied so that the light is on about 50 percent of the time. It will have to be readjusted every time the volume on the stereo is changed.

COLOR ORGAN

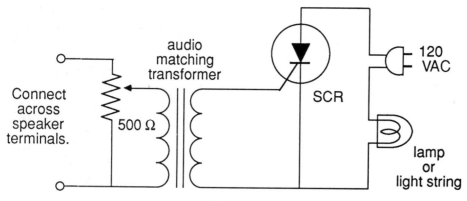

FIG. 22-3.

FAST STOP FOR AC MOTORS

A DC voltage applied to an AC motor will make it stop spinning instantly. This could be a useful way of stopping a tool that would otherwise take a long time to come to rest. Shown in FIG. 22-4 are two ways of sending a brief shot of DC voltage to a motor. The switch in circuit A is a three-position SPDT toggle switch with one position having a spring return to the center. Switches like these are available from surplus mail order companies. Use the spring return position as the STOP position. The other two positions are the standard ON and OFF that you would expect a power switch to have. To stop the motor, switch it from the ON position to the opposite side and let go—the switch will automatically return to the center OFF position after briefly giving the motor a shot of DC. Another way of doing the same thing with a pushbutton and regular switch is shown in diagram B. In either circuit, be sure to use a diode whose current and voltage ratings exceed that of the motor used by a wide margin.

However, be careful where you apply this circuit. On some equipment, a fast stop could be dangerous. When the spinning load is heavy or off-center, repeated instant stops could lead to premature wear of the motor and bearings. Of even more cause for concern are tools that are attached to the motor shaft with a screw thread. The threads are directed so that in normal operation the attached tool can only get tighter. But sudden stops are not part of normal operation. When the motor shaft stops dead, the inertia of the attached tool can cause it to unscrew itself and fly off. It's hard to imagine a situation where this wouldn't be dangerous. But despite these warnings, the fast-stop circuit does find applications with motor-driven gear trains and with high speed, low mass tools that require frequent changing of bits. If you see a tool begin to unscrew itself when the shaft stops dead, quickly click the switch to ON again, instead of simply looking on and preparing for disaster.

FAST-STOP CIRCUITS

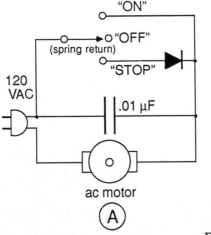

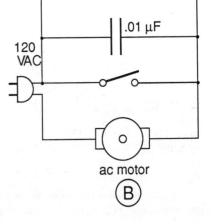

FIG. 22-4.

245

FLIP-FLOP

FIGURE 22-5 shows two circuits for activating relays and triacs with pushbuttons. They each have two buttons—one for ON, another for OFF—and use a normally open pushbutton for each. Circuits that use just a single button for both are common, but they require more parts and usually need a low voltage power supply. There are also mechanical latching relays that perform the same function. The circuits in FIG. 22-5 have the advantage that they can also be turned on and off electronically from within a circuit. A transistor connected across one of the pushbuttons has the effect of pressing it when it is biased by a brief current through its base/emitter junction. Either circuit could also be activated by an appropriate voltage pulse applied directly to the bottom of the ON pushbutton.

FUSE MONITOR

FIGURE 22-6 shows how to hook a neon light across a fuseholder so it will indicate when the fuse is blown or not in place. When the fuse is installed correctly, it shorts out the neon so it can't light. But when the fuse isn't in the circuit, current can flow through the neon and either the rest of the circuit or the 100-kilohm resistor, indicating that something is wrong with the fuse. The resistor is necessary for the bad-fuse indicator to work when the power switch is off, but could easily be omitted. Enough current would flow through the device itself to light the neon.

LEDS

LEDs are versatile low voltage indicators but don't have to be limited to just that. They can be used as 120 VAC pilot lights with a 5-kilohm, 1-watt resistor and a diode, as shown in circuit A of Fig. 22-7. The resistor does get somewhat warm however, and should not be mounted in a crowded area. Circuit B is for using a flashing LED like the Radio Shack #276-036 as a pilot light. It requires a slightly higher voltage and the filter capacitor to provide a smooth DC supply.

LED VARIABLE COLOR POWER INDICATOR

A two-color LED can be used with circuit C in FIG. 22-7 to indicate the relative output level of an AC power control circuit as it was in Chapters 1 and 2. Phase-control circuits, autotransformers, and other circuits that control AC power and have a load connected to their outputs can be monitored using the special LED. The LED changes gradually from green to yellow to red, giving an indication of the power output of the controller as the accompanying chart shows. When the load is open or disconnected, the LED lights up red only.

NEON LIGHT CIRCUITS

Here are two alternatives to standard neon indicator lights. Circuit A in FIG. 22-8 flashes a single neon lamp. Circuit B alternates between two. In each case, the flash rate is determined by the values of the resistors and capacitors and can be varied from one flash every few seconds to well within the audio frequency range.

When operated off DC as these circuits must, the neon lamps won't glow as brightly as they would if they were operated from an AC supply the way most pilot lights are.

246

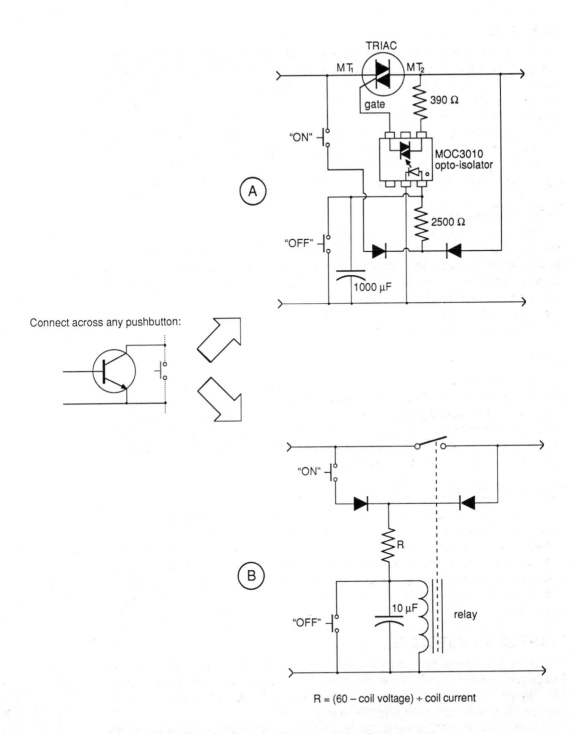

TRIAC

MT₁ MT₂

gate

390 Ω

"ON"

MOC3010
opto-isolator

A

2500 Ω

"OFF"

1000 μF

Connect across any pushbutton:

"ON"

B

R

10 μF relay

"OFF"

R = (60 − coil voltage) ÷ coil current

FIG. 22-5. *Two pushbutton-activated flip-flop circuits.*

247

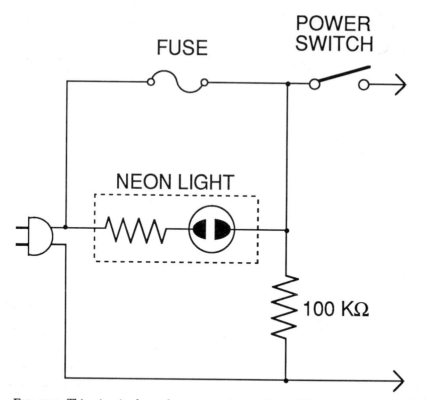

FIG. 22-6. *This circuit shows how to monitor a fuse with a neon indicator.*

With a DC supply, only one of the lamp's electrodes glow, whereas with AC, both appear to be lit. But because they are flashing, the neon lamps in these circuits attract more attention than standard indicators.

Both circuits contain a small DC supply made up of a diode and filter capacitor. The diode can be any rectifier diode with a reverse voltage rating above 200 volts. The capacitor should have a voltage rating of at least 200 volts as well, but its capacitance can be low. With a higher capacitance, the neon lamps in either circuit will remain flashing for several seconds after power is removed. This might be desirable in some cases, but not in others. Experiment with the value of the filter capacitor to get results that suit you.

Circuit A is called a *relaxation oscillator*. The 0.1 microfarad capacitor charges through the resistor until it reaches the breakdown voltage of the neon lamp. At that voltage, the neon gas between the electrodes inside the bulb ionizes and forms a conductive path. The capacitor discharges through the lamp, producing an orange blip. The lamp becomes dark again and its resistance increases when the capacitor's voltage drops below that necessary for it to sustain ionization. This lets the capacitor recharge and the cycle repeats itself. The flash rate can be varied by changing the value of the resistor, but don't go below one megohm or the neon lamp could burn out.

Circuit B goes into operation because all neon bulbs have slightly different breakdown voltages at which they begin conducting. When the circuit first receives power, the volt-

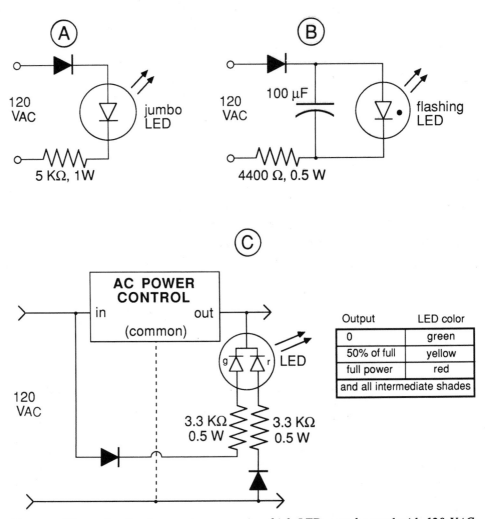

FIG. 22-7. *These circuits show various ways in which LEDs can be used with 120 VAC.*

age across C1 quickly rises. One of the neons will turn on first. Assuming NE1 turns on first, the capacitor C2 charges through R3 and the much lowered "on resistance" of NE1. The lowered resistance of NE1 diverts current around NE2, keeping it dark. When the voltage across the capacitor reaches the turn-on point of NE2 however, it lights that lamp instead and begins charging in the opposite polarity through it and R2. As it charges, it eventually reaches NE1's turn-on point and NE1 lights again. The cycle repeats with the frequency of oscillation set by the values of R1 and C2.

Neon lamps require a lower firing voltage when they are illuminated by ambient light. Pilot-light holders let some light through their lenses, and any application where a neon is used as an indicator is likely to do the same. But if for some reason you are using a neon lamp in a circuit for its electrical properties, make sure the increased turn-on point of the neon is considered if the project is to be enclosed in a dark place.

POTENTIOMETERS

Often a potentiometer is made to function like a rheostat in a circuit by using only two of its terminals. When connecting it this way, short the unused end terminal of the potentiometer to the wiper as shown in FIG. 22-8. This will slightly reduce the noise it produces as it is rotated, especially when it gets old and worn. With the additional connection, the potentiometer presents only its maximum resistance to the circuit instead of becoming completely open when the wiper momentarily loses contact with the resistive track or is touching poorly.

REGULATORS

The LM340-XX and 78-XX series of voltage regulator ICs are available in a variety of commonly used voltages. They are easy to use, reliable, and are quite inexpensive by mail order. But a better alternative to fixed voltage regulators is the LM317 adjustable voltage regulator. With a very simple circuit, this one IC can take the place of any fixed voltage regulator from 1.25 volts to 37 volts, eliminating the need to keep several different values on hand.

In addition to greater flexibility, the LM317 offers better performance than fixed regulators. It has better load and line regulation, presents a lower output impedance, and can achieve higher ripple rejection. The full overload protection circuitry contained in fixed voltage regulators is also present in the LM317, making it just as rugged and immune to mistakes.

The circuit labeled A in FIG. 22-9 shows how to use an LM317 IC as a voltage regulator. It has three connections to it, corresponding to the input, output, and ground terminals of fixed voltage regulators. The 5-kilohm trimmer potentiometer is used to set the output voltage initially and needs no adjustment after that. A zener diode could be used in place of the potentiometer as another way of setting the required voltage. The output voltage will be approximately 1.25 volts higher than the zener voltage.

Although the circuit looks more complicated than using a fixed three-terminal regulator, all the components except R and the potentiometer can be left out and performance will still be greater than fixed voltage regulators can provide. But for even better performance, the extra components are recommended. Capacitors C1 and C3 suppress transients, reduce any tendencies to self oscillation, and improve high frequency performance. Taking advantage of the IC's accessible adjusting terminal, C2 improves the ripple rejection. Any ripple present at the adjust terminal would otherwise be amplified by the IC and appear at the output. Diodes D2 and D3 are for protection, while D1 lets current from the load flow back to the supply when driving reactive circuits. The diodes should be rated for at least three amps and 50 volts. An effort was made to show all the ground leads connected to a single point in the schematic. This practice should be followed in the actual circuit as well, because it will result in slightly better regulation.

Both the fixed voltage regulator ICs and the previous circuit that can replace them are limited to 1.5 amps. For more current, the circuit labeled B can be used to permit either regulator to share current with a PNP power transistor. Along with the increase in current-carrying capacity it provides, the circuit substantially reduces output impedance, which is important when driving audio loads.

NEON FLASHERS

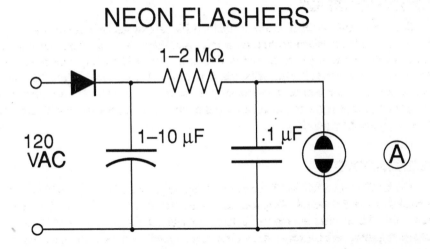

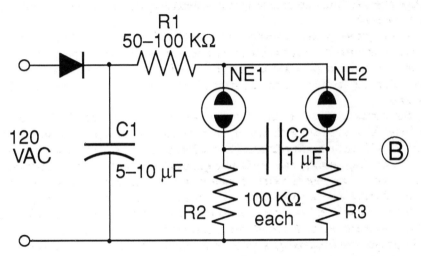

POTENTIOMETER HINT:

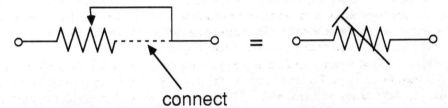

connect

FIG. 22-8. *The two neon light flashing circuits and a
diagram showing how to connect a potentiometer as a rheostat.*

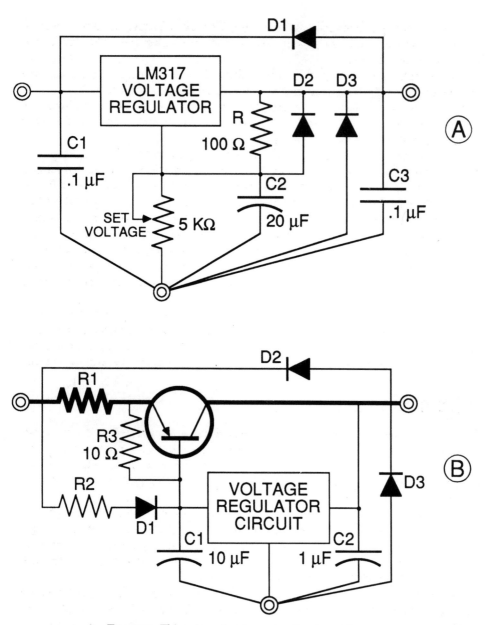

FIG. 22-9. *These two circuits are voltage regulators.*

The resistor ratio R2/R1 sets the ratio of current shared between the transistor and the IC. The total current capacity is equal to the sum of the current carried by the regulator and the transistor. The transistor must be able to handle the required current and power dissipation, however. Select a transistor whose wattage rating WT is sufficient to ensure that WT/WR > R2/R1, where WR is the wattage rating of the regulator (about 20 watts in either the case of a fixed regulator or an LM317 circuit). The resistors should be rated for the current they can carry as well. Typical resistance values are 1 ohm for R2 and less than an ohm for R1.

It is essential that the transistor, the regulator IC, and D1 be mounted on the same heatsink to keep them at the same temperature. The case of the transistor and the IC must be electrically isolated however, because they are at different points in the circuit. As long as these precautions are followed, the overload protection of the regulator IC extends to the output of the current-sharing circuit as well.

The resistance and wattage of R1 and R2 depend on the amount of current the circuit is designed to supply. Outputs currents in excess of 20 amps are possible, but the current-sharing circuit is used mainly for supplies under 10 amps. Diode D1 should be rated for 3 amps at 50 volts. The rating of diode D2 depends on the load expected. Diode D3 protects the circuit from reverse voltages applied to its outputs. It can be omitted, but if included, it should have a current rating at least half that of the fuse used to protect the circuit. The values of C1 and C2 are not critical, but be sure their voltage ratings are sufficient. When used with circuit A, they take the place of the smaller value bypass capacitors specified there. As in that circuit, all grounds are connected to a single point for better regulation.

Keep in mind when using fixed or variable three terminal regulators in any circuit that they will not deliver their rated current unless they are well heatsunk. Another thing to beware of is that different manufacturers of regulator ICs use different pin designations and sometimes connect the case to a different pin. Always check the data to be sure.

SOLID STATE RELAY

A more reliable alternative to old-fashioned electromechanical relays is a solid state relay. Because it has no moving parts, a solid state relay is silent, longer lasting, more compact, non-arcing, and does not produce as much electrical noise. More and more solid state relays are being used in applications where standard relays were previously used or couldn't be used because of their stated drawbacks.

Of course it's possible to buy solid state relays already assembled and packaged, but it's cheaper to make your own. The relay circuit in FIG. 22-10 uses a low voltage DC input to control AC power with a triac. The power-handling capacity depends only on what size triac you use and that it is heatsunk well. For any input voltages, use a value of R given by: R=Input Voltage × 50.

The triac driver opto-isolator makes the circuit quite simple. It has an LED input that will operate over a 15 to 50 milliamp current range, so the exact value of R is not critical. Similar opto-isolators accept input currents as low as 5 milliamps. The capacitors suppress high frequency noise that might otherwise trigger the triac. For overvoltage protection, add a low voltage zener diode and fuse as shown in the schematic.

This relay is suitable as an extension switch for controlling large loads. It can be located right next to the device being controlled, with thin DC control wires run to a remote battery and switch. The advantage of this is the avoidance of long high power wiring runs that cost more to install, develop a voltage loss, and are governed by electrical codes. Because the low voltage control circuitry is electrically isolated from the 120 VAC, the relay is

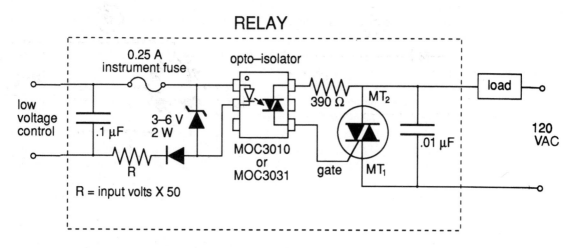

RELAY

low voltage control

0.25 A instrument fuse

.1 μF

3–6 V 2 W

R

R = input volts X 50

opto–isolator

MOC3010 or MOC3031

390 Ω

gate

MT₂

MT₁

.01 μF

load

120 VAC

FIG. 22-10. *Circuit for the solid state relay.*

ideal when safety is important. One of the frequent uses of low voltage relays like this one is for switching high power lights and fans from in or near showers and pools.

VOLTAGE BOOSTERS AND CUTTERS

Situations sometimes occur when you want to supply a nominally 120 VAC device with a higher voltage. For example, a soldering iron rated to deliver 27 watts at 120 volts will deliver approximately 33 watts when it's powered at 147 volts. It shouldn't burn out either, as long as the supply is kept within 125 percent or so. Other devices can also benefit from higher supply voltages. Or, you might want to use a lower supply voltage to power some circuits.

Either of these is possible using the circuits shown in FIG. 22-11. If the device you are powering doesn't require AC but can work equally well from a DC supply (loads like light bulbs and heaters), you can use any of the three circuits. If the application demands AC (motors, equipment with transformer power supplies, phase-control circuits), then you're limited to circuit C.

Circuit A supplies 60 volts DC rms with no capacitor across the output. But when capacitors are added in parallel with the output, the effective supply voltage can be increased to a maximum of 170 volts DC. The amount of capacitance needed for a particular load and desired voltage is easiest to determine experimentally by measuring the voltage at the load with various capacitors. Circuit B uses full-wave regulation. It can provide a 120 to 170 volt DC output but requires roughly half the capacitance that circuit A does. Make sure the capacitors you use in either circuit are rated for at least 170 volts DC because that is the voltage they will see if the load is disconnected.

Circuit C shows the secondary of a low voltage transformer connected in series with the 120 VAC line. Depending on which way it is connected, the secondary winding is either in or out of phase with the supply. By reversing the connections to it, you can add

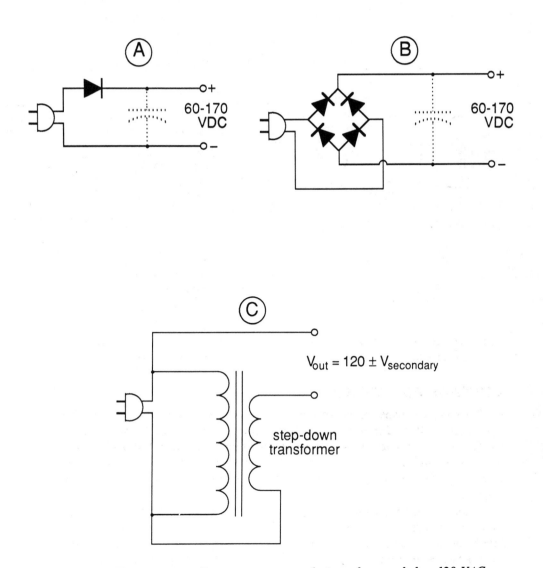

FIG. 22-11. *These circuits allow you to operate devices above or below 120 VAC.*

the secondary voltage to the line voltage or subtract from it. This way the output voltage can be boosted or cut by whatever secondary voltage the transformer has. The maximum output current is limited to the secondary current rating of the transformer. The advantage of this circuit is that the output remains a 60 Hz AC sine wave.

ZERO CROSSING

The best time to switch AC power on or off is in one of the 120 fractions of each second when the voltage is at or near its zero point in the sine wave. This reduces RF noise and the potentially dangerous electrical spikes that occur when inductive loads are switched on and off in the middle of a waveform. It is also particularly good to switch transformers off at the zero–crossing point in the AC supply, because that leaves their core in an unmagnetized state which creates less of a current surge when it is next turned on.

There is no way to assure zero crossing switching with an ordinary mechanical switch or relay, however. These devices are completely indiscriminatory about where in the AC waveform they switch on or off. But when a triac controls AC power in a project, the use of an MOC3031 triac driver opto-isolator instead of an MOC3010 automatically builds in zero-crossing switching. The MOC3031 waits until the 60 Hz sine wave it is controlling is crossing the zero voltage point before it switches on or off.

In this book, the MOC3031 triac driver opto-isolator was only recommended in the chapters where it is necessary—in the computer outlet box and in the power supply circuit for the straight wire without gain. But it can be used in the other circuits as well. It only costs about 30¢ more than the 3010 but is slightly harder to find.

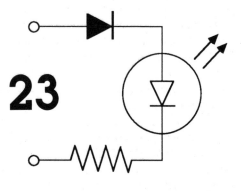

23

Parts
Sources

If you build a lot of electronic projects, you will find it's best to buy most components from mail order companies. They stock a wider variety and have better quality parts at lower prices than retail stores do. The better ones are very quick and convenient as well, challenging the only remaining advantage of retail stores.

Mail order electronic suppliers can be roughly divided into two categories: one group sells mainly new, prime quality components and the other deals mostly in surplus parts. Listed below are the mail order companies where all the parts for the prototypes were obtained. There are others, and this list is not intended to cover them all, but the ones given below represent excellent choices. It is a good idea to get on their mailing lists and keep your catalog collection updated, because the components these companies stock change, particularly the surplus items.

NEW PARTS

ACTIVE
P.O. Box 9100
Westborough, Mass. 01581
1-800-343-0874

*Prime quality semiconductors, good
prices, wide variety*

DIGI-KEY CORPORATION
P.O. Box 677
Thief River Falls, MN 56701
1-800-344-4539

*Semiconductors, passive components,
connectors, opto-electronics*

GLADSTONE ELECTRONICS INC.
1585 Kenmore Ave.
Buffalo, NY 14217

Parts and modules not found elsewhere

HANIFIN ELECTRONICS CORPORATION
P.O. Box 188
Bridgeport, PA 19405
1-800-523-0334

*Hard-to-find components, good variety,
some surplus and less-than-prime
components as well*

JAMECO ELECTRONICS
1355 Shoreway Road
Belmont, CA 94002
(415) 592-8097

Excellent prices and variety, semiconductors, tools,
 computer electronics

MCM ELECTRONICS
858 East Congress Park Drive
Centerville, Ohio 45459-4072
(513) 434-0031

TV service parts and tools, Japanese semiconductors

MOUSER ELECTRONICS
Catalog Mailing Services
P.O. Box 699
Mansfield, TX 76063
(817) 483-4422

Semiconductors and passive components, good prices
 on some hard-to-find items

PEERLESS RADIO
19 Wilbur St.
Lynbrook, L.I., NY 11563
1-800-645-2268

Passive components, a very helpful catalog

Also consult Chapter 13 for some suppliers of high quality audio components.

SURPLUS PARTS

ALL ELECTRONICS CORPORATION
905 South Vermont Ave.
P.O. Box 20406
Los Angeles, CA 90006
1-800-826-5432

BCD ELECTRO
P.O. Box 830119
Richardson, TX 75083-0119
(214) 690-1102

EDLIE ELECTRONICS
2700 Hempstead Tpk.
Levittown, L.I., NY 11756-1443
1-800-645-4722

ETCO
North Country Shopping Center
Plattsburgh, NY 12901
(518) 561-8700

H & R CORPORATION
401 E. Erie Ave.
Philadelphia, PA 19134
(215) 426-1708

HI TEK SALES
119r Foster St.
Peabody, MA 01961-3357
(617) 532-2323

JERRYCO INC.
601 Linden Place
Evanston, IL 60202
(312) 475-8440

JOHN J. MESHNA JR. INC.
19 Allerton St.
Lynn, MA 01904
(617) 595-2275

MARLIN P. JONES & ASSOC.
P.O. Box 12685
Lake Park, FL 33403-0685
(305) 848-8236

R & D ELECTRONICS
1202H Pine Island Road
Cape Coral, FL 33909
(813) 772-1441

TECHNICAL ELECTRONICS
P.O. Box 2301
Woburn, MA 01888
(617) 279-0800

WHAT TO BUY NEW

Buy all semiconductors new. Surplus houses usually won't offer better prices or selection for semiconductors, and those they stock are often of inferior quality. As a general rule, shop new for anything whose value is invisible to the eye. A good IC and a bad IC look the same on the surface, so don't take chances; buy from companies whose business is mostly new components from large-name brands. These companies usually have a toll-free number for charge orders and ship out their orders in a day or two. This makes them more convenient and only slightly slower than shopping at retail stores. The savings and quality is worth waiting a few days most of the time.

WHAT TO BUY USED

A chassis, outlet, line cord, etc. cannot generally fool you—it's either good or bad and anyone can tell the difference right away. Your best bet for items like these whose value is immediately discernible upon inspection or by reading a description is buying them from surplus dealers—either mail order or local stores. In addition to those listed previously, check for surplus dealers' ads in the backs of electronics magazines and write to get on their mailing list.

RETAIL STORES

Look in your local yellow pages under Electronic Equipment and Supplies. Listed there will be the stores in your area that deal in new and used electronic surplus. If you get to know the local ones and what they stock, you might find rare bargains that aren't available through the mail. Also, retail stores are the only alternative when you need a particular component in a hurry.

Radio Shack is particularly convenient because their stores are numerous and their free catalog lists and describes everything they sell. Unfortunately, the number of hobby components they stock seems to diminish each year and their prices are higher than the mail order companies and even some independent retail stores. Watch the sale flyers, though. Radio Shack comes out with a number of new components between their big yearly catalogs and occasionally have a real bargain in one of their clearance sales.

MORE SOURCES FOR PARTS

A good source for raw parts is old equipment. Often you can find junked electronic equipment at dumps or recycling centers. People also sell used electronic equipment at garage sales and flea markets. When you take apart old equipment, remove all the useful components like the line cord, switches, and other controls but leave the circuit boards intact. Gradually, you will accumulate a bunch of circuit boards packed with parts. They don't take up much space this way and allow you to look for just the resistor or capacitor you need before removing it. Removing all the parts if you're not going to use every one is a waste of time. Of course, when dealing with old parts from discarded equipment, it is wise to check them first before building them into any projects.

Some of the parts for the projects in this book didn't come from electronics parts dealers but from other unlikely sources. One of these is department stores where sales and rebates often combine to make some appliances quite inexpensive. Nowadays it is often cheaper to buy commercial products for the parts they contain than to buy the parts separately. Manufacturers can get parts so much cheaper than hobbyists can that sometimes it is worth buying assembled products only to take them apart.

For some applications, mass-marketed products like calculators, clocks, timers, etc. are attractive alternatives to building certain circuit elements from scratch. For example, to build a timer to control an AC device, it is much easier to buy a household digital timer and figure out how to interface it to a relay than to design your own timer circuit from scratch. To make a simple counter, a calculator can often be used with the appropriate modification. Construction articles in electronics magazines are a good source of ideas for modifications like these.

In the future, it is likely that creative experimenters will start seeing mass-marketed products as likely sources of parts for their projects. Hobby electronics will become more the skill of integrating these and other commonly available modules to make them do new and unusual things, rather than working soley with discrete parts as in the past.

Index

555 timer IC, 221

A
acrylic cement, 229
activating circuit, 221
  alternative, 223
  construction of, 222
  use of, 223
active minispeakers, 193-206
  accessories for, 204
  amplifier circuit for, 194
  audio monitor use for, 204
  board and crossover circuitry
    of, 198
  building amplifier into, 196
  calibration of, 200
  component arrangement
    diagram for, 199
  parts list for, 205
  portable carrier for, 201
  schematic for modification of,
    195
  tracing hum with, 204
active stage, 149-150
adhesives, 229
alphatic resin glue, 229
aluminum, working with, 234
ammeter, 207
amplifiers, 193
  circuitry for, 194
  impedance in, 142
audio circuits, straight wire
  without gain for, 128-155
audio output transformer, 124
audio taper, 84
auto-transformer, 207
automatic power switch, 95
  circuitry schematic for, 96
  construction of, 96
  use of, 99

B
balance control, 133, 148
battery charger, 24, 241

automotive, 32-33
  nicad, 33
  schematic for, 242
bike light, 123-127
blown-fuse indicator, 207
boxes, 232
breadboards, 229-230

C
capacitor bypassing, 242
  across larger capacitors, 243
  across switching contacts,
    242
  schematic for, 243
chemicals, 238
circuit breaker, 207
color organ, 244
common ground, 134
complementary metal oxide
  semiconductors (CMOS),
    handling of, 231
components, 235
conduction, 67
connectors, 238
construction hints, 229-240
contacts, 135-136
continuity tester, 207
controller
  solid state, 3
  uses for, 9
conversions, 53
crimp-on connectors, 238
current regulator, 27
cutters, 239

D
DC adaptors, 24
diacs, 16
digital multimeters (DMMs),
  180, 237
digital panel meter, 188
  calibration of, 190
  parts list for, 192

  schematic of, 189
distance measuring system,
  43-55
DPDT power switch and relay,
  207
drive circuit (see tide clock),
  116

E
EI core transformers, 175
electric hand dryer, 217-228
  activating circuit for, 221
  alternative activating circuit
    for, 223
  cutaway side view of, 220
  design considerations for, 217
  modifying hair dryer for, 218
  motion detector for, 223, 224
  parts list for, 227, 228
  schematic for, 219
  uses for, 226
electromagnetic interference
  (EMI), 90
electronic distance measuring
  system, 43-55
  bicycle attachment for, 50, 52
  circuitry for, 43
  construction of, 46
  improvements to, 54
  measuring wheel for, 47, 48
  modified calculator for, 44
  modifying calculator for, 46
  parts list for, 55
  resolution for, 49
  schematic for, 45
  uses for, 51
electronic exercise incentive,
  163-171
  circuitry for, 164
  construction of, 167
  control unit of, 167
  exercise machine wiring to,
    168

internal parts arrangement for, 167
parts list for, 171
schematic for, 165
television hook-up of, 169
use of, 170
enclosures, 232
labeling of, 233

F

fan, refrigerator, 75
fast-stop circuit, 245
fast-warm feature, 4, 8
flash lamp, 56
flip-flop, 246
fluorescent bike light, 123-127
circuitry and parts for, 124
construction of, 125
exploded view of, 126
parts list for, 127
schematic for, 125
use of, 126
frequency counter (see tide clock), 120
full-wave phase controller, 11
fluorescent light dimmer, 20
schematic for, 14
uses for, 13
voltage/output time relation of, 14
fuse holders, 232
fuse monitor, 246

G

gain stage, parts sources for, 151
generators (see fluorescent bike light), 123
glues, 229
grounding, 137
star type, 139

H

half-wave phase controller, 11, 12
schematic for, 15

uses for, 15
hand dryer, 217-228
heat transfer, 63
heater control, 11
heatsinks, 67
installation of, 71
hemostats, 239
high-pass filters, 38
modification of commercial, 39
schematic for, 39
hot-melt glue, 229
house wiring tester, 207

I

impedance, 142
infrared remote control relayer, 35-42
circuitry for, 36
construction of, 38
further uses for, 41
installing relayer in, 40
modifying high-pass filter for, 39
parts list for, 42
schematic for, 37
input wiring, 137

L

labeling project enclosures, 233
lead benders, 239
LEDs, 246
120 VAC use of, 248, 249
monitors using, 9
mounting, 6
variable color power indicator using, 246
light dimmer, 11, 13
line-in-use telephone accessory, 104-110
logarithmic response, 84
low voltage cutoff circuit, 77
parts list for, 81

M

magnetizer/demagnetizer, 172-179

measuring wheel (see electronic distance measuring system), 48
metals, 234
minispeakers, 193-206
monitors, LED, 9
motion detector, 223
circuitry for, 225
construction of, 225
parts list for, 228
schematic for, 224
uses for, 226
motors
fast-stop circuit for, 245
speed controller for, 11, 12, 13
synchronous, 111
multi-sensor digital thermometer, 180-192
adding digital panel meter to, 188
calibration of, 187
circuitry for, 183
construction of, 185
parts list for, 191
printed board arrangement of, 186
schematic for, 184
sensors used in, 182

N

neon flasher circuit, 251
neon light circuit, 246-247

O

odd values, 235
oscillator, 114
oscilloscopes, 120, 237
output voltage controller, 207

P

parts sources, 257-261
Peltier, Jean, 63
phase control, 1, 11-13, 207
phase reversal, 134
plastic, working with, 235
plug-in tester, 207-216

calibration of, 212
circuitry for, 208
construction of, 210
internal component
arrangement of, 213
parts list for, 215, 216
schematic for, 211
use of, 212
point-to-point wiring, 6
breadboards and, 230
portable refrigerator, 63-81
120 VAC power supply
circuit for, 77
construction of, 70
control circuitry for, 76
cutting cooler for, 70
direct conduction type, 67
ice chest modification,
cutaway view of, 68, 69
ice chest modification, side
view, 66
incorporating fan into, 75
installing heatsink, TEMs,
and aluminum parts in, 71
interior heatsink and fan type,
65
making power supply for, 78
optional low voltage cutoff
circuit for, 77
parts list for, 79
required materials for, 67
small size, parts list for, 80
two methods for, 65
portable speaker battery supply,
201
diagram of, 202
parts list for, 206
portable xenon strobe, 156
battery charger for, 160, 161
circuitry for, 156
construction of, 159
further uses for, 161
layout diagram for, 160
parts list for, 162
parts sources for, 157
schematic for, 158

positive temperature coefficient,
4
potentiometer, 250, 251
volume control with, 140
power controller, 11
power indicator, 246
power inverter, 100-101
power supply circuit
120 VAC, 77
straight wire without gain,
155
preamps, 88, 129
printed circuit boards, 231
protected outlet box, 90-103

R
radio frequency interference
(RFI), 90
refrigerator, portable, 63-81
regulated voltage and current
supply, 24-34
circuitry for, 25
construction of, 28
current regulator circuit in,
27
panel drilling guide for, 29
parts list for, 34
schematic for, 26
use of, 32, 33
voltage regulator circuit for,
25
wiring diagram for, 31
regulators, 250
relaxation oscillator, 248
relay, solid-state, 253
remote controller, 35-42
remote volume control, 82-89
adding automatic power
switch to, 95
adding power inverter to, 100
alternate uses for, 88, 102
basic circuitry for, 92
block diagram for, 83
circuitry for, 84
construction for, 86
internal parts arrangement

for, 87
no-frills version of, 92-95
operation of, 88
parts list for, 89, 103
printed circuit board for, 86
schematic for, 85, 98
resistors, 147
resolution, 49
rheostat, 251
ringing telephone alerter, 56-62
circuitry for, 56
completed circuit diagram
for, 59
construction of, 59
parts list for, 62
schematic for, 58

S
safety, 237
SCRs (silicon controlled
rectifiers), 12, 17
selector switching, 131, 139
semiconductors, 64
sensors, 182
separation control, 133, 148
simple projects, 241-256
soldering
contacts, 136
tools and techniques for, 236
solderless breadboards, 230
solid-state controller, 3
solid-state electric blanket
control, 1-10
alternate uses for, 9
circuitry of, 4
component wiring diagram
for, 7
construction of, 4
features of, 1
finishing, 6
mounting components in, 6
parts list for, 10
point-to-point wiring in, 6
schematic for, 5
use of, 8
solid-state relay, 253-254
speed controller, 11, 12, 13

spray chemicals, 238
star ground, 139
stepped volume control, 140
  circuit schematic for, 143
  kit for, 148
  programming for, 144
  resistor values for, 147
stereo systems
  remote control for, 35, 82
  straight wire without gain for, 128-155
straight wire without gain, 128-155
  active stage circuitry for, 149, 150
  adding selector switches for, 139
  balance control for, 133, 148
  channels in, 129
  chassis for, 148
  construction of, 135, 148
  contacts in, 135, 136
  features of, 135
  front panel layout for, 138
  functions and operation of, 129
  grounding for, 137
  input wiring for, 131, 137
  internal component arrangement for, 138
  materials sources for, 151
  parts list for, 153
  phase reversal in, 134
  power supply for, parts list of, 155
  schematic of one channel in, 130
  selector switching for, 131
  separation control in, 133, 148
  stepped volume control for, 140
  tone control for, 134
  using programs with volume control in, 141
  volume control for, 132, 140
strobe light, 156-162

switching circuit (see tide clock), 115
switching contacts, 242
synchronous motor, 111, 114, 121

T

tank circuits, 173
tap and drill set, 239
telephone accessory, 104-110
  alternative uses for, 109
  circuitry for, 105
  construction of, 107
  internal layout for, 108
  parts list for, 110
  phone line connections for, 104
  schematic for, 106
temperature compensation, 2
test equipment, 24, 207, 237
test leads, 238
thermistor, 3, 4
thermoelectric cooling modules (TEMs), 64, 67, 71
thermoelectric effect, 63, 64
thermometer, 180-192
thermostats, 76
thryristor, 12
tide clock, 111-122
  calibration of, 120
  circuitry for, 111
  clock face for, 118
  construction of, 115
  drive circuit for, 112, 116
  internal component arrangement of, 118
  oscillator for, 114
  parts list for, 122
  power supply for, 112
  schematic for, 113
  switching circuit for, 115
  uses of, 121
timer circuit, 221
tone control, 134
tool magnetizer/demagnetizer, 172-179
  calibration of, 178

circuitry for, 172
construction of, 173
heavy-duty switch in, 177
heavy-duty wiring in, 176
parts list for, 179
schematic for, 174
use of, 178
tools, 238
transformers
  audio output, 124
  EI core, 175
  output controller for, 11
  use of, 38
  video-matching, 38
triac, 6, 8, 12, 16

U

unsoldered contacts, 135

V

variable ac power controller, 11-23
  alternate uses for, 20
  circuitry for, 17
  completed, 22
  component wiring diagram for, 21
  components for, 16
  construction of, 19
  parts list for, 23
  schematic for, 18
ventilation, 237
video systems, remote control for, 35
voltage booster and cutter, 254, 255
voltage regulator
  circuit diagram for, 252
  circuit for, 25
volume control, 82-89, 132
  programmed, 141
  standard potentiometer for, 140
  stepped, 140

Z

zero crossing, 255

Edited and Designed by Lisa A. Doyle